THE
BETTER
BUSINESS
BOOK

VOL. 2

AUTHORS
UNITE

Published by Authors Unite

www.authorsunite.com

Edited By

THE
MASTER WORDSMITH
Masterpiece Services for Entrepreneur Authors

www.themasterwordsmith.com

Contents

CONTENTS

CONTENTS

CONTENTS

Section Two: Management and Culture

CONTENTS

Section Three: Well-Rounded Skill Sets

Part Three: The Journey Of Business

Section One: Point A To Point Business

CONTENTS

Part Four: Mind, Body, And Spirit

Section One: A Sound Mind In A Sound Body

Section Two: Getting Better Every Day

CONTENTS

CONTENTS

Wanna chapter in
The Next Better Business Book?

FOLLOW THIS LINK to get on the waiting list:
http://authorsunite.com/waitinglist

Dedication

To all the contributors in this book. You changed my life.
I will always be here for you.

Introduction

Welcome to Volume 2 of The Better Business Book.

This series started as a way to take 100 business books, reduce them to the 100 most important nuggets of wisdom, and put them all in one place. What we didn't realize was that it would turn into far more than that. Yes, it's a library of lessons, but it's also a community. Over 100 very different people came together in the shared desire to pass on their value to you, the reader, and to each other.

And then something amazing happened: we did it again. Several of us joined close to 100 new authors to share even more value in this second book. And others are already getting ready for a third book. What started as a compilation and became a community is growing into a movement. Maybe one day soon you'll be part of it.

We hope you enjoy reading this book half as much as we enjoyed creating it for you.

Love,

Us

Part One

IN THE BEGINNING

Section One: What Every Entrepreneur Needs To Know

The Marketing Trap You Must Avoid If You Want Success

JIM ESTILL

"Marketing is a battle of perceptions, not products."
—Al Ries and Jack Trout

Inexperienced marketers are easy to spot in a crowd.

In a moment, I'll tell you how you can do this. But first, who am I and why should you listen to me?

My name is Jim Estill. I'm the CEO of Danby Appliances – a compact appliance distributor and manufacturer in North America. Before selling bar fridges and wine coolers, I sold computers. My first company was a technology distribution business I started out of the trunk of my car while in University. I grew that company to $2 billion in sales.

I've retired twice – both times unsuccessfully. As an angel investor, I have advised and invested in many technology companies, including a founding board member of Research in Motion/Blackberry, before the company went public.

I share this so you know I've grown through all stages. I have started from zero and grown companies to billions. My goal today is to help you become a better marketer. Marketing is my biggest strength and it's the one skill that's helped me scale every one of the companies I've run and advised.

The good news about marketing is it's not difficult to do well once you understand how it works.

If you can avoid one of the major pitfalls in marketing I'm about to reveal, you'll give your business its best chance at success.

As I said, inexperienced marketers are easy to spot in a crowd. One way to tell is by how much emphasis these marketers place on measuring their return on investment (ROI) for their marketing efforts. Experience teaches that ROI in marketing *cannot be measured accurately*, and we are fooling ourselves if we think it can.

The main reason ROI in marketing is virtually impossible to measure is that most effects from marketing are not instant. Many effects and results of marketing are caused by accumulation of impact over time.

Think about this example. Did you buy the pair of Nike shoes because you saw the ad on a billboard? Because you saw the ad on Facebook? Because you saw the ad on television? Because the store clerk suggested them? Was it the ad this month or last? Or was it the ad you saw when you were 12?

The answer is you don't know exactly why you buy the shoes when you do. It is a combination of all these factors that make up marketing that cause the consumer to take action. Marketing effects happen over time. Good marketing creates the perception needed to cause purchasers to buy. It can also create the warm feeling towards the company or product that prompts the purchase.

If you are selling water and there is no perception that your water is any different than anyone else's water, then a marketing campaign or promotion or price reduction can potentially shift share from a competitor. Look at FIJI water or any bottled water you buy in airports.

FIJI does a good job differentiating their product. It is much easier to sell "Natural Artesian Water" over "bottled city" water if Natural Artesian can sell the refreshment and health benefits of the brand. Airports also have a unique advantage because there's low competition. You can get away with charging $4 for a bottle of water when no one else is selling or allowed to sell water in your marketplace.

Because of all these variables, measuring ROI becomes nearly impossible. As a result, some companies will stop marketing. This is great news for those that keep marketing. In time, share will shift to those that continue to invest.

Another danger lies in moving all your marketing to channels where there's the *illusion* of measurability. Just because the Facebook ad you ran to cold traffic converts, does not mean the ROI you calculate is accurate. What ads did your prospect see before your ad appeared in their newsfeed that day? What emails did your prospect open before yours popped up in their inbox?

Marketers are desperate to know how to measure ROI and this desperation is being exploited by better and savvier marketers online. The value you place on measurability comes from a perception that other forms of marketing – ones less measurable – are inferior. This is good marketing working against you.

To be clear, I do still believe there is value in trying to measure ROI in marketing. If I didn't, it would be like saying since we haven't found a cure for cancer, we should stop trying. The point I'm making is you shouldn't base *all* your marketing decisions on whether or not you can measure an ROI.

Remember, marketing is a battle of perceptions and just because ROI in marketing is impossible to measure accurately, does not mean marketing has no value. Just because we desperately want to know how to measure ROI in marketing, does not mean it can be done. And just because the measurement is not accurate, does not mean we should not still try to measure it.

Let's Make A Deal

JARET HENHOEFFER

Having completed over 150 deals selling companies, acquiring companies, joint ventures, investing and completing capital raises, I've learned the hard way how NOT to close a deal.

Here are a few lessons from the school of hard knocks.

A DEAL IS NOT A DEAL UNTIL SIGNED ON THE DOTTED LINE

I recently agreed to work on a transaction for Kevin, a fellow member of a large entrepreneurs' group. It was a difficult negotiation – the kind of deal I love. After months of creating selling documents and endless calls to a targeted list of prospective buyers, I finally found a motivated buyer willing to pay greater than the valuation Kevin agreed to at the start of the process.

Driving home I was excited and mentally celebrating the handshake exchanged between buyer and seller. But it turned out I'd gotten ahead of myself. (If you have ever watched the sports bloopers where the football player celebrates the touchdown for the last 5 yards and accidentally fumbles the ball, you understand what I mean about avoiding premature celebrations.) Here's the two phone calls I received after the handshake:

"I'm starting to rethink my valuation and believe it might be worth more than we originally agreed .... I have run some numbers and we are starting to realize we will miss running expenses like a car through the business ... maybe we should hold off a few more years."

"I talked to my tax accountant and he says it should be a share sale not an asset sale as we originally agreed to ensure tax efficiency, so the buyer is just going to have to change what they offered."

Just like that, the deal was off. I'd dropped the ball just before the end zone.

Fortunately, it got my attention, and in time I was able to figure out pretty much everything I did wrong. Here's what to do instead:

1. **Set realistic price** expectations early. Lock down "the minimum number" that the seller will accept. Verify the seller's number is realistic given what buyers will pay and what comparable businesses have sold for in the recent past. If it is not, walk away.
2. **Get the Tax Guys in Early.** Tax issues have become a sticking point in almost every deal I've done. Sellers should base their minimum acceptable price based on how much money they will put in their jeans *after* the IRS gets its share. It's the dealmaker's job to bring the tax guys in early to avoid a monkey wrench at the 11th hour.
3. **Prep Psychologically for Sticking Around After the Sale.** Once a buyer opens their wallet and pays the seller, the relationship fundamentally changes. After the cash hits the seller's jeans, the buyer will still expect the seller to be around for a transition period that might be anywhere from 6 months to 3 years. This mental shift is not easy. Negotiating employment agreements with someone who is used to being the boss is challenging. Hire a business coach to assist with the adjustment to this new world. If the seller won't commit to staying during the transition, or isn't able to adjust, the deal may die on the table.

QUICKIE DEALS: GIVE UP SOMETHING OF LITTLE MATERIAL VALUE THAT THE SELLER VALUES

When I was a kid, Monty Hall hosted a game show called Let's Make a Deal. Hall offered 'Quickie Deals' to audience members if they had random items on hand such as a pocket-sized paintbrush or a peppermint.

During a recent transaction, I learned the value of Quickie Deals. After much back and forth, Sandra (the seller) advised she was feeling good but not great about the negotiation. I like my sellers to feel great about the deal, so I asked what it would take to get here there. She named several items, and each item was like a pocket paintbrush for Monty Hall – of little cost to me, but of significant perceived value to the seller. Keep an eye out for these in your negotiations. Your pocket paintbrush might be letting them keep the company cell phone plan or giving access to personal IT support from the company for a few years. Something that's easy and cheap for you, but invaluable to them.

WATCH OUT FOR FISHERMEN

There are plenty of folks around the globe who pretend to be a fish when you throw out the bait. My friend Doug is an avid fisherman – he tells me to watch for nibbles that will steal your bait and swim away. The same is true when you sell your company. I've had nibbles from competitors hoping to scoop confidential information but who have no intention of buying. If you aren't careful, you may get numerous unqualified buyers presenting themselves as legitimate. Doing research is critical for sellers to drive up their closing valuation. You have worked hard to get where you are – flush out the real bidders to maximize value on your exit. To flush out real bidders, insist on Non-Compete/Non-Solicitation agreements along with deposits or other fees early in the process.

BE REALISTIC ABOUT WHAT YOUR BUSINESS IS WORTH TO OTHERS

What is your business worth? The simple answer: **Your business is worth what someone will pay for it.**

That means my friend Rod is an important person in any sale. Rod works in his pajamas yet always seems to deliver the most value in any transaction for a simple reason. He is relentless at researching, identifying and qualifying possible buyers, and contacting them repeatedly until they respond. Every good auctioneer knows getting qualified, interested buyers to the auction is the only way to guarantee a higher sale price. There is no use having a valuable business and an ideal sales document but not finding all the buyers. So make sure that you talk to as many potential (legitimate) buyers as you can find! Hire someone like Rod to do the research for you if you need to.

PAY IT FORWARD

I value mentorship. When CEO GLOBAL launched a mentorship program for members of Entrepreneurs' Organization, I signed up immediately and Mentor Ed was assigned to mentor me. We developed a friendship and I learned a lot. The next year, Mentor Ed asked if I would mentor his daughter. Mentor Ed's daughter wanted to buy a business and when Client Joe hired me to sell his company, it just happened to be the perfect opportunity for Mentor Ed's daughter.

Similarly, when my neighbor advised he looking for a new challenge in mentor

Ed's industry, I made the introduction. Now, Mentor Ed has a potential new employee, while my neighbour gets to explore a new opportunity. Mentor Ed eventually sells his company, I expect he will call me. I've never advertised, yet I have more business than my team can handle. Remember to pay it forward and eventually it will come back to you in spades.

If you remember these five tactics and practices, I promise you that your business will close more deals more frequently and more profitably than anyone who doesn't follow them. Best of luck!

http://www.penguinpower.ca/

Quit Is Not In Your Vocabulary

K. BILL DOST

Being an entrepreneur is in essence a license to have someone punch you in the face on a daily basis.

I heard that sitting in a forgotten meeting room in a forgotten venue listening sadly to a forgotten speaker so many years ago (where I'm sure you've also sat before), but that message stuck with me.

I think it's because I'd had a particularly tough month of it and I was looking for ... something. Call it hope, call it faith, call it my dream. I'm not sure. I know I was severely lacking that day and I latched on to what that guy said, I left the room when he finished speaking and went home to my wife and I repeated those words, and often when I'm on stage I say them too. But unlike that forgotten speaker, I add hope to it – and my desire here in these next few pages, is to give you hope as well.

Maybe you're at the end of your rope? Maybe the obstacles look too big? Maybe your COO / Executor / No.2 just resigned and you don't know what to do? Well I'm going to tell you what to do:

Put one foot in front of the other, and keep moving forward.

You see, no matter where you are, what you're doing, how bad it is, how unique your situation is ... it's still too early to quit. It's not the last round of the fight – Rocky hasn't been punched in the face enough times, he hasn't looked at Clubber Lang and said those magic words "It don't hurt so bad, it don't hurt so bad." You CAN take another hit, you CAN get knocked down, and then you CAN get up again. Another round is about to begin and you may just win that one. Keep getting up and you WILL win the fight. You just have to believe in yourself.

Now I appreciate our lives, your life, it isn't a movie, you aren't Rocky. However, we can look to so many real life examples of teams and people that just needed to hang in a little while longer to get their "win." They just had to stick it out a little while longer, and believe me, chances are if you are reading this, you just need to do so as well.

Rudy Ruettiger of the movie *Rudy* is perhaps one of the most famous examples of sticking it out. He was told he was too small, that he could and would never play for Notre Dame Football, but not only did he play for them in the last game he was eligible to play, but he sacked the quarterback!

Frank O'Dea, in his book *When All You Have is Hope*, describes in painful detail how he led a wayward life, was broke, was a failure and then after much heartbreak, including his parents, created Second Cup Coffee in Canada.

Bob Parsons, the founder of GoDaddy, famously watched as his entire "win" from his first sale dwindle down to almost nothing, even going away on holiday to decide what he should do. Close the company down? Keep it going? He recounts seeing a happy parking lot attendant and then determining that he could park cars for living if he had to. He eventually sold 70% of GoDaddy and became a billionaire in doing so.

So often we look to the people who quit too early. Stop doing that, look to the people that refuse to quit, get your inspiration from them! I did a podcast a few years ago for Paper Napkin Wisdom and I stated the following – Sometimes you wake up and you think you're going to lose it all, it's on those days you need to get a double helping of faith – in yourself, in your family, in your business, in your maker.

While it's great to fail and tweak your business, it's terrible to quit and give up, so I tell you this, that the best is yet to come! Believe in yourself, take stock in how far you have come, in what you've accomplished, in the growth and change and success that's already occurred and now just imagine the future is going to see that occurring ten times more!

You can do it, you just have to believe it.

Dr. Denis Waitley used to say it best: "if you think you can you can, if you think you can't you can't." It's all in the power of believing in yourself. Do you? If you do, great! If you don't, borrow someone else's belief in you until you do. Invariably, a spouse, a child, a friend, someone does believe in you, so take them at their word, trust them, and start believing in yourself. When you start doing that you'll understand that there is no such word as quit. It doesn't exist. It's for other people.

Just keep putting one foot in front of the other, and you'll be amazed at where you may just end up! Success is just around the corner. It's too early for me to give in and it's too early for you to give in. I look forward to seeing you at the finish line. Here's to the win!

In Business As In Most Things — Culture Is Everything

MICHAEL MCCOURT

Every company has a culture. The only question is whether or not management takes a hand in shaping it. I have learned that it is too important not to at least try to shape it. We have had our culture go sideways before and it is not fun. Sometimes it is a bad apple who gets hired into the bunch. Sometimes  we just lose our focus on culture and it gets away from us. We are stronger together and culture is that glue that binds us in a common cause. I want my company to have engaged people who feel their stake in the business. I want my company to have a spirit of camaraderie where we have fun together and have each other's backs in time of need. Finally, I believe that true success comes when you own your own technology so I need a "Yes We Can" attitude.

A Culture of Engagement

Many companies try different methods to build employee engagement. I believe the best way is to be a little free with key performance indicators. At our company our main product is billed hours. Not very sexy I know, but it is the truth. The numbers of hours billed every day, month, week and year  are directly related to our financial success as a company. We can't track hours billed daily but we can track them weekly. So the number of hours we bill every week we call UpTime. An email goes out every Thursday showing the numbers of hours booked for the previous week and percentage of hours we billed against the number of hours we could have billed if we had clients and PO's for it. UpTime tells everyone in the company every week if we are winning or losing. To make it more fun we set UpTime goals and when we achieve them everyone in the company gets a $50 bill. Not a check with source deductions taken off, not two twenties and a ten, but a $50 bill. There is a little magic in giving out $50's and I love doing it. We also have a SuperGoal which is set just a little out of reach. A stretch goal. This reminds the team that we plan to grow and hire. When we hit these everyone gets a $100 bill. UpTime and SuperGoals have been instrumental in building our culture of engagement through consistent information on performance (consistency builds trust) and real rewards for achieving targets.

A Spirit of Camaraderie

Hand in hand with UpTime goes FunTime. In the early days at D&D I as President chose every team-building event and managed it every time. The problem with this is that I ended up doing all of the work in order for everyone to do what I wanted to do – not what the team wanted to do. We experimented with a social committee as most companies do. This only made sure that the committee did all of the work and the events were what the committee wanted to do.

Enter FunTime. Each quarter the company puts a fixed amount into the FunTime pool. This money can be spent on any event that anyone wants to lead. We have done a lot of fun team-building things like paint-balling, go-karting, and archery tag. We had a snooker night and bought an online poker server for weekly poker nights with the entire team across the globe. We have also gone as a group to hockey, baseball, lacrosse and football games. An employee decides on an event they submit it to management to ensure that it is legal and appropriate. Once it clears these hurdles it is up to the entire team to vote on it. As long as 50% of the company votes and 66% of those who vote are in favor of the event it goes ahead. The employee is now responsible to his/her peers for the event and the budget. Both of these are great leadership skills to develop. To make matters more interesting we also add a chunk of money to the FunTime pool when we hit UpTime goals. The best part is that our employees have voted each year to use some of the FunTime pool to help families in need. Now that is a spirit of camaraderie.

"Yes We Can" Attitude

Everyone is talking about innovation these days, but precious few are doing it because it is a very hard thing to do. We have tried many things, including creating a Seal Team with special training in facilitation of innovation. We realized that people aren't comfortable trying new things and just dreaming at  their desks, so we built a special area in our offices called Shark Tank.

(Notice the nautical theme.) We filled the Shark Tank with the latest technologies and made it a safe place to try new things. From it we developed our VERA (Vision Enabled Robotic Assembly) technology and we continue to create new and exciting things.

My favourite driver of our culture of innovation was the time we built a RoboCoaster – basically a 300 mph racing seat mounted to the end of a large robotic arm. We did this for our 20th anniversary in business and it was wildly successful – not just in creating a great buzz but to prove that we could do it. When I first announced it to my team I was met with nothing but skepticism. I wrote down all of their concerns on a big white board. I reviewed all of the reasons that it couldn't be done with them. When they were fully satisfied that it could not be done I told them point blank that we were going to do it  anyway. The team dug in and the energy built until we had it running. It was awesome. In doing what the entire team thought was impossible we made a monumental leap forward in our Yes We Can Attitude.

This is the tip of the iceberg with kinds of programs that any company needs to run and run well to shape a positive culture. Many of the ideas are not original to us and were stolen from other companies with great cultures. Feel free to steal these ideas and fit them into your own business! Your company culture – and success – will thank you.

mmccourt@ddauto.com

Stay Out Of The Mud!

COLIN LAKE

"Never wrestle with a pig. You both get dirty, but the pig likes it."
—George Bernard Shaw

Knock, knock. The salesman walks through the door and lofts a heavy but well-designed opening line. The client is interested enough and offers the salesperson a chance to sit down. The salesperson quickly asks a "nails down the chalkboard" question/statement like "tell me a little bit about your business" or "is that a picture of your wife and kids?" And the client realizes that the salesman isn't really interested in them, but is regurgitating lines he's rehearsed and used hundreds of times.

Have you ever sat across from that person? Or worse, have you ever *been* that person? I'm pretty sure we all have. It's like wrestling with the aforementioned pig – both parties get muddy, but either you're the one not enjoying it, or you're the pig.

So often when we meet someone new – in business, at a cocktail party, a networking event, on a social media site or anywhere else – we're so quick to tell our story or "sell our wares," we forget the good nature and intention of a social interaction. The key that opens the lock of a successful social or business interaction is simply be interested and don't worry so much about being interesting. So many salespeople and entrepreneurs are too focused on getting something from the conversation rather than enhancing their lives through connections.

When the goal of a conversation becomes a strong connection and the aptitude to understand whether you and/or your company can provide a value or service, the nature of every conversation you have will change forever in your favor.

What does that even look like?

Ask them something they probably haven't been asked before. Or better, ask them something that forces them to think, rather than give you the same answer they've given the last 20 people who asked the same question. For example, "What are the two or three most important things to you and your business today?" A question like this, when asked with real interest, launches a conversation around real goals and the needs that surround those goals. From there we have the freedom to ask more questions and myriad of ways to make recommendations, offer services or make connections to enhance their business and ultimately their lives.

Another great tactic is to ask a question that 99.9% of your target audience is going to say yes to. "You know how small business owners are always looking for more referrals from their existing clients?" Clearly the other person will agree, so now you're afforded the opportunity to solve for this challenge through our experiences with their peers or services you/your firm offers – and to prove that you're not one of the "social media experts" and "web development specialists" on the prowl with nothing real to offer.

Ask more than one or two questions. And take notes (after asking permission, especially if using a tablet). Nothing shows the willingness to listen more clearly, than taking notes based on the most important factors of each sales interaction. The average human speaks 125-175 words per minute, within 24 hours of any conversation we retain less than 50% of what we heard and within 48 hours 50% of that is gone! In other words, we often comprehend/retain only one-fourth of what we hear.

Various studies stress the importance of listening as the key communication skill. A University of Missouri study points out that many of us spend 70 to 80 percent of our waking hours in some form of communication. Of that time, we spend about 9 percent writing, 16 percent reading, 30 percent speaking, and 45 percent listening. Yet studies also confirm that most of us are poor and inefficient listeners. Why?

Several reasons are likely.

1. Listening training is unavailable to most people. Even though listening is the communication skill we use most frequently, it is the skill in which we've had the least training. We know we've had much more formal training in the other major communication forms (the first twelve years

of schooling) – writing, reading, speaking. But outside of professional counselors and therapists, very few persons have had any extended formal training in listening.

2. We think faster than people can speak. We have the mental capacity (brainpower) to understand someone speaking at up to 400 words a minute. This gives us the false sense that we have time to daydream in the middle of a conversation; thinking two, three and four steps ahead of our clients or friends as they tell their story. We forget to listen to what's being said, missing the opportunity to ask the next logical question which will determine what's most important or exactly what they mean by what they said.

The next time you find yourself debating the issue of why your product is better or why the extra fees that your firm charges are worth it, remember: the client you're "selling" will continue to wrestle around in the mud with you, ultimately appreciating the end result of getting you out of the office quickly and not having to commit to anything.

All people we interact with, especially your clients, are hungry for someone to listen to them and work with them to resolve their issues. When we do, we'll get everything we've ever wanted out our relationships – business, family, friends, and more. So listen for the sake of learning. When the point of connection becomes about the interaction not just the transaction, the connection becomes real.

And your clothes won't have mud all over them.

Section Two: Getting Off The Ground

Where To Begin?

MEREDITH JAYME

Beginnings are often the most difficult part of any journey. The first steps that we take can frequently be some of the most important ones. I have found that taking those first steps with three driving factors in mind is key to ensuring that these crucial beginnings lead you in the direction that you want to be going and ensure future success.

1. Passion

Passion makes just about everything in life better. Ask yourself: why you are truly doing something? What drove you to pursue this idea? Has this always been something that you've loved or has interested you? If you can truly say that you're passionate about what you're doing, then pour yourself into it. If your motivating factor is that you see this as an easy opportunity to make money but don't really care about the idea, that should be a sign to reevaluate. For some it can be hard to know what you love and want to do if you haven't done it yet, so focus on doing things that motivate you, that inspire you, that move you forward, or that you see yourself using as a stepping stone to evolve your career forward.

2. Positivity

Maintaining a positive outlook is essential not only in business, but in life. Make the most of where you are and use every opportunity to prove yourself. Make genuine connections. Do anything like you would do everything – even the seemingly most mundane of tasks can be done with excellence. Let rejections move you forward and accept that there is something better awaiting you. It's important not to let the "no's" pull you down. It just takes one "yes" to lead you to your dream opportunity. Look at mistakes and negative experiences as lessons learned and chances to turn things around. Practice finding at least one positive outcome of any seemingly negative situation that you may find yourself in. Things could always be worse. Use every opportunity to prove yourself and do the best that you can. Your best is always enough.

3. Progress

It's important to realize that everything takes time and that every journey is different. You may not think that you're moving quickly enough or accomplishing as much as you'd like to, but baby steps are still steps. Remember to celebrate the small successes and reward yourself for the progress that you are making, while continually striving to be better, do better, and take your business and your self to the next level. Don't be afraid to be unconventional. Remember to analyze your goals and work towards the next steps. Make a timeline for your future but don't lock yourself into an unreasonable plan. It is important to be realistic and honor the steps that you are taking as long as they are moving you forward. Along with this, don't be afraid to say no to the wrong opportunities. So many people are eager to jump to accept the first job that they are offered, for example, when there are still so many other opportunities waiting to be discovered.

We all have to start somewhere. Moving forward with a foundation built on passion, positivity and continuous progress will ensure that you're taking the steps necessary to accomplish your dreams and meet and exceed your goals.

Full disclosure, I wouldn't say that I feel like I've "made it" yet or am living the dream life that I imagine for myself, but I am definitely working my way there. I think that it all comes down to trusting your own path and pursuing your own dreams regardless of whether or not you know how to get there. Whatever it is that you really want to do, do it. Whoever it is that you really want to be, be that person. We don't have to have it all figured out, and I don't know if we ever do, but I think that we figure out a little more with each day, with each new opportunity, and with each new experience that we expose ourselves to.

Every day is a new beginning and the future is infinitely bright. Why can't today be the day that changes the rest of your life?

meredithjayme@gmail.com

Love Of The Game

DANIEL J. BOCKMAN

I was once asked by a newspaper reporter, "How did you become so successful?" In haste to come up with something very enlightening, I answered, "*I just kept thinking there are no more reasons I shouldn't be.*" At the moment I answered this question, I thought it was a generic answer, but looking at it now I really like my response to the question.

But the question *How did you become so successful?* makes me think: how does anyone become successful at business?

To become successful at business, you must have love and passion for what you are doing, yes – but there is another aspect of business a lot of startups forget about: you must have love of the game! The game I'm talking about is the game of business, from what you love about it to the things that suck! It's very easy to have love and passion for the kind of business we are practicing and the products and services we are selling. But it is something much different to love the actual game of business. Being a business owner is fun because we get to live our dreams and make money at it, but inevitably, there are things about business that are not so much fun! The bills, taxes, government regulatory, HR, paperwork, reports ... I could go on. No one enjoys those parts of the game. Yet there is a certain type of people that do enjoy every aspect of business, even the things we traditionally think suck about it. These people truly love the game – and often are the most successful businesspeople.

Let me ask you this question; how do you beat a winner? You know the kind of people I'm talking about. The ones that never seem to lose, and everything they touch turns to gold! They never seem to struggle and they always come out on top of every business deal. How do you beat someone like that?

It's a trick question. You can't beat those people. But when you love the game, you can become one of them. The winners have a love of the game. They find pleasure in fierce and formidable competition because it creates innovation and persistence in their own organization. They like it that business is hard. Not only do they love their work and craft, but they also love everything most people hate about business! How unfair is that? The good news is, there are no laws or regulations against passion for your craft or the game of business. When you learn to love the game, you can join these people in their successes.

I often say to new entrepreneurs, "If it sucks for you, then it sucks for your competitor too." I say this to encourage them to take the initiative. Taking the initiative is the cornerstone of all success in the business game because success is not going to just fall in your lap one day. Seizing the opportunities and advantages you already have in your life and thinking like the winners of the world by doing a few simple things and changing the way you think, can help you find love for the game of business. I found the love of business when I started looking at it like a big real-time game. Almost like playing sports. I wanted not only to enjoy my craft but I also wanted to enjoy the "business world venue" where my crafted was being practiced. Here are six ways you can do this.

1. We humans are competitive by nature but modern society and social norms have taught us over time to be a bit more sophisticated and not act like cavemen fighting over a kill. Deep down in our primitive subconscious brain lies a desire to come out on top and survive above everyone else. Tap into that competitive side of yourself and get a little "raggedy" with your mind. Champion your thoughts of success and being number one. Challenge yourself to fight a little harder, to work a little longer, to be a little better every day.
2. Use your fear of losing the game as energy and fuel. Fear is one of our strongest emotions that can be used to our advantage. Knowing you might lose the game will force you to re-strategize and get back into play.
3. Think only about how you are helping people and creating impact in your industry and not about the money. Working for the money alone is like winning the Super Bowl for the trophy only, and not the title of world champ. You can buy a trophy from a trophy store and make it say whatever you want, but that alone won't mean anything. Win the title and no one can contest your success (at least till next season).
4. Embrace your competition. Feel the spirit of the game and approach each day with a mind prepared to win. Channel anger into fuel and extinguish thoughts of jealousy and envy of those more successful than you. Appreciate the fact that you have competitors that try and beat you

and be flattered that they try and steal your ideas. You are significant to them and you have an impact on their operations.

5. Enjoy the fact that nothing comes easy to you and that business is hard work. You have to work at this game and use laser focus to get what you want. Nothing worth doing was ever easy. If you choose the easy path, life becomes hard – if you choose the hard path, life becomes easy!

6. Empower your risk-taker instinct. There are two types of risk takers in the world: 1) the foolish risk takers that gamble in casinos and buy lottery tickets and hope for longshot luck, and 2) the strategizing calculated risk takers of business. Risk is not that "risky" if you are planning, strategizing, and looking for opportunity everywhere you go.

Take these six principles and view the business world as a game. Use them to make business fun and play the game as hard as you can. The game is rigged in the favor of those who want it the most and to those who will destroy the concept of the rules. The game is unfair and unkind at times but when you learn to love it – all of it – you will never be down for long.

Moving On From Complacency

CLAIRE ALLISON

Have you ever tried to convince yourself that you love your occupation while in another pointless meeting, at a "team bonding" event, or just a typical Monday? I know I have, but every job, no matter how big or small, comes with its own pros and cons. If anyone were truly happy with every single aspect of their profession, then I'd love to meet them.

When do you know that it's actually time to move on? How do you know when you're staying where you are out of dedication and when you're staying out of complacency?

I've learned to ask myself these key questions when considering a career change.

- *Am I happy?*

This is the most important question. The answer to this question should directly correlate with your final decision. Some people tie this question to compensation, but according to a recent study, more than a third of employees would give up part of their salary in order to be happier at work. When you think about everything you dislike and what you would like instead, make sure you're thinking about important and meaningful changes. Wishing there were better lunch options or "jeans day Fridays" should not be the driving force here. Do you feel discouraged to bring up innovative ideas in meetings? Does your boss make you feel inferior next to the new intern? Do you get paid less than your colleagues with fewer responsibilities? These are the types of questions that will affect your long-term happiness.

- *Am I passionate about what I do?*

If you no longer care about what you do and the impact it has, then what's the point? When you take passion out of the equation, then you're simply going through the motions. You're just another robot in a corporate uniform.

Conversely, if you are still passionate about what you do, then maybe it's simply time to find the right employer that will appreciate you and what you have to offer.

- *Does my job inspire me to be better?*

When's the last time you were given a significant responsibility from your supervisor? When is the last time you were truly challenged? If your employer doesn't consistently take you out of your comfort zone and push you, then you're probably in the wrong place. It would be easy to do the same tasks day in and out and become complacent, but the monotonous routine would personally drive me insane. Without challenges, you will not grow and without growth, you will not reach your full potential.

So if you can answer "yes" to all three questions, it's worth staying put at least for the time being – but if not, you might be ready to move on.

To put it another way, allow me to tell you a story: A man was out on his Sunday afternoon run and saw one of his neighbors cleaning out a birdcage in the front yard. He was amazed that the top was off of the cage, but the bird sat there contently as its owner cleaned the cage around it. The jogger slowed his pace and asked his neighbor, "Aren't you afraid the bird is going to fly away?" The bird's owner laughed and said, "I don't think she knows that she can."

How many times have we remained where we are because we believe we can't or shouldn't leave? Complacency can only affect your life if you choose to accept it. So if you're feeling caged, take a look around and make sure the door isn't standing open.

What I Learned Not To Do In Business

BRAD CLIMER

There are some lessons in life and business we are going to learn the hard way. I'm not sure we will get it any other way. We have mentors, self-help courses, and gurus, but yet we still miss the point sometimes until it hits us in the face. For me, the thing that kept me out of some good business deals and experiences was arrogance. Arrogance is defined as having or revealing an exaggerated sense of one's own importance or abilities. It literally blinds you to many wonderful people and awesome opportunities. I'm sure many readers have experiences and have stories similar to what I am about to share.

It was the late 1980's and I was a young salesman for a paper company. It was a great business to be in. Paper was in abundance then and the digital age was years away. There was no internet. There were no smartphones. Reports were still done the old-fashioned way, on a sheet of paper. Companies always ordered and reordered paper for invoicing, reports, letterhead and more. So building strong relationships with clients to get that business and those repeat orders was the objective. Once the company was signed, you could sit back and watch the commission checks roll in. I was always on the lookout for this type of company.

Here's where the arrogance comes in. I was young and feeling my oats. I knew I could sell to anyone. No company was too difficult to approach. There was one particular company in my city, however, that I was determined to land. This company was a high-volume user of paper products. They did quite a bit of invoicing because this city location was their headquarters. But for some reason, no one from our firm had ever sold to this company. It intrigued me so I was told that I could try, but good luck and don't get your hopes up.

I called the company many times. Finally, one day I got to the main buyer. I was ecstatic! I did my best to be professional. I used every technique I had ever read from every sales book that was available. Guess what? I did it – he promised me fifteen minutes. Fifteen minutes. More than enough time to make the sale.

I remember wearing my best suit. I knew I could not be defeated. I was not going to be denied. I went in for the appointment. Within fifteen minutes he said the magic words that every salesperson lives for: "Let's do it." I sold him! I was stoked! The buyer signed the order and slid it across the desk to me.

I could not wait to get back to the office to share my good news. I was the wiz kid. I was "The Man." I was on top of the world.

I cannot explain what occurred next. Nor can I explain what was going through my mind or what I was thinking. In my excitement, I guess I wanted him to know how successful I was. My ego took over and my logic left the room.

During my pitch, I'd noticed he had a Rolex watch. Upon further examination, I realized it was a replica and not authentic. I, however, was wearing a real Rolex. So I asked him if I could look at his watch. I proceeded to examine it. Then he noticed I had a Rolex and his face dropped when he saw my second hand sweeping. His was ticking – it was the obvious sign of a fake Rolex.

He leaned forward and said to me, "Hand me the order back. I need to get approval from another department." I handed the order back to him. He said, "Call me tomorrow and I will have the order signed and ready to go."

This was the largest order I had ever attained and the residual income was going to be very good. I was very excited. In fact, I had already spent most of the money in my head. Plus I was the first person from my company to close a sale from this buyer. I went back to my office and promptly informed my boss and the rest of the office that I had "bagged" this account. I felt amazing. There were plenty of high fives and back slapping. But in the back of my mind, I was worried about what had happened with the watch.

The next day, I called to make arrangements to pick up my signed contract. The secretary informed me that the buyer was not available and that he would call me back. He did not call that day. The next day I called again. I was informed that the buyer was not available and I would have to call him back. I finally drove over to his office, only to be told he was too busy to see me.

After two weeks of calling and dropping by, it had dawned on me: that moment with the watch had ruined my sale. I had embarrassed and humiliated the buyer. My out of control ego had cost me the biggest sale of my young career.

I kicked myself for being so arrogant, and I tried to apologize, but I never got back into that account. The buyer never took another call from me. It was a tough pill to swallow.

To this day, I reflect on the arrogance and massive ego I displayed. I have since learned to be humble and to really monitor how I interact with all my clients. I've learned to ground myself when my ego tries to take over. I reflect daily on how my feelings affect my actions. And I never try to convince a client I'm better than them. But I will never forget learning that lesson the hard way.

So when you're young in your career, I urge you: think through your actions. Do the work to be better. And when you do make mistakes or let your ego take over, be prepared to learn a few lessons the hard way.

You Are Never Prepared Enough

WENDY A. BARBA

You are never prepared enough to get the dream job or start your own business.

This doesn't mean that you shouldn't prepare. Preparation can be good. But over preparation can paralyze you and keep you off your main goal. Focusing on every step of the way may take you further from your own goal and discourage you. Instead, learn to listen to your inner child passionate voice, own your outrageous craaazy goals (aka your wildest dreams), and welcome failure with a big smile. To do this, here are three things to focus on besides preparation:

Passion: Build your business like a six-year-old

Selling is my passion. I remember at the age of six I sold stickers. These were not cool or trendy stickers, though. These were ordinary product labels (imagine Johnson & Johnson shampoo). I would sell these to my classmates so they could make cool notebook covers. Once a week, after school I would walk to the manufacturer to collect the leftover or damaged labels from their recycling bin. Yep, I built my business at the age of six. I didn't stress over the issues or consequences. I didn't worry about how prepared I was or wasn't. I just saw the opportunity and took action. Why? At that time, I wanted to be a veterinarian and save starving and sick animals. So with 25¢ per label, I bought food for the street dogs in Venezuela. I guess you could say I built my first non-profit at six. This illustrates the potential of nurturing your passion and transforming fear. Build your business like six-year-old you.

Not sure what your passion is? Think of what brings butterflies to your stomach. This could be feeding street dogs or consulting in social media or opening a catering company. Only you know your passion and only you can nurture it.

Planning: Set outrageous goals and plan to reach them

Have you heard the phrase, "a goal without a plan is just a wish?" This is so true. Sometimes we are so focused on the final product that we forget how to get there. It's like expecting to finish in the top 10 of the Boston Marathon but not ever training for it.

I am a planner. My plan was to graduate with a double major in International Business and MIS, work for General Electric, make a lot of money, earn my MBA while working full-time, lead the Latin America region, gain international sales experience, and build skills to negotiate at all levels. Once I mastered these skills I would open up my own business.

The funny thing about my plan is that when I shared it, people thought I was crazy. These were my closest friends, mentors, professors, colleagues and other business peeps. They laughed at me. They discouraged me. They instilled doubt into my goals and my plans. But the more they tried to discourage me, the more I stuck to my plan.

Sometimes people have the notion that this was easy or that I was lucky. I don't see it that way. I was simply determined to follow my plan. Someone once told me; you will never work at GE while living in Miami and absolutely no chance of working from home. "You need to move to a town with GE Headquarters like Cincinnati, Ohio," I was told. I applied to General Electric Company 16 times. I actually started to enjoy the interview process! It gave me a rush of adrenaline. I even developed a manual on how to tackle each question. Even interviews, like our goals, require a plan.

I finally joined GE in 2005. I led the GE Appliances Latin America region and developed international negotiations skills. I was right on track for my plan. I remember one of my managers said, "don't you think you are moving too fast? You will get burned out." I smiled and thought how bizarre that comment was. I was exactly where I had planned to be.

Once I got into GE, I had a checklist of accomplishments that I needed to fulfill in order to prepare me to start my own business. But my plan started to derail. I became so focused on running up the corporate ladder that I passed on several opportunities to start my own gig.

Self-doubt and fear of failure took over. Why now? If you remember, my plan ended with *"start my own business."* I hadn't planned for that yet! I realized that no plan is perfect, there WILL be adjustments. No plan is enough by itself; each plan brings you one step closer to your goal. Your plan will never prepare you enough.

I don't regret my path. I just know that I needed to work hard, to stay focused and to take a leap of faith on opportunities that would get me back on track instead of dwelling of how I could have, should have, and would have done things. In life like in business, fear of failure is inevitable. You just have to keep that in mind, learn from your mistakes and keep on moving forward.

I wholeheartedly recommend that you make a plan, stick to a deadline, and own your plan. Remember that success doesn't just fall on your lap (and if it does, run with it you fast tracker). You must plan for success and work hard.

Push: Take calculated risks and execute

If the plan that you hold yourself accountable for does not work, that's okay. Don't get discouraged. Keep your head up, smile, tweak the plan and keep on going. Remember, like our friend Winston Churchill would say: "success is stumbling from failure to failure with no loss of enthusiasm."

The moment that you face the fear of failure, will be the moment that you commit wholeheartedly to your goals and enter the life of entrepreneurship. Embrace failure and fear, my friend. Make them your BFFs – or as I like to say: "keep your friends close and keep your FEARnemies closer." Dealing with failure brings solutions. Dealing with fear stimulates your creative mindset. These two will provoke decisions, force you to execute and teach you how to be flexible; while bringing you closer to your passion, which is the reason you got started. Don't be afraid to execute, because like Thomas Edison said a "vision without execution is just hallucination."

So empower yourself by being flexible. Learn from each opportunity and embrace fear of failure. Remember that "life begins at the end of your comfort zone," so what's holding you back? Find your inner six-year-old voice, plan your outrageous goals, and get comfortable with the fear of failure. You can do it!

wendy@napavale.com

How To Know When It's Time To Take The Leap

ASHLEY WARD

Ever wonder if you're ready to be an entrepreneur? I used to wonder that literally all of the time. Until one day, I became one.

My career began as an employee, like most entrepreneurs. I juggled being a fulltime employee and developing a digital marketing agency on the side. Normal work weeks turned into 80+ hour weeks. I wanted to quit the day job, but I was afraid. I didn't think I was ready. That fear got the best of me and settled with me for a very long time. It prevented me from becoming the entrepreneur I had always dreamed of becoming. It wasn't until five and a half years later that I took the leap.

Knowing when to sacrifice a secure form of income to become a fulltime business owner is one of the most difficult decisions I have ever made, clearly because it took me over five years to do so. Giving up a steady paycheck, benefits, paid time off, and security aren't always the easiest things to factor out. So, I continued to push my dream down the drain as I waited for a big red banner to drop down saying, "Okay, you're ready!". The same red banner, the sign of approval and permission, that most entrepreneurs wait for.

Not once did that banner appear. Five and a half years I waited for it, but nope, no banner. Eventually I realized: it was never going to show up, *and I didn't have to wait for it to stop being afraid.* And here's the thing: neither do you. If clocking in, having a structured schedule, and doing repetitive tasks to benefit someone else's business and not your own is driving you mad, you can stop waiting for a banner or anything else to tell you you're ready.

Instead, ask yourself these questions:

How Comfortable With Change Are You?

As an entrepreneur, you'll have to change your business model to adapt to success, and frequently. If one plan isn't working, you'll have to scrap it and start over. Failure happens often, but can quickly turn into success with a little change. Very rarely does an entrepreneur succeed with their original business plan right off the bat. You need to be open and willing to adjust in order to better serve your business and customers.

When I took the leap and quit my job, I knew I was going to have to make a few immediate changes to my agency. One was the pricing and package structure. The original structure was created to accommodate small business, high maintenance clients. After reaching out to 3 different mentors for advice, I ended up restructuring the types of services I offered to better accommodate my new type of client, my "dream" client. This meant first figuring out what my dream client looked like. I knew working for very small businesses wasn't going to pay the bills long-term or allow my business to grow.

So, I increased my prices to target medium to larger-sized businesses and only offered the services that I did best for those clients. For my agency, that meant removing website development, email marketing, and content management from my list of services – even though I was good at all of those offerings. It also meant not spreading myself so thin and taking on so much. If I was going to charge more, I needed to invest more time for my clients, which meant fewer clients.

Removing half of my suite of services was an incredibly difficult change to make. I don't like saying no to new business and dislike even more not being able to help out my clients 100%. Which meant I needed to find a resolution to accommodate this change for my business and for my clients. The solution? Instead of sending potential clients away because I no longer offer the services their seeking, I created relationships with website developers, email marketers, and bloggers that I could trust and could refer my clients to. I now have multiple referral relationships that work both ways and allow my business to offer what it does best.

With every change comes testing. Some of the new prospective clients loved the change and responded well, while others ran the other direction looking for more structure and more services. And I'm not done making changes – I never will be! It's an ever-changing battle, but it's one I'm open to because my ultimate goal is not just to succeed at what I do, but to for my clients to succeed. That means adapting, a lot.

Can You Accept Advice From Others?

Pride is a thing. A really large, always-in-the-way type of thing that can make or break an entrepreneur. When you start to tell family and friends that you are thinking of becoming a business owner, you're going to get mixed opinions. Some of the people closest to you may not think it's a good idea. They'll even *beg you* to think otherwise. Here is where it's okay to have pride. In fact, you'll need it when everyone around you says not to take the leap, but your heart says go for it. Pride helps you stay committed to your business decision, regardless of whether or not people believe in you as an entrepreneur.

Where pride gets in the way is when you're too full of yourself to accept feedback. Having a business mentor (or more than one) is something that is incredibly helpful, for instance, but only as long as you're willing to listen to them and implement their advice. The mentors may not always be right, but they almost certainly know more than you, so keep an open mind.

A friend of mine went from business mentor to business mentor because he didn't like what he was being told by each mentor. It wasn't until he found a mentor who supported what his current plan was and didn't challenge him that he finally committed to a mentor. Is that mentor going to help him push the boundaries and expand his business? Most likely not.

You need to be able to have a moderate level of pride as a business owner, but also be open and willing to listen to advice that allows your business to grow.

Do You Have a Backup Plan?

A backup plan isn't a requirement. In fact, most entrepreneurs take the leap without one. But having a backup plan, or two to three, is more helpful than not.

What pushed me to finally take the leap was when I evaluated these four things:

1. I don't have a mortgage right now. We rent.
2. I don't have any children (but I do have a dog who sometimes feels like a child).

3. I have more than one business idea if my first one fails.
4. I have what it takes to get hired if worse comes to worst and I need to seek employment again.

If I "failed" as a business owner, my risk was pretty low. Does this mean that if you have a mortgage, a family, and aren't that hireable you shouldn't take the risk? Not by any means, but it does mean you should have some other kind of backup plan and direction of where to go if things start to go south. Give yourself a timeline to evaluate the success of your business. For me, I decided to give myself a year and if I didn't hit my expected income range, then it'll be time to evaluate whether I'm not doing the right marketing, the right pricing, the right services, etc., or if the business itself isn't working.

Will I ever need to pursue any of the backup plans I made for myself? Most likely not, but having them gave me the confidence and security I personally needed to pursue taking the leap.

Being an entrepreneur is messy. It's far from a glamorous 9 to 5, secure salary, paid benefits type of lifestyle. In fact, it's usually far more than 40 hours a week, doesn't come with great healthcare options, and you have to check emails on vacation. But that's okay. Being an entrepreneur is the most rewarding, and hardest, thing I've ever done. I've worked the longest hours, had to think critically and outside of the box like never before, and am continuously learning how to balance my personal life with this entrepreneurial life. I've also worked with dream clients, made relationships within the industry that I never would have before, and now have the opportunity to travel the world doing what I love most.

The entrepreneurial journey is a beautifully challenging one. It's one I think certain individuals like ourselves are born ready for. Being an entrepreneur is something that's built deep inside of us and doesn't leave our thoughts until it's pursued. Sometimes you just need to wake up, smell the coffee, and take the leap.

Nothing But A Number: Forget Your Age, Offer Value

MATTHEW PALM

How old does this guy think I am?

I remember thinking as I sat in front of Robert, a top healthcare executive, trying to convince him to work with my company.

Not kidding, that was all that was going through my head. No questions about his business, pain points, overall strategy, or anything else I was trained to ask. I couldn't even come up with a canned pitch about the services I represent. Hell, I wasn't even thinking about my go-to line about the weather (which is crazy, that one works every time).

No, all I could think about was how Robert has been in the business longer than I have been walking this earth, and he *must* see right through me for the young con artist that I am. What could I possibly tell this guy that he has not already heard from every other 23-year-old sales rep that has sat in front of him throughout his career? Sure, I had spent over a year obsessing over learning every single thing I could about my industry and had already started building my own book of business, but that could not possibly matter.

I shouldn't even be here, I must be wasting his time, I convinced myself.

But then something happened that changed the way I view myself, and more importantly the way I will view my business for the rest of my professional life.

Before I had time to blurt out "You got me, I'm only 23!" to the made-up question I had earlier fabricated, Robert started asking *me* questions. Actually ... not just questions, he was asking me for *advice*!

"How do you go about x?" and "What has been your experience with y?" he asked while on the edge of his seat, seeming truly interested in my knowledge of the industry and organization I represented.

Now let me say that I typically do not have an issue keeping my composure in unexpected situations, but I will admit that for a split second during this conversation I was at a loss. My mind was racing with how I could possibly answer his questions, and why he would even take the time to address 23-year-old me as an equal. *Was he just messing with me? Was it April Fool's Day?* I glanced down toward my watch. *Nope, June 14th.* I also saw that we are 5 minutes into the meeting and he hasn't made a comment about my age yet, what is the deal?

And then, before I could totally derail the conversation by blurting out one of these insane thoughts, it slowly became obvious that not once had the question of my age even crossed this man's mind. I began to realize that, as was likely the case with countless meetings I had been in before this one, I had completely constructed this age barrier for myself. I was horrified by the fact that I must have been missing opportunity after opportunity simply because I could not get past the fact that I was younger than almost all my peers. In that very moment, I made a deal with myself that I would not let trepidation around my own age prevent me from success ever again.

So, I took a breath, looked Robert in the eyes, and unloaded 23 years of wisdom on him (okay, that is a bit of an exaggeration, but I knew I had good insights to share). I was not apprehensive about asking him questions, I was not afraid to admit when I did not know an answer to his questions, and I openly discussed my experiences (both positive and negative) in my business with him. Our conversation went thirty minutes over our allotted time, and we built a rapport that has now grown to a level stronger than ever, almost a year later. Thanks to Robert, I am able to view myself not as an early 20-something professional, but as a sales professional who is an expert in his field.

And that is the real takeaway from all of this: to my clients out in the field, I am a true expert in what I do. They do not live and breathe my product, day in and day out, as I do. Just as they have made long-term commitments to their careers, I have dedicated so much time to learning and understanding my business that I would be doing them a disservice by not sharing that competency with them. And most importantly, I am representing something that can be the solution to serious business problems they are having, and by being self-conscious of my age I am obstructing my own opportunity to help find them a solution. How selfish of me to be concerned about my age when I have all this valuable experience just waiting to be shared!

Robert made it unacceptable for me to not deliver the value that I am capable of delivering, and I have carried that mindset with me in every step of my career since this momentous meeting. No longer will I sit in front of client waiting to be exposed as a 23-year-old fraud, but instead I walk in with a smile on my face and experiences to share.

For all the young professionals reading this, do not allow yourself to wait for your own Robert to appear. As a matter of fact, let's just solve this right here, right now. I will be your Robert: you have put the time in, you understand your business, you have value to share, your clients need you. Now forget your age and go make yourself irreplaceable!

Oh, and one last thing. I went back and asked Robert how old he thought I was a few months after our initial conversation. His answer: "Maybe ... 29? I don't know, why would I have been thinking about that?"

Exactly. If they're not thinking about it, why are you?

mattpalm92@gmail.com

Three Lessons For Getting Out Of Somewhere You Hate

CHARLOTTE IGO

I'm basically a hospice nurse. And I love hospice, I really do. Once upon a time, however, I worked at a hospice facility that I hated with the burning passion of a thousand suns. Most employees spent an inordinate amount of time planning their escape, myself included. My path to salvation came as a flippant offer from a doctor who had just been ridiculed at a staff meeting. His question was a simple one: "is there a way to do this business without hating it?"

Long story short, he asked me to go into business with him to open our own hospice. I told him despite my education and experience, I had 3 kids in college and no finances to spare for a startup proposition – but that if he started it, to keep me in mind. Then came the offer that changed everything. He said, "I'll finance it, you get 20%."

My initial answer was still no. I further explained that I could not be all things or do all things, but I knew the people who could. I told him the only way I could do it would be to pay at least three other people at least 5% each to cover the skills I didn't have. His short answer was, and I quote, "I don't care what the f*** you do with *your* 20%." This quote ultimately encapsulates the first lesson: **know who you need, and don't be greedy.**

I knew we needed these other roles to get a hospice off the ground, so I quartered my 20% to bring them on board. I know, it sounds incredibly altruistic (or incredibly stupid) to gift that kind of an opportunity. I saw it as an investment. I literally earned millions of dollars for other people in my role. I may be a nurse, but I'm a nurse with a business background that can make spreadsheets sing like an Italian diva. I knew what other roles were needed, and I knew having them would be the difference between getting 5% of something and getting 20% of nothing. I gained much more, both literally and figuratively, than I would have attempting this on my own. A little more expenditure to get the right people can gain exponentially higher profits in the long run.

So I invited three other players and we were in essence the Power Rangers of hospice. We grew to be quite successful, won awards … and then had a rather ugly work divorce in the end. This led me to the second lesson: **know your business partners well**. As a collective the hospice power rangers believed in investing in the people we worked with, and like all investments there was a monetary value associated. The doctor wanted more of the profits to go into personal bank accounts. The rest of us felt differently. Things imploded from there.

Partnerships are very similar to marriages. Divorces happen every day, and it's always a good idea to discuss things like children, faith and home ownership dreams before you get married. It's an equally good idea to have a few discussions before you sign an operating agreement. Oops. My bad. We should have dated a little longer, as it were.

The final lesson comes from developing the new hospice in contrast to the hellish old one: **it's okay to expect the best**. The companies I own now are not all the same. But they do all have the same three non-negotiables for quality performance.

- Be Good.

I don't care what the position is. Be good at it. In fact, be great. Nurse? Be a great nurse. File clerk? Be astounding at alphabetizing. If you want a great organization, hire good people and expect great things. By and large people will rise to the occasion.

- Be Compliant.

Again, I don't care what position, or even what industry. Follow all rules, guidelines and laws. Dot every "i" for Medicare. Don't speed when driving. Always pay every for every minute of overtime. Following the rules every time makes it easier in the long run. Don't be sleazy, cheap or cut corners. It's bad for business.

- Be Nice.

I've let really great clinicians go because they were a**holes. I work a lot. I want more than a great agency; I want one I enjoy working at too. When the assumption is everyone is doing their best, but mistakes still happen because we are human, there should be no reason to lay the finger of blame on anyone. When everyone is working for a goal rather than for recognition, it's easier to work together. It shouldn't be the Hunger Games, for Pete's sake.

This final lesson has been the most meaningful in my long-term success. I have learned it's not too much to ask because every day the people I work with meet these expectations. The fact that they do makes it possible for me to reach further professionally, which ultimately benefits everyone that works for me. We all invest in each other.

So if you've had enough and are ready to strike out on your own, remember these lessons as you do. They helped me; they'll help you.

Your Talent Is The Gift That Keeps On Giving

KIMBERLY ALLEN

Don't sit down and wait for the opportunities to come. Get up and make them!
                                                    —*Madam C.J. Walker*

At our core, writers desire three things: the ability to write what we love, get our work published, and be fairly compensated for our efforts. But if you haven't authored a book–even a badly written and/or edited one–you're likely not considered a "real writer" in some circles. I bought into this notion for a while, pigeonholing myself into believing there's only one road to writing success. This works the same way for most entrepreneurs – until you've done X, you're not a real coach, a real business owner, a real success.

How does one overcome this mindset? By remaining open to all of the ways your talent can be employed, and using those experiences as stepping stones towards your ultimate goal.

You can start by making the necessary investments of time and money into your craft. Whether you choose to attend college or gain knowledge in other ways, get educated on what it takes to sustain working as a successful writer or whatever you are and the different ways you can get there. Don't be afraid to branch out of your comfort zone. Invest time with people who share similar ambitions and interests but above all else, seek out those who are already well versed on where you want to be. Always positively visualize and speak life to your aspirations, and take logical, deliberate steps towards that end.

While en route to your purpose don't dismiss opportunities that correspond with your goals, even if the packaging happens to look a little different than what you originally imagined. For example, working in a newspaper setting was never something I aspired to. However, the opportunity to write for my college newspaper also offered the chance to try my hand at editing, where I learned many useful techniques that still resonate. This led to my first paid job copyediting book reviews and recommending those suitable for publication.

These initial experiences introduced me to the world of editing, a role I now enjoy as much as writing.

Those experiences also opened the door to my first post-college writing gig: authoring a weekly blog column for the *Atlanta Journal-Constitution*. Again, this was not the career path I envisioned, but it allowed me to continue writing, get published, and operate in my gifts.

Don't Give Your Gift Away. Despite getting hired for the only two writing/editing-related positions I'd ever applied for at the time, when I began my freelancing career I either worked for free or at less than the going rate.

I once offered to write for a local community magazine for free to help shore up the area's image. The publisher refused. As a fellow creative who had given away her fair share of talent, she firmly believed in paying people for their work. She was right; thinking back on the times that I did work for free, when asked to do extra I resented it and rarely delivered my best. Her invaluable lesson coupled with mutual respect led to years of writing for this publication, and I was eventually promoted to managing editor.

Free labor is acceptable in some situations, such as internships, to gain experience and exposure. But just know there will always be those looking to siphon your talent as long as you allow it.

I attended a seminar where the speaker waxed poetic about how women let others take advantage of – and effectively steal – their talents and gifts. If women knew their worth, they would always demand pay worthy of their skills, she said. Inspired, I approached the speaker afterwards and introduced myself (we shared a mutual client who consistently pays me for my work, so my name was recognized). I offered my business card, asking to be considered for future projects. Seemingly impressed, the speaker promised to get in touch. But when we reconnected, the speaker "cried broke" and asked me to edit an entire book at such an absurdly reduced rate I may as well have worked for free. (And had this person caught me a few years earlier, I probably would have!) So much for the message of demanding worthy compensation.

At its core, the creative realm is no different than corporate America. People will make promises they have no intention of keeping in order to tap into your talent and/or connections. Whenever you consider working for free, remember that there is nothing more fulfilling than getting paid to do what you love, so don't sell yourself short! You *will* cross paths with the right client(s) who values everything you bring to the table.

Recognize That Your Talent Is Personal. Whether you are a writer putting words to paper or an artist brushing colors onto a canvas, creative types express–and expose–themselves through their work. Sharing your work with the world doesn't always feel as satisfying as the process of creating it.

The point of being artistic – or entrepreneurial – is to share something unique and distinct that only you can produce. But the bottom line is, not everybody is going to respect your style or appreciate your talent. Don't let others drown out your voice based on their limited understanding of what they believe your type of creative should sound like.

Further, no matter the source, negativity can induce procrastination and a level of perfectionism that ensures you never complete a project. Does criticism feel good? No, but constructive feedback is necessary for improvement. So instead of getting discouraged, use those feelings to fuel your own personal inferno. If the advice received hinders instead of helps, absorb what is of use and seek balanced opinions from trusted sources–even if you have to pay an expert to get it. Take a step back and channel that energy, passion, and sometimes even frustration, into your project.

The tools needed to successfully maintain your investment include dedicating time not only to writing, but also networking and education. I attend at least one writing/editing related event per month to stay in the loop professionally and socially, because you never know where your next opportunity or idea will come from. Find a supportive yet honest writing group or friends/family that will hold you accountable while offering opinions you can trust. But most importantly, keep creating. Pursue your passion relentlessly and your gift will eventually return in kind.

www.KAllenCommunications.com

Section Three: Uncommon Knowledge

Working With People

JEREMY MARGENT AND ADAM MARGENT

Growing up, kids want to work as something different every month. Adam wanted to drive trucks and Jeremy wanted to design video games. Then we both wanted to be athletes, and then coaches. One might assume they will live where they are being raised, or dream to live in an exotic or popular city. When you graduate high school or college you reach a crossroads where you need to define your path. Often overlooked, as everyone stresses about their job title or salary or what company you will work for, is who the management and colleagues are that you will be working with. Regardless of where one may end up and how intelligent or hardworking an individual is, those outlying factors are just as important. Over the course of our careers, we have found that the business relationships we have had, both good and bad, have taught lessons that are integral for success and happiness. A person needs to be very dynamic when developing business relationships in order to make any working or employment situation work well and remain enjoyable!

The first lesson we learned is the importance of connecting with others. Teachers often emphasize the importance of networking and collaborating because "that is what it's going to be like in the real world." They stress the fact that once you graduate you are going to have to meet different individuals and personalities from all backgrounds of life, regardless of where you are. Lo and behold, universities are right (just look at all the different collaborators and authors of this book)! As your career progresses the people you have to work with, build relationships with, and trust become a very wide-ranged, eclectic group of professionals. Those connections can lead to a job, an employee, or even a feature in a book!

The second takeaway from our business relationships is harnessing the power of synergy. As much as we like to believe we can get almost anything done ourselves, the truth of the matter remains you achieve greater things working with others. It is important to be flexible and have a dynamic personality when collaborating with your peers, colleagues, and management. Everyone has something to bring to the table, so you have to be open to everyone's opinions, and understanding to where they are coming from. This way you can learn how to listen and respond effectively. You will often find that even if you may disagree with a suggestion or opinion, there is an aspect of it that is helpful.

A third important lesson we've extracted from our relationships, and which has been emphasized by working with family, is the importance of communication. As the business structure among family members takes place it is important to communicate clearly and effectively. When you begin any new job, or relationship for that matter, you must be patient and recognize the person you are dealing with, and in what particular setting the relationship and communication is going to take place in. A wise woman once told me "It is not what you say, it is what they hear." If you know someone is stressed out, it might not be the best to be overly aggressive when speaking or directing them. If someone does not work hard and needs motivation, you might have to be a bit more vocal and repetitive to get them to do the tasks at hand. You must communicate properly in each different setting.

The last takeaway I have from my business relationships is one specific to working with family. When working with family, you have to be able to separate the business relationship from the personal relationship. This is a lot easier said than done, but is vital to keep in mind to make sure one relationship does not affect the other. You hear stories all the time of families working together that end up torn apart, and other stories of families successfully growing their business together. If ego and stubbornness get in the way your family most likely will not have a success story. Those are personal traits that have to be put on the back burner when discussing business, to make sure the best decisions are made for the business. Arguments might ensue, but there is a hierarchy in place as to who approves the decision. If it is your job to just make suggestions, leave it at that.

We own and manage a short-term leasing company operated through AirBnB. We have a very similar mindset of operating a business from the way we were brought up, but there are often times an unforeseen circumstance arises that has to be figured out. After a short discussion we generally know what has to be handled to remedy the issue, and who is responsible in doing so. Giving and understanding the set of responsibilities among team members is crucial when problem solving (regardless of whether or not they are family). Jeremy tends to deal with the day to day operations of the AirBnB business, while Adam focuses more so on maintenance and home improvement. We both enjoy driving around and prospecting new properties and ideas, but we understand the expectations that have to be done to make the business run. This way too, if a disagreement does arise, there comes a time where one person does take the lead and the other one has to listen a bit more.

Most careers take a very unpredictable path. As a business person you will have to encounter many different business partners in a variety of settings. Some of your business relationships might be very brief, and only business oriented. You might just know that person as a voice on the other phone line. Other business relationships might last a lifetime, until the other person is a great friend or even feels like your family member. As in life's relationships, business relationships are dynamic, and so you must be too! Family or not, whether your business wins, loses, or draws, the relationships you form will remain vital to future success.

What Will You Fall For?

JAMES RANSON

Hey, did you know "gullible" is written on the ceiling?

Ha! Made you look.

Okay, maybe not – we all probably heard that one back in second grade. But in business and entrepreneurship circles these days, this prank is alive and well – and it's about as funny to fall for as it was in second grade, only worse. Because the punchline isn't "made you look" anymore. Now it's "made you pay."

Raise your hand if you've ever bought an information product, joined a mastermind or training group, attended a conference or event or retreat, hired a coach, or paid for an online program because of a clever sales page, a persuasive speaker, or an excited mass email from a high-profile expert.

Now keep your hand up if whatever you bought didn't turn out the way you thought it would. The product or program was unhelpful, the mastermind was a glorified Facebook group, the training was elementary, the conference was a vehicle to sell you more things, the coach was distant or impersonal or didn't fit you, and above all none of them got you the results the sales page, speaker, or email led you to believe they would.

Keep your hand up if you still had to pay for that thing no matter how little it helped you, either because you signed a contract saying so or you were just too lazy or forgetful to take advantage of a 60-day refund guarantee. Keep it up if you went into debt to pay for it. Keep it up if paying for the thing is still impacting your financial situation today. And keep it up if you haven't just done this once, but several times.

Is your hand still up?

Mine is.

It's really easy to be a gullible entrepreneur today. Aside from the fact that those sales pages and speakers and mass emails are designed to sell us things, there's something about being entrepreneurs that makes us *want* to buy what they're selling.

Part of it is the dream of quick and easy success, of course. But many of us also feel like we're *supposed* to buy these things – like it's what entrepreneurs *do*. There's major peer pressure around this kind of spending. We entrepreneurs compare notes on the groups we've joined, the retreats we've attended and the coaches we've hired the way high schoolers gossip about essay grades and prom dates. We treat four- and five-figure program purchases like badges of honor – all the more so if we go into debt to cover them. We even came up with a perfect euphemism for this kind of spending: "investing in ourselves." (Because when you're investing in something, that implies you're going to get a return – and that makes the up-front and/or ongoing costs worth it, right?)

All of this combines to create a shared mindset among entrepreneurs that tells us *the more money we spend "investing in ourselves," the better we are at being entrepreneurs*. Our very self-definition becomes wrapped up in how gullible we can be. Each new purchase tells us we must be doing it right, even as we struggle to pay off the last ones. We're unable or unwilling to see that what we're really doing is wandering a giant casino floor, and each email or sales page or speaker is just one more flashing slot machine.

But our own minds are only half of the problem. The other major factor is that there are far too many slot machines: experts, gurus, speakers, coaches, authors, bloggers, podcasters, and yes, entrepreneurs, whose focus is *selling things to you* rather than *creating things that will benefit you*.

This is a subtle but powerful difference. When the goal is sales, the seller doesn't typically care if the product or service is right for you, if it fits your individual situation or needs, if you're comfortable working with them, if you can afford it, if you ever actually use the product or service, if it gets you any results at all, or if they never talk to you again. The only thing about you that matters is whether you pull out your credit card. This is, perversely, why so many sellers put so much effort and money into sales pages, speaking to sell, and cross-promotion to their acquaintances' email lists. The goal is to find as many gullible people as possible and appeal to their gullibility from a distance, so none of them ever get a real face-to-face chance to see through the salesy smokescreen (at least until after they've paid).

Conversely, entrepreneurs with the goal of creating something that benefits people are much pickier about who they sell to. These people want to see their customers *succeed*, not just pay. They'd rather turn down sales than work with the wrong people. They may write or speak or advertise to a degree, but they're often too busy working and creating (and yes, making good money) to spend a lot of time promoting themselves. If you want to buy one of their offerings, they'll take the time and effort to find out how (or if) that offering will get you the results you want and be worth its high price tag – and if it won't, they won't let you buy it.

Who would you rather buy from? And who do you think would help you be a better entrepreneur?

The truth is, being a good entrepreneur has nothing to do with how much you spend. Instead of looking at your business "investments" as a metric for success, try looking at how much value you're giving to your customers and whether that value is translating to actual income. If you do find a coach or a program that *really* works for you, it's probably worth paying for. But you're perfectly capable of building a business without those things – and you don't need to hamstring yourself trying to pay for them just because a speaker or sales page tells you to.

The well-known adage says that if you don't stand for something, you'll fall for anything. And in our early days of entrepreneurship, when we're still figuring out what we stand for, it's easy to fall for the "made you pay" tricks of the first kind of seller – sometimes at a huge financial and emotional cost. But fortunately, once we fall for a few it gets easier to spot them coming. And as we learn to stand for ourselves, our needs, and our integrity, the gullible desire to buy our way to success gradually falls away.

themasterwordsmith.com

Contrarian

SCOTT ANDERSON

con·trar·i·an, n. – someone or something opposing or rejecting popular opinion

"Be greedy when others are fearful and fearful when others are greedy."
—Warren Buffett

This is the greatest advice and oftentimes the hardest to take. Who else do you think of when you hear contrarian? Perhaps Bill Gates, Steve Jobs, Richard Branson, John D. Rockefeller, Oprah Winfrey, Henry Ford, Roger Bannister ... the list goes on.

The list is enormous and is synonymous with lists such as the world's billionaires, the people who built America, titans of industry, etc. These men and women were the ones that broke the mold of being normal. They achieved greatness by putting themselves out there for ridicule and carving out a new path never before traveled; they took the risks others were not willing to take.

Being a contrarian takes great patience, self-discipline, and an iron will that can't be defeated by the naysayers, skeptics and pessimists that will always try to tear it down. One must dig deep and determine exactly why it's their mission in life to resolve "this problem" or they will find themselves down a slippery slope of depression and self-doubt. If your vision is not strong enough, you won't succeed. The reason you're pushing forward towards this solution must have such depth that only incapacitation or death will stop you.

Elon Musk is going to colonize Mars. When asked if he has ever thought he might fail, he responded, "no, failure is not an option. Not unless I'm dead or incapacitated."

Imagine putting farmer, software entrepreneur, real estate investor and venture capitalist into the same biography? Well, I'm a farm boy who fell in love with business when watching Warren Buffett and Bill Gates speak at the University of Nebraska while I was there for college. My path from farming to investment banking on Wall Street to returning to the farm was far from the norm; then add in starting a financial software company for farming and doing venture capital and real estate investments all over the United States. That's pretty far from any one of those individual paths, however it's what I decided would be the best way for me to achieve my vision as a businessman.

You too have the same opportunity to bend your path to your own vision. It's not necessary to follow the same track as others have before; rather blaze your own trail regardless of whether or not it makes sense to others. If you want something bad enough, you must be willing to lose it to get it. I don't know how many times people have tried to tell me "it won't work," "that's not normal," and "I don't get what you're doing."

I share my path with you to inspire you to take risks, put yourself out there, and follow your vision. Don't be afraid to follow a path less traveled and diversify, especially if people tell you that you can't do it or it's impossible. People thought it was impossible for the human body to run a mile in under four minutes until Roger Bannister did it. Then thousands more did it. You can go as far as you can see, then once you get there, you'll be able to see further. Go and make your vision a reality and the impossible the normal. Society and evolution depends on visionaries with crazy ideas and unusual paths – the contrarians, if you will. I encourage you to go be one.

Invaluable Or Insignificant: Undeniable Skill Not Required

ANDREW PRATER

Game changers in sports and business separate themselves because they recognize the process to becoming an invaluable asset while most, unfortunately, quietly remain insignificant. I learned this truth firsthand as a professional baseball player, which created an awareness and belief that we can all become an invaluable asset in any environment regardless of whether or not we possess undeniable talent or skills.

In baseball, coaches play the best nine for *that game*, not necessarily the best nine players. I benefited from this, because early in my professional baseball career I was labeled a defensive specialist. As much as I wanted to be an undeniable force on offense, and was not satisfied with my one-dimensional label, I didn't focus on things out of my control. Instead I stayed focused on the process of becoming an invaluable teammate and one of the best nine on the roster. A defining moment occurred early one season, when some uncharacteristic success at the plate was becoming a distraction. My batting average was at a brief career high and I was getting excited. One afternoon our hitting instructor that season stopped by my locker to remind me to stay humble and stick to the process because .300 hitters *always* hit .300, not just for a few games. It was early in the season and he knew that if I started to focus on sustaining success as a hitter I could easily become insignificant.

I don't own a t-shirt that says, "Baseball is Life," but I am very thankful that, in spite of myself, I learned the process to becoming an invaluable asset – which in turn helped extend my playing career well beyond what my talent deserved. The process has three parts: **Be On Time, Focus on Substance Over Image, and Build Relationships.**

I believe in making a strong impression as often as possible. If you are satisfied with just making a strong *first* impression, you are selling yourself short. The mindset for making sustainable strong impressions starts with being on time *all of the time*. This is an absolute to the process and requires no special skill or ability, it simply requires effort. "Life happens," but when arriving on time is an absolute, no one knows you had a flat tire because you called a cab. When you are not on time,you become a distraction, become the focus of negative unwanted attention, and are forced to begin conversations with an apology or an excuse. Invaluable professionals are driven by punctuality and understand that punctuality is a fountain of free positive publicity. I had a coach in college that said, "Five minutes early is five minutes late." He demanded that we discipline ourselves to give enough time to make adjustments with the unforeseen, because he knew that five minutes early was cutting it too close. Punctuality breeds productivity, and both are fingerprints of an invaluable asset.

Image will attract but substance will sustain. My transition from *playing* baseball into the *business* of baseball was built on the principle of building substance before image. I observed others promote their sexier baseball career achievements or their baseball cards and glossy 8x10's, only to find that neither were helping their customers achieve results or reach personal goals. Instead of trying to compete with the image portrayed by my competition, I focused on the substance of my brand. I quickly became an invaluable resource by prioritizing preparation and predictability. Clear and timely communication is a byproduct of preparation and allows you to operate in a predictable manner, allowing both employees and clients to thrive. I further separated my brand by developing a unique hitting program, which drew attention to the substance and content I had to offer rather than my image and personal achievements as a hitter (or lack thereof). I could not go back and rewrite my resume, achievements, or batting average, but I could draw from my past experiences to create an invaluable component of my brand.

Developing authentic relationships is another huge component to becoming an invaluable member of any team, in business or sports. Relationships will challenge your sense of entitlement and should not be predicated on what you will get *gain* from them; rather, on what you *bring* to them. Early on, I learned that the value of building relationships could make the world smaller and provide instant validation and credibility when needing to open doors or make a connection. In my circle, I am surrounded by so many unique individuals whose personal testimonies through different life stages could help me navigate my path more clearly. I was fortunate during my transition from player to businessman to cultivate several authentic relationships with successful people who helped me begin the foundation for my brand. One mentor would make the subtle statement, "read about it," from time to time, reminding me that if you are going to put yourself out there and do something, then separate yourself with front-page-worthy innovation, effort and news; essentially make it your own. Success in business is about people. Transactions and deals will fall apart, but relationships will weather the storm in business and in life.

Whether you're playing baseball or running a business, these three lessons will serve you well in becoming invaluable – no matter what skills you bring to the table.

aprater@baseballsolutions.com

Five Keys To High Performance
No Matter Your Industry

TODD SNYDER

Being an entrepreneur is rewarding, but definitely has its challenges. I own six businesses – all quite different – from professional racing to cosmetic dentistry to software. And each experience has taught me some fundamental rules that I encourage any entrepreneur to apply to be successful, to have fun and to not burn out.

The following five keys to success have allowed me to benefit from each business, and keep a work-life balance:

1. Know Your Limits, Strengths and Weaknesses

You can't be everything to every business. Businesses need marketing and promotion, sales, finance, human resources – even if you were an expert in all of those things, there are only so many hours in the day.

Concentrate on what you do best, and delegate other responsibilities to professionals with the expertise you either do not possess, or don't have the bandwidth to handle. Your business will be better for it.

And it's important to know your own strengths and weaknesses. You may think you're great at marketing, or that finance and payroll are easy. But if the data and results don't support that opinion, it's time to change it.

Work with people you trust, and ask for their honest feedback. Surrounding yourself with "yes" men and women will be detrimental to your ability to determine your strengths and weaknesses.

2. Have Passion for What You Do

It may sound cliché, but there's a reason why you so often hear "love what you do." If you can't wake up every day excited about what you're promoting, selling or investing in, how do you expect your employees and customers to be excited?

I enjoy something different with each one of my businesses, which clearly are varied. The passion is obvious with racing – what a rush! But with dentistry, it's a different kind of exhilaration, and extremely rewarding, to help people smile and have confidence in themselves. And I lecture all over the country to help other dentists be successful, which has its own rewards as well.

Do I love every aspect of every business I own? Of course not. That's an impossible expectation. But as long as you have passion for at least some aspect of your business, and it will come through in your results.

3. Invest in High-Potential Growth

Passion is of course important, but so are profits. No one wants a business that isn't profitable and growing. When I look for businesses to start up or invest in, I look for growth potential, measured by how low the overhead is to get started and the scalability of the business.

Can it start small and grow big? Will I be able to support that growth through early profits? How many people do I need to get it off the ground, and what are the start-up costs? Can we create the product on our own at first, then eventually outsource as orders increase?

Some entrepreneurs thrive on high-risk ventures – I thrive on high potential with lower risk, and it's worked out very well for me. Do your homework and be sure to examine every angle before jumping in.

4. Create a Competitive Advantage

In order to succeed, you have to possess advantages over similar companies in your market. To discover your competitive advantage, you need to ask yourself a series of questions regarding your business.

Who is your audience, and what problems does your product solve for them? Put yourself in your customer's shoes – what is the advantage they gain from your product or service? How can you create a winning business model based on a unique offering to stand out against your competitors?

The secret to gaining a competitive advantage in any business is to find a niche where you can be either the best – or the only – company with the product or service. Find out what everyone else is doing and then do something different. Your competitive advantage can be based on a unique skill, product, intellectual advantage, or offering unique hours of operation.

The alternative to uniqueness is to be ordinary, and sell the same product or service with the same price as everyone else. For example, many general dentists seem to offer the same services, and then offer their services at a reduced fee. Their only competitive advantage is price, the same as a Walmart or Costco. A true competitive advantage for a dental office could be that they offer an identifiably different type of care, service or product; such as cosmetic dentistry – which is more profitable, requires more training, different branding/marketing, and few offices offer. It's a reason for patients to choose that office over all the others – and even pay more for that choice! That's' a true competitive advantage.

5. Focus On Mental and Physical Health

Too often, hard work can compromise relationships, opportunities and life quality. It's extremely important to take time to revitalize the mind, soul, muscles and heart, especially if you're working hard. You should be eating right, getting enough sleep, exercising, building strong ties with friends, family, and community. And, as much as possible, minimize your stress!

The most important relationships in your life are with yourself, your family and friends. So treat yourself well and make life worth living. You want to look back on your life's accomplishments and success in not only business, but in relationships and your effect on the world. Offset hard work with well-deserved play time in your areas of interest, as well as with friends and family. When reinvigorated from time off one can make greater strides in business. My favorite escapes are family time and endorphin-releasing, adrenaline-filled sporting activities like surfing, snowboarding, working out and professional car racing. "Recharging the personal battery allows for higher sustained performance."

You don't have to own multiple businesses like I have, or be delving into several different types of products and services, to follow the five pieces of advice I've laid out here. They can apply to any business of any size and purpose. Best of luck in your endeavors.

www.drtoddsnyder.com

Staying Unscripted In A Copy/Paste World

GEORGE MOCHARKO

The bulk of my work over the past decade of my career comes down to one action: Copying and Pasting.

No, not with scissors and glue like you did for Kindergarten projects; I mean punching the keyboard keys CTL + C, then CTL + V. This action of extending my left pinkie and tapping down my left-hand index finger happens so much when I'm using a computer, I do it without thinking anymore. I use it when I want to look up a subject I want to search for in Google, or when I want to save time retyping my email into an online form.

When I first started working as a communications professional, I thought that there would be an abundance of time for me to sit and concentrate and focus on writing, composing work of original thought – thus giving me the unique ability to hone my chops as a writer to create beautiful prose on command, and on deadline.

The reality was not as glamorous. My job demands required that I copy/paste information from a pre-existing bit of content, to then surgically insert that copy into a newer document. My job was, in short, to do whatever it took to keep the organization's message consistent, grammatically correct, and keep from reinventing the wheel.

Usually it was a website, newsletter, or brochure. Sometimes, it was a long-form technical document, business proposal, or a press release. Almost never was it anything creative.

To be clear, using copy/paste is not plagiarism. That's only when you copy/paste someone else's ideas and pass them off as your own. We never plagiarized other sources; we merely plagiarized ourselves.

I use desktop publishing software for work. I'd find a Word document on a server to find some copy to recycle and then copy/paste it into a word box and flow it onto the page. Then, I'd save and print the document for a never-ending round of proofreading edits. After making those changes I'd send the document to the printer and put the publication "to bed" – a bit of jargon editors like to say self-satisfyingly when they unwittingly think a project is complete.

Never mind that phrase. These documents kept waking up, because I'd always find twelve minor proofreading errors when checking against the blueline that came back from the pre-press operator. Using copy/paste to compose something wasn't all that efficient because I'd still have to go back and make changes to the copy before it was finally done. I swear I would have caught those mistakes myself if I hadn't been so bored reading the same damn message over and over.

So why do we use copy/paste as professionals? The standard answer is to keep things consistent. Yet that word consistency sticks in my craw, because underlying this little word reveals a larger idea: such as why large organizations are unable to be the first to do anything original, or even deal with change. There's an "if it ain't broke, don't fix it" attitude at nearly every organization, and it comes down to them making sure that nothing comes across as "off-message."

Late in my career, it struck me that I wasn't the only one doing this copy/paste routine for my job: Nearly everyone is on autopilot using copy/paste for their careers:

- We Copy/Paste our presentation styles and PowerPoint slides so we can be taken seriously.
- We Copy/Paste the dress clothes we wear to work so we can fit into our office culture.
- We Copy/Paste our behavior in the Boardroom to get the results we want.

(Oh, and by the way, when I wrote that, I copy/pasted the first section of each bullet.)

Every time we copy/paste something, it means we're scared of sticking out and trying something new. Communicating with originality helps people remember you, because your authentic way of seeing the world and expressing yourself helps create your unique personal brand.

It's not easy: Office culture has a way of making people scared. The pressure to know the right answer. The pressure to keep things clinical, and our personal attitude distanced from the subject matter at hand. Copy/paste keeps us behaving in this manner without revealing anything about ourselves.

Most corporate messaging uses this distancing language – whether through business jargon, overly technical documents, and white papers. When a colleague or coworker uses this language, they're missing a real big chance to hear in your own words why something is important and truly create a bond with you.

We all know people who "walk-the-walk" and "talk-the-talk," to use a tired cliché. These folks look good on paper, and say all the right business buzzwords, yet for some reason their words don't communicate anything. Their pre-loaded scripts funnel into one ear and out the other, with your brain hearing a lot of white noise as a result.

That's because words lack a certain energy when they're parroted back. It's like a copy of a copy of a copy; the last iteration becomes degraded. And it's because that person sounds even sounds like they are reading from a script, not speaking from their innermost thoughts.

Once you've found your voice, make sure to raise it often so people can know your true worth. We are all so similar, and yet so different. Find what makes you different and connect from that place. The people that stand out to me that I've worked with, were the ones who were willing to go a little off-script for a moment. They were the colleagues I'd have personal conversations with. The ones who cared about me as a whole person and not just as a worker.

Sometimes knowing exactly what to say can help because you want to know your stuff, but let's not copy/paste everything in life. Say what's on your mind, in your own voice. You may not be saying the right words, but at least they'll be from the heart.

Stay unscripted. Because the heart oftentimes communicates better than the mouth.

george@geotechconsulting.com

Five Rules For Life

AISHA WAHAB

Life never goes as planned. You can't control every situation or interaction but you do have control over what you can do and how you move forward in life. There are Five Rules that will benefit anyone in any situation. These Five Rules can be applied to your individual life, professional life, and overall mindset. The goal of these Five Rules is to keep your eye on the prize and maintain constant progress forward in all aspects of life.

Rule 1: Always Invest in Yourself

This is the most important rule to live by. If you are juggling a family, a career and a social life, it is important to always remember to invest in yourself. Whether that investment is time alone at a gym or spa, a day off to get some rest or relax or do chores, or if you want to pursue a degree part time to build you up for the next phase. It is important to invest in yourself in all areas of life. Treating yourself to a new house, car, degree, or vacation allows you to treat yourself and be momentarily happy. Even if the investment is material, the investment pays off because it serves its purpose for you. If you are well rested, you will be more productive and alert. If you catch up on chores or the gym or something like that you will have peace of mind and know that you have invested in keeping your life balanced or your health a priority. If you pursue education, you will always learn something new, you will stimulate your brain, and you will gain attain knowledge. Each is an important way to invest in yourself.

Also, with regards to relationships, if you feel that you are investing too much time and energy into someone, pull back. This feeling is the same as chasing a shadow, you will never catch it and always be in the dark. But if you move towards the light in your life, the light that makes you happy and smile, the shadow will always follow you.

Rule 2: Never Settle

Never settle for the current setup or circumstance of life. If you have been at a job for years and are a master of what you do, there is always a way to improve a process and be more efficient. Constantly try new things, learn, and see what you can change. This will allow you to continue to use brain power even when you are not being challenged, it allows you to have new experiences, and constantly grow as a human being even when your circumstances are stagnant.

Rule 3: Only Compete With Yourself

We often overvalue other people's achievements and undervalue our own achievements. Whether you are a minority, have a less than stellar education, or something else, we often focus on the deficiencies that only we see. Comparing yourself to another person often results in depression, self-esteem issues, or even jealousy. The reality is that no one has walked a day in your life. Each person is deeper than another considers. Your life is unique, your journey is your own, and your future is what you make it. So always keep one eye on your past and one on your future. Your story is the only one that you need to be concerned with.

Rule 4: Always Help Others

It is important to give back to society. Whether you give your time every day or once a month, it is important to give back to the community you live in. There are many people struggling in life. Struggling to find themselves, struggling to survive, struggling in different capacities. Donating your time to your local non-profit, place of worship, schools, or community organizations, will not only help them but it also helps you. It helps you by giving you a sense of purpose, a sense of appreciation for what you have, and a sense that you can make a difference. People help others for many different reasons. Find something you enjoy and think you can help others with. For example, if you are a successful business person, you can always offer to help with resumes or business plans and in that area to those seeking guidance. You can apply this to any skill you may have or just help with current efforts at a local organization. Giving back builds relationships, cultivates community, and helps people that need it, just like you did at one point in your life.

Rule 5: Own Your Story

Don't ever shy away from who you are. Whether you are a woman, foster child, person of color, or didn't go to an Ivy League school. You are special.

You will run into people who treat you differently for many different reasons, people that are not kind, people that think they are better for no reason. Implicit bias is not easily recognized by anyone and the reality is that life and people are not always fair. The reality is that you are unique and not everyone knows your story or cares. If you meet someone with prejudice or a bias, you can't change them, but you also can't change who you are. You have to own it. Once you unapologetically own your story another person's opinion won't matter. Standing up for yourself forces others to respect you. Once you have made peace with who you are, where you come from, and what you overcame, you will be confident. With confidence, no one can dim your light.

These Five Rules are important to incorporate in your daily life because they allow for the pauses in life to be temporary. Your personal life, professional life, and overall mindset might be impacted by different circumstances but everything is temporary but the trajectory of the direction you are going is more permanent. Life is constantly changing and as you take the good with the bad, these Five Rules will keep you on track.

aishawahab.com

Trust And The Long Haul For Competitive Advantage

EDWARD FARRELL

Nearly 800 days ago I went out on my own. This act was less result of my own choosing but as a result of the influences of the market in Australia. In the early days I questioned what I had done; the money wasn't flowing, the work didn't feel right and a sense of isolation had overwhelmed me. However, I stuck to it and over time the reasons why I started manifested themselves into what has become a testament of who I am and why I went out on my own.

My name is Edward Farrell, I run a cybersecurity based in Sydney, Australia. I'm not a businessman, I'm a computer security enthusiast who happened to find himself as an accidental proprietor. Starting out on my own was an interesting choice. I'd left my former employer for a number of reasons but perhaps my core justification is more about how I chose to manifest myself and contribute to the industry I work in. Ultimately I wanted something meaningful to work in and where my work was valued. There are three qualities that kept me in good stead; presentation, trust & aiming for the long haul. When anything has fallen by the wayside, these have kept me going.

Image and outward presentation are far more complex than what we are all too often presented with. I'm a security nerd, this is my image without exaggeration or flamboyance and people rely on it as a source of trust. Today I dress in a suit, tomorrow I'll be in jeans and a comfortable business shirt. In my team there is no posing, no prima-donna approaches and no drama. Presenting an insincere image that focuses on stereotypes or domineering drama is a misinterpretation of our work and ultimately leads to a fatigued customer. I've always approached things the way I learnt in my 14 years as a volunteer lifeguard: walk into the situation cool, calm and lucid, this will alleviate more issues than contributing to the panic and stress that is often associated with cybersecurity. It also communicates a command presence and confidence, from which one can build trust.

A trusted relationship is the foundation for any firm where services, individual well being or security are involved. Security has been dominated by a 'fire and forget' product approach that means that a one-off sale is all that's required, and as a professional a vested interest in maintaining any semblance of quality or assurance is not required. This model serves no one but the salesperson pushing a self-fulfilling prophecy that eventually consumes a business through fear. I've tried to form a trusted relationship with my customers over the years that negates this model, and relies on paying for time as opposed to installing a product that may generate a sizable income but will do no good for anyone. It may sound enslaving, but this is where an individual like me lives. I intend to be here in many years to come, and this longevity has a greater purpose.

I also work in a technology industry; it comes and goes, it'll go into recession at some point or worst yet they attract individuals looking for a quick sale and a buyout. Information Security, or Cybersecurity as it has evolved into, has become something of a behemoth. I often find myself seduced by the image of a quick sell, an immediate win or some other impetuous end game and yet I know certainty and trust will be more valued. My father has been providing technology consulting services for 34 years, my accountant has been in business for a similar period, my mechanic worked on my parents' cars back in the 1980s. These are not big shot salespeople with whitened teeth and overpriced haircuts, they're real people who have dedicated their lives to a craft. It is something I feel we've lost in western businesses, a desire to go the distance over the immediate win.

While I often battle with the questions of showmanship, taking advantage of people or selling out, I come back to the things that have grounded me and I find solace in what I do. I ask myself what kind of world do we create when our motivation is purely financial? Can we not, as the tradespersons before us, find joy in something we're good at and translate this into something that sustains us and the world we exist in? This stoic approach might not yield millions of dollars or given any measure of success as we're all too often presented, but it has led me on a phenomenal journey that I intend to continue.

A business with sincerity and integrity at its core will win in the long run, and if nothing else, it's not a bad way to live, learn and leave this world a little better than we found it.

Six Lessons Learned In Starting, Running, And Selling A Business

ABED MEDAWAR

The following lessons are some of the most important ones I learned as the sole owner of an international shipping company I formed in 2000.

1. Partnership

The business was formed with a good friend. However, soon after we opened our doors, it was clear we had different sets of priorities and visions, and it was best to go our separate ways. I bought him out and continued on as a sole owner until the business was sold. In the years that followed, I learned to appreciate the enormous value of a business partner. My wife was always a great source for a bird's eye perspective on things, and I had key employees I could count on for specific issues, but I missed having a business equal who had as much to lose as I did. Someone to provide balance, help see the other side of an issue, and that can help make something happen or stop something ill-conceived or poorly thought through from happening. Some of my earlier decisions or actions were made out of emotion rather than careful deliberations. I was learning through trial and error, and in retrospect I am certain mistakes could have been avoided if I had the right equal partner.

2. Failure

Failure can be a very valuable teaching tool. I learned that as long as I stuck to my core values, exercised proper due diligence and believed in the concept, the subsequent failure of something was not as a reflection on who I am or my values and standards, but rather simply the failure of that project and for reasons I needed to understand. For example, a customer who controlled large volume of business was working for someone who was allegedly mismanaging his company and she was looking to leave. I saw an opportunity to open our first branch office in Dallas, TX built around her and her business. But how would we manage that remotely from our NJ office?

There were questions, there were risks, but there was also potential for great reward against reasonable expenses. About 6 months later, the project was clearly a failure. This person was very difficult to work with, very messy and disorganized and we decided to terminate our agreement and close that office. In terms of expanding the business and branching out, this was our first attempt and it was a significant failure. In the months that followed, I reflected on this attempt to open a branch office and learned some valuable lessons that we applied to another effort in Denver, CO at a later time. I learned to not allow the failure to shake my confidence and continue to believe in the fundamentals of the business and keep taking measured risks without the fear of failing.

3. Follow up

As a business owner, I was the director and producer of the show. If something didn't get done, if a vendor failed to give me what I needed by a certain time, if a customer failed to confirm that order by a certain point, if an employee didn't get back me, the first question I had to ask: did I follow up before it was too late? Did I persist? Was I driving the process? Was I proactive or reactive? I learned to not leave the fate of an important question, an inquiry, in someone else's hands but drive the process, to be in charge of whatever timeline needed to be followed. For example, I flag every email that requires a response for follow up and it sits in a separate folder along with other flagged emails. I go through that folder several times a day and I persist until I have what I need – especially if a customer is waiting on me. The last thing I want the customer to see is me reacting to their request for whatever action or response is pending from the vendor. I used to trust that others would get back to me and quickly learned that often just doesn't work. Blaming someone after the fact doesn't get me anywhere except to perhaps make me feel better that it wasn't my fault. In business though, that doesn't really matter. With time generally being a major component of everyday business, and often a valuable component in the formula of success, I learned I increased my chances for success when I proactively pursued results.

4. Opportunities

I learned that the worst of times can often lead to the best opportunities with a positive outlook. In my business, a failure by a vendor was often an opportunity to impress a customer with a timely fix. During the recent economic recession, we found key vendors that in past years would not even bother to return our calls or emails were struggling to find new business, and so were much more interested to work with us. We took advantage of those opportunities and formed new relationships that continue to this day.

5. Strengths and weaknesses

It didn't take long early on while growing the business to really figure out what I did well, that was the easy part. I enjoy service, I like to give it and I care a great deal about getting the job done the right way, pleasing the customer, and quickly moving on to the next task. The hard part was figuring out what I didn't do so well, such as accounting functions and human resources. I don't have the aptitude for in-depth financial analysis nor the patience for matters relating to human resources. I learned to play to my strengths, and work on my weaknesses whether through education and personal growth or tasking someone else better equipped with that particular responsibility or simply asking for help. That takes total honesty and can be brutal, but in the final analysis it has to be about what's in the best interest of the business.

6. Preparing to sell the business

The process of completing the sale of the business once the decision was made was daunting, but it didn't necessarily have to be that way. Throughout the years, we documented transactions very well. What we didn't do well was tie different aspects of those transactions together into clear and accurate reports as it wasn't a priority in our decision-making process. Our systems did generate some reports, but they were nowhere near detailed enough. Opportunities and forecasts drove decisions rather than a review of historical data. But to an investor, that data was significant, so selling the company without it proved a lot more difficult than anticipated. I learned the value of keeping extensive and detailed records – beyond basic financial reports – should I start another business.

Starting, running, and selling a business was a personal journey that taught me many more lessons than I wrote in this chapter. If you allow it, the growth and learning never stops. Throughout the journey that included potentially catastrophic events such as a lawsuit thatthreatened to close the business, a historic recession, and multiple wars, I always reminded myself of this quote by Eleanor Roosevelt: "The future belongs to those who believe in the beauty of their dreams." Perhaps the biggest lesson of all was to persevere through the most difficult of times as long as I believed in the beauty of my dream, like Eleanor said. I hope that lesson, as well as my other six, will help you as much as they have helped me.

mobileabed@gmail.com

Section Four: Powerful People

Your Rearview Mirror

GREG PLUM

How did you get your last job? How about the one before that? If you are like most, you got it from a referral by a friend, colleague, old boss, or maybe even a family member. Why is it, then, that each month over 100 million people turn to online services, such as Indeed.com, when they find themselves seeking their next career move?

According to the International Association of Employment Websites (IAEWS), most general employment websites see 11 – 30 applications per job, and unique monthly visitors numbering north of 50,000! How can you possibly expect to stand out in a playing field of this magnitude ... a playing field of people who don't know you?

If you take this path, I can promise you one thing: you will get rejection after rejection (if any response at all) for positions that you could easily do in your sleep. You will start to question your abilities and possibly even your own self-worth. Not a place any of us wants to be.

The more logical alternative is to recognize and nurture your network of advocates. Of course, we do this when we need to. When we need something – like a new job. But what about now, when we are gainfully employed? Why not maintain on-going, authentic, contact with those from our past? These people have worked with us, gotten to know our strengths, and lesser strengths, and they know, first-hand, the value we bring to any situation. These are the people we should be focused on. It is almost as if we are peering into a rearview mirror to see our way forward.

Think of it as a bank where you regularly make deposits. We make deposits to save for the future, when we will eventually reap the benefits of these deposits. We all know the concept of the time value of money ... what about the time value of *relationships*? Real relationships take years to develop, and become the true asset that can help shape your future, but only if you take the time to invest in them as assets. If not, those relationships will merely become people that you used to know.

There is another benefit that goes way beyond the future withdrawal ability from your relationship bank. Think back to the last time you re-connected with someone from a "previous life". How did that make you feel? How did the other person feel? It was likely a highlight of the day for both of you. Why not make it a habit?

But, we're busy ... how are we supposed to be able to cram in reminiscing sessions into our overflowing schedule? Simple, make it a part of that schedule. A process that is vital to your future success deserves a slot in your calendar.

A Real-Life Example

I have a friend, Glen, who is in the throes of a career conundrum. He spends 15 of his waking hours every weekday as a slave to a job that he has come to despise. As an outsider observing his situation, it seems obvious to me that he needs to take action, and quickly. While he wants to make a change, the challenge is how to even consider taking additional hours away from his family time to seek a new career opportunity. His situation is further complicated by his questioning his chosen career path.

In a recent conversation, we discussed his options. Together, we decided on an actionable plan – one that fit into his already hectic schedule. Glen committed to contacting his network of colleagues, former co-workers, and friends for a few minutes each day. The purpose of this would be to share his current situation, learn about what his contacts have been doing since they last connected, and identify possible ways to help each other. Yes, each other. While Glen is currently in need of assistance, he could absolutely help his counterpart in some way.

Like investing for retirement, the earlier you start, the better, but it is never too late to start investing in your future nest egg. But Glen is not a "networker." Can you relate to this? Many cringe at the thought of networking! This is different, though: simply keeping in touch with those that you have met in the past, and had developed a positive and healthy relationship. Period. Nothing scary or sleazy about it!

Where can Glen start? We decide he is going to take 15 minutes every morning, before he gets busy with his job, to send a simple email to 5 people from his contact list. EVERYONE has a contact list, regardless of the form that it has taken ... a software system that keeps track of contacts, a simple spreadsheet, or maybe even a good old-fashioned rolodex. Remember those?

Anyway, back to Glen ... by emailing 5 people each morning, people who know him, and hopefully like and respect him as a person (if not, why are they still in his database?), he will likely spark a dialogue with at least 2 of the 5. That is 10 new conversations per week, or 40 per month! These are 40 conversations with advocates who may be able to assist him, or give him an opportunity to assist them. If not, they certainly have their own networks of people who may have a need right within Glen's wheelhouse. Notice that we are expanding our scope by focusing on *people* and *not* a particular job type or industry. Glen's skills, much like your own, are easily transferrable to other industries, addressing his desire to explore new frontiers.

The Numbers Don't Lie

According to Lou Adler, author of Hiring and Getting Hired, "85% of critical hires are filled by networking." Why spend a single minute on a strategy that yields only a 15% success rate? Stop trying to convince strangers of your professional ability and your innate work ethic, and focus on those that already know you. The path to your future can best be seen by looking into that rear view mirror and focusing on your advocates, your champions: the people who already know you.

greg@plumUC.com

Entrepreneur Voices From A Corporate Past

SAM JACOBA

In early 2015, I hit major a crossroad in my life when I took an early retirement from Intel Corp. For several weeks, I struggled to decide on whether going back to corporate or to finally take a leap of faith and become a full-time entrepreneur.

I've explored several corporate roles in tech and other industries, but felt that my heart and mind are not leading me there anymore. The call of entrepreneurship is stronger now compared to my first early retirement in 2009 with Microsoft after twelve and a half years being in the company. During this time, I consulted with friends, other entrepreneurs, family members and my spouse about whether taking the leap will be the best for me.

Weighing their collective voices, I still struggled to make the decision to jump into the unknown. I'd gotten so used to corporate life having spent almost twenty years there that there are voices inside me that keeps on anchoring me to that world.

However, amidst these voices that kept me in my comfort zone, other voices in my corporate past urged me to move forward. The first came from Mike Hard, my hiring manager and first GM of Microsoft in the Philippines. We were in Atlanta for the Microsoft Global Summit when my colleagues and I saw Mike after he moved back to the US. Most of us felt uncertain after Mike left and during our conversation, Mike kept on telling us "do not be afraid." That assured most of us that everything is going to be all right even without him at the helm of the company.

I then recognized that fear is what kept me from crossing over and I faced it by learning more about what lies beyond. Fear grips everyone who ventures into the unknown, and the best way to conquer this is by learning more about it. So I dug in, devoured market insights, crunched numbers, analyzed studies, plugged into digital and physical mastermind communities, sought the wisdom of industry and business experts and aligned what I learned with my passion, purpose and potential. My fear was slowly replaced by excitement as the full picture of where I want to go unveiled before me.

Successful entrepreneurs I know have experienced fear at least once in their journey, and they have used that as fuel to pursue their dreams. Fear is what kept me in my comfort zone and out of my courage zone. Eventually, I made the jump, ran head on and bootstrapped two technology startups.

After several months of long nights and extended work hours, I was exhausted and another voice from my corporate past came back to me. "Always look after yourself," was what Richard Francis, third GM of Microsoft Philippines told me in his last day in the country. Richard was also my golf buddy and he always has a lot of advice whenever we play the game, more so when he's hitting pars and birdies.

Looking after oneself in the corporate world can have various dimensions but I needed this reminder when my health was deteriorating due to the blistering pace of launching startups. So I stepped back and became more mindful of balancing my work and leisure hours, and soon my health improved. I also took note of my energy peaks and tackled the biggest challenges during those times. This approached allowed me to systematically overcome the major obstacles that we faced as we introduce our services in our chosen markets.

There was also one point in my entrepreneurial journey that I felt giving up, when I was suddenly left in charge of our house when our house help retired prematurely. Since my wife works full time in corporate, I had to juggle managing housework, taking care of our three kids, and the two startup businesses. It was such an overload that I almost gave up on my entrepreneurial dreams.

It was at this critical stage that another corporate mentor from my past spoke to me. "Just enjoy life, Sam," Uday Marty said. Uday was Vice President and Managing Director of Intel Southeast Asia and he reminded me that you could find joy in any aspect of your life. He was always full of life, in and out of the office, and one of the smartest and kindest people that I know. His passion is to climb mountains and he was set to climb Mount Everest. He perished doing what he loved most. He was on a climb in Mount Rainier in Seattle in 2014 when an avalanche swept his whole team while they were sleeping at their base camp.

So for almost six months, I juggled housework with startup work. Due to the reminder from Uday, I began to view housework as acts of love to my wife and kids, rather than chores. I again valued the physical work and had fun by adding play elements like imaging that I was a river dragon spewing geysers whenever I water the plants in the garden. Or roleplayed that I was Anthony Bourdain whenever I prepared dishes in the kitchen. Eventually, we found dependable house help and I became more mobile again, and continued to work with my partners to grow the businesses.

Looking back, I'm glad that I listened attentively to Mike, Richard, Uday and all my other mentors in the past for they have given me relevant lessons that I now follow in my entrepreneur life. Today, I have new mentors and I always pay close attention to what they say and observe closely what they do, taking heart that they have been ahead of me and have paved the way for me to have a higher chance of success in business and in life.

Why I Buy Beers I Can't Afford

CHRIS SNOYER

When you're a young, broke student, beers are like gold. In college dorms, they're an entirely separate currency. I'll never forget the tallies that were diligently kept as we all passed beers around based on who was flush with "textbook money" or whose parents had most recently visited and left behind a case or two (Love you mom!). The difference between then and now (I hope) is that as adults, we don't have a general ledger tracking who owes who a Budweiser, two rum and cokes, or three bites of a footlong sub.

When I graduated and joined the working world, I made fast friends with a man who seemed to have no issue stepping in to buy that first round for the fellas (shocker, right?). I knew where he worked, and could reasonably assume he wasn't made of money, so one day I inquired about his apparently frivolous beverage budget. I was met with an interesting theory. He figured that about half the people he covered would repay him with a drink. 40% would conveniently forget him (or the group) on the next order, but that the remaining 10% would pay him back tenfold one day, via drinks or otherwise.

This piqued my interest, because it was clear that this was not some long-con he was playing to accumulate a wealth of whiskey sours. He was not keeping track of who fell into which categories, or of his total outlay. He was simply doing what he could to ensure the people around him were having a good time. (Oddly enough, we're still great friends to this day.)

As we mature, we tend to form more friendships outside of the bar than in, but this generous approach is quite transferable. I don't mean that I keep a sharing flask on me at all times, but I always try to provide value wherever possible, and have no expectation of a return. This can mean making an introduction for a friend looking for a new job, referring new business to a former employer, or helping a peer test the beta version of their new app.

Again, I don't keep a ledger, but I can reasonably assume that the more time I spend propelling and supporting others, the more people there are on this earth who want to see me win. I know this, because I'm lucky enough to have had many great friends and mentors of my own, and I'd love nothing more than to see THEM win. It's this feeling exactly that makes me wonder why so many people are so timid to ask for help. All of those people who are in a position to help you? They didn't get there alone. They'll have a laundry list of people who played a part in their success, and if they don't have amnesia, they're looking for a chance to jump in and pay it forward. (Okay, this isn't true of *everyone*, some people are just jerks ... but more people want to pay it forward than not, I've found.)

Successful people seem to have a common understanding. Unlike the number of drinks you can have in a night, or the number of drinks you can buy without missing rent, success is **not** finite. Success can take many forms and is not black and white, so we do not need to spend our time and energy trying to pry it from the grips of our peers. Rather than fighting over slices, we can grow the pie together. Go into "the red" on time invested in others (and the beers that may accompany this activity). Get past the small talk and take the time to understand what gets them out of bed in the morning. Help them if you're able (you always have something to give), and don't forget to ask for help. Vulnerability can yield a powerful connection!

Plain and simple: Helping another achieve their goals will do nothing to hinder your own. Whether you're buying rounds or making introductions, living a generous life will make you the person that people want to be around. If you do the math, you'll see that's payback enough.

Oh, and those jerks who are in it for themselves? They might end up with a nicer sailboat than you, but trust me, they'll be jealous of your crew.

Thanks for reading! The next round's on me.

www.withspiffy.com

The 33 Rule

SCOTT CARSON

The biggest lesson that I like sharing with fellow entrepreneurs is what I call the 33 rule. We all have a tribe of people that surround us. I'm a big believer in Seth Godin's idea that we also have different circles of influence. We all have families, friends, peers, colleagues, co-workers, and people that we're connected with online and in social media circles and things like that.

My basis for the 33 rule is the fact that of all those people in your life, you're only really going to make 33% of them happy automatically. Those are the people that like you, they love you no matter what. On the other side, you're going to have 33% of people in your tribe, group, followers, that don't like you. It doesn't matter what you do, they're going to dislike you. They don't like that you're a guy, a gal, your weight, you're too skinny, you're too pretty, you're too ugly, you're too loud, you're too quiet, you're too extroverted, too introverted, your breath stinks, your breath doesn't stink. Often, these people are jealous because you're out striving, trying to make yourself better, accomplishing goals, and trying to live a dream, when they don't have the drive to or the passion or the need to better themselves.

What we as entrepreneurs and business owners often get into is the problem of, if we do a marketing piece or something out there, we tend to gravitate towards those people, the few people out there that have something negative to say. But when we realize that we will never have 100% of people love us and want to work with us, we become a lot happier. Unfortunately, sometimes that 33% to the far right are some of our closest friends, family, relatives, spouses, and sometimes we should stop spending time with them or eliminate them from our lives for a period. Sometimes it is permanently. I have been down that road where I've had to eliminate somebody permanently. It's not easy, but you must realize one thing. If you really want to accomplish something big as an entrepreneur, you want to do something big as a business owner, sometimes your dream is bigger than the people that you surround yourself with.

So when we can forget the 33% that hate us, we can better appreciate the 33% that love us … and focus our business efforts on the middle 33%.

The middle 33% are the people that are on the fence. The people that you don't know or people that don't have an opinion of you. These people don't love you or hate you, but they want to find more information out and if you do the right things to reach out to them and do it on a consistent basis, you're going to convert that middle 33% to your side. So, then you're dealing with 66%.

Now, what happens after a time if you do this is the 33% that are on the bad side will gradually come around, too. You'll often find people that were once your biggest critics or biggest haters, they're going to fall into two categories.

One, they're just going to keep hating you and not talk to you and be eliminated from your pool and your network, which is great, or two, they'll come to your side. They'll eventually swallow their pride and either start saying good things about you like, "I knew you back when you were just this," or they'll ask you for help, "Hey. I'm so proud of you for overcoming your limitations or your drawbacks. How can I do what you did to get where you're at today?"

That's really a very powerful moment is when some of your biggest critics have become your biggest advocates. That almost always happens in time if you just stick to what you're doing. But you'll never get to that point if when you do something, you worry about the 33% of the people that don't care. Unfortunately, some of us don't have a thick enough skin to begin with and we build that thicker skin by dealing with people saying negative things. Don't go there. Instead, realize their opinion doesn't matter. Tell yourself "I don't care what their opinion is because I'm only going to focus on the people that I can really help and do the most amount of good for: the people that love me and the people that are on the fence. That's the groups that I want to spend my time with, my focus, money, and energy with. Those are the people that will make me happy."

That's my biggest gift or biggest, best advice ever been given to me and it helps me every day in what I do. I don't mind being myself. I'm much happier being myself than trying to be something that I'm not. The people in my 33% that love me and the middle 33%, they can either like or they respect me.

Maybe a few hate me, but that's okay. You can't get anywhere successful in life with everybody loving you. Then when people start to hate you, you know you're doing something right. You can't have the sweet without the sour. Just remember to focus on the loving and middle 33% blocks. The rest will take care of itself in time.

Manager, Mentor, Or Me?

STEPHEN R. SIMMONS

This is a story about being fully present and attentive in every moment, being clear about what you want and need, and never forgetting that you are working with other complex human beings, whether you are managing or being managed.

When I was just starting out, my first manager once told me that, as a manager, he generally gave his team members "enough rope to hang themselves." Despite the slightly negative connotation of this statement, it would prove an invaluable lesson for me, as time revealed its fuller meaning.

As an entrepreneur, you might very well be a control freak. I know I am. This ailment can make it easy to forget to give your team enough "rope" to show you who they are. Over-management can be as disastrous as lack of management, and can prevent uncovering the most effective ways to collaborate with, and get the best from, your team. This can be especially poignant in a startup, where roles are still evolving. Does one of your team need less structured management than others? Is another team member a few months of mentoring focus away from rock star greatness? The rope metaphor teaches us that management is not a "one size fits all" proposition. You'll do best to find out where you can help, and where each individual can be most impactful with their contributions, by being observant and providing them a spacious enough sandbox.

Another thing this same manager told me during a performance review was that one of my strengths was having a knack for knowing how far I could go on my own, and when it was time to ask for guidance. This resonated with me, and I took it to heart that being respectful of his time and pushing myself to solve problems was working well. This lesson ultimately provided a guideline for considerate collaboration that I've carried with me ever since. From conducting efficient, goal-driven meetings, to calling on colleagues with clear objectives already in mind, opportunities to apply it in practice present themselves almost daily. Know your limitations, and always challenge yourself to expand them, and be thoughtful about tying up others' time. Things tend to run more smoothly.

Together, these tidbits of wisdom would coalesce to form much of the basis of my approach to professional collaboration, whether managing, mentoring, or being managed. I count myself lucky, and I'm forever grateful to have received early influence from a successful and attentive manager, who clearly had my personal success in mind as one of his objectives. These ideas would percolate in my psyche over time, and help me to find greater success as a manager or member of the several teams I've been a part of in the years since. And, the mentoring I was given prepared me to mentor others in a way that finds that more often than not, when you give folks the right amount of rope, they don't end up hanging themselves after all (and even if they do, you're there to catch and support them).

There's also the Me approach to management, where progress and success are measured primarily through the lens of task assignments, and not much exists beyond crossing items off of the manager's personal task list. As severe as this might sound, it's all too common in companies of all varieties, and generally falls short, often creating a toxic environment in the process. The most successful professionals take a more holistic and engaged approach to interacting with their team, realizing that it's not just about Me.

Flash forward a few years to my new job as lead engineer at a prominent startup incubator. Working closely with the Director of Technology, I was tasked with overseeing a team of engineers that I had never worked with before. This was an ideal place for the lessons that I'd learned to find a way into practice, since I was managing and being managed in roughly equal measure.

I loved my job and the company, things were running smoothly with the tech team, and my working relationship with my boss was stellar; however, over time, I found myself wanting more. I'd come to the realization that I could envision my talents and interests being better engaged within the organization. More specifically, I wanted to more evenly straddle the worlds of the technical and business thinkers, widening my focus from the purely technical. Essentially, I wanted my boss's job.

This might have been a non-starter, or maybe the moment when the Me in the room could have taken over by hatching some kind of scheme to climb the corporate ladder. In less healthy environments, or with someone who hadn't learned the lessons that I'd learned, this might have been what transpired next. However, not long after coming to my realization, I was having lunch with my boss, and although I hadn't at all planned to, I somehow became inspired to ask him "So, where do you see yourself in 6 months to a year?"

This is also a testament to the fact that I'd gotten lucky again, because I once more had a manager who was good at it. He was accessible, attentive, and engaged, but not overly so. So, the atmosphere that he had created set me at ease to be clear and honest.

He asked me why I was asking. Then, before I could stop my mouth from moving, I came out with "Because I want your job." After a bit of a pause ... and I'll never forget his exact words, he said ...

"We can make that happen."

And, he was serious. Unbeknownst to me, it turned out that he had his sights set on moving into a more purely business-thinking role. So, after some consultation with the higher-ups, about 3 weeks later we'd made the shift, and I had a new set of business cards.

This was one of those great professional moments when it all just came together, through a collaborative foundation that had been built from those early lessons, which had by then become muscle memory. And, by finding enough presence and clarity to speak directly to the one person who could help me get what I wanted, it came quickly to fruition. Suddenly, we were just two people simply collaborating openly to find the best outcome.

So, "Manager, Mentor, or Me?" It's clear that the answer is: "All of the above, in the right measure." Successful collaboration requires a manager who is engaged but not imposing, a mentor who is flexible and attentive, and a Me that operates with clarity and intention to identify synergies.

Now, many years later, as I'm currently building a new team to drive my first solo venture, I'll continue to strive to foster this kind of atmosphere ... and I'm looking forward to the day when one of my engineers tells me s/he wants my job.

Mentors: The Secret Sauce That's Right In Front Of You

SHANE YEAGER

"I think a role model is a mentor – someone you see on a daily basis, and you learn from them." —Denzel Washington

Every business book you pick up these days talks about the importance of finding a mentor, immediately creating a picture of a gray-haired sage, locked away somewhere in the mountains. We fantasize this heroic journey to find them, and when we do, they have all the answers guiding us to fame, riches, and happiness.

That won't happen. But the good news is, it doesn't need to. In reality, mentors are all around us.

The problem is that we are distracted into looking too far and too wide. Stardom and social media has us listening to "experts," reciting their latest tweets and taking their advice. Will you ever meet these people? Hopefully, but let's be realistic here. It makes sense to already work the network you have of the people you have actually met, before going for the Forbes Top 100 list. Here's how to do it.

What I'm about to show you is an exercise of deep thought, reflection, and forgiveness. You will need to be open and unbiased about the last 10+ years of your life. Be honest with your mistakes and your successes. Try to remember every meaningful interaction with people you've come in contact with and assess their strengths and weaknesses. By critically analyzing your environment, you will lay the groundwork for expedited growth, self-understanding, and mutual respect for those around you. This will help you identify your own personal shortcomings and greatly help you in finding friends, partners, and passions.

Begin by creating a list of names of people who have impacted you, both good and bad. Then work your way down by listing one positive and one negative lesson you learned from them – either by direct learning or observation. The positive part of this chart is for actions or traits that you admire, or have produced strong results. The negative part of this chart is for actions that have produced poor results. Your positive lessons should seem like compliments and your negatives constructive criticism. You should be comfortable telling the person what you learned and how you feel.

I encourage you to reach out and actually tell these people how you feel. You'll be amazed at what happens when you are open with them, even your idols.

You can copy my form below.

Name	Positive	Negative
Mom	Stay positive even when times look the worst.	Delegate frequently or be overwhelmed.
Craig	Kindness & fairness to your labor force doubles output and loyalty.	Equipment maintenance and reliability is directly linked to profitability and morale.
Mike Love	Reflection and meditation is the secret to a calm mind and body over long periods of stress.	Life passion, business, and personal relationships need to be carefully managed.

To help with your thought process I'll give you a little backstory on each one of these.

My mom has been an amazing woman and influence in my life. She's always handled the toughest of times with a smile and a laugh. From observing how that attitude makes people light up, I learned to do the same: always stay positive.

She ran her own hair salon and would work long hours. Knowing how hard she worked I always wondered what would have happened if she delegated more, freeing her up to do the things she loved. Taking what I've learned in my own experiences, entrepreneurship requires expert delegation to be scalable and successful.

Craig was a local farmer and my first employer. Through his leadership I learned to work! We'd bail hay, pick corn, and clean chicken houses. He employed many local kids and always treated us fair and with respect, even at 15 years old. I noticed how I always wanted to go back to work for him, despite the jobs being dirty, labor intensive tasks. I knew he cared about us, and that was enough.

As we worked, equipment would sometimes break down, halting the entire workforce. Every time the hay baler would break, a group of 5 of us had to sit and wait, our momentum would be stopped and we'd get lazy. I learned that maintaining core equipment was essential in keeping profitability, but more importantly, keeping morale high.

When I started my career I was lucky enough to travel with the Beach Boys on and off for half a year. Through that experience I was able to see what long time celebrities go through day to day. Extensive travel, fans, and distance from family can take its toll.

From observing frontman, Mike Love, and talking with members of the band and his family, it became clear how much this man had personally gone through. Despite his stage persona he's actually a quiet, calm and collected guy. He's an active meditator and reflector. Watching how he handled stress was incredibly important, as there are times when entrepreneurship and life will greatly test you. You need to be strong.

Seeing the complicated dynamics of success was also an interesting lesson. All the band members were managing their personal, business, and life passions as they toured. It was a laborious task and something I noted to prepare for. It was essential to define clear boundaries in each of those categories or risk significant hardships.

As you complete your chart, however long you want to make it, reflect on your past years and appreciate where you've come and what you learned. When you face times of success and moments of unbearable stress, pull out your chart and take a look at who could help you most. You'll see, the mentor(s) you've been looking for, have been there all along.

It's easy to take life for granted and forget about the small moments, but your mentors, if examined carefully, will leave you with boundless wisdom and courage.

Networking For Better Business — Web Vs. Social

AVI HUBERMAN

Halfway across my journey I was fortunate to create a golden opportunity – to stop for a moment and think what the best way for me to make a difference. Until my mid-40's the perception that led me was what most people do when they listen to their parents: Study a "respectable" occupation, have a "dignified" work that will both outcome in receiving a high salary and lead to a "Great Satisfaction" with no risks taken.

Two Engineering degrees, a respectable job in the security/military field, combined with: state of the art electronics in the industry, supply chain management, worldwide procurement, human resource development and more – certainly respectable.

But one day I went to ask the advice of a famous Rabbi, who said simply: "Management levels and ranks do not matter. Your role in this life is to help people." The timeout that I received after retirement from my government job a few years ago – led me to think more closely about that advice, and to review what can actually lead to a significant change in life – not just for me, but also, and especially, for others.

One possibility that came up was from my brother, who at the time was in the middle of his quest, was: "how to reach decision-makers in the most engaging way and make them interested and anxious to respond" through social B2B digital networking. I adopted his idea almost immediately and together we established a company dedicated to doing just that. Why? It is the heart's desire of every business owner seeking to develop their business and each employee seeking their next challenge – what a way to help others reach their goals!

Adopting behaviors of digital networking was new to me. Leaving the old fashioned way of communication between people seemed to be missing something – I had to take a step back to determine what it is. The use of social networks in the past decade was more in the personal social world, but can it help in the business world as well? It turns out that in a few good steps, defining correct and precise goals you want to reach – you can touch decision makers, and systematically raise the conversion rate of replies to your messages.

On the other hand, I've found that the digital world of today can degenerate us slowly if we use it in an exaggerated and exclusive manner. Our social skills and ability to communicate directly with our connections will eventually decay if we do not keep the "social fitness" in the sense of direct communication with those we see as a potential future customer or our "Dream Job" employer.

The ability to communicate with people digitally can lead both sides to communicate, but at the end of the day, in order to sign on business agreements we will need to meet together and talk, look each other in the eyes and shake hands firmly – all of these are not currently possible with any social network.

In the continuous efforts to search for business contacts/leads, one special lady has crossed my path – she had invited me 3 years ago to participate in an early morning business networking arena of the BNI (Business Networking International) organization. From that day – I've met business owners, shook their hands, studied their business, connected together for business relationships and generated business leads with actual results. The ability to help people directly, sharpen your message to them, and create fluent speech in front of an audience (which is the no.2 fear after death), continuous learning of how to improve your networking capabilities, adopting and executing the statement "the givers will gain," all led me forward!

After almost three years in the BNI organization, being the chairman of the largest and fastest growing chapter in Israel and becoming an ambassador in the organization, I'm helping more business owners than ever succeed and make more money from being a part of BNI.

Some of the basic steps which I think are a must on the way to develop your business, by integrating both digital and facial networking, include:

First – Show yourself in social meetings, networking events and 1:1's: look at yourself – how you dress up, how you stand before an audience, how others see you – this is the first impression someone sees. At the same time – your digital infrastructure – must possess both excellent visibility and professional content. Most people miss one or both phases (above) and wonder why they do not get results.

Second – define the target audience for your business (for your products and/ or services). What is the targeted market segment? Maybe private customers? Businesses? Who are the companies / professionals you want to reach out to? What is the best way to reach those people socially? What's the best way to reach them digitally? How best can I do both?

Third – engage with your target audiences:

Digitally – the message you're sending to the reader on the other side must be short and precise.

Human interaction – attending a conference / social event, a meeting with a friend / family / business owner / colleague – how to do it in the most impactful way? Start first with small talk rather than straight to business. When you do get to "the point" – Introduce yourself to your partner in a concise manner: who are you? What are you looking for? Which ringing "bells" should your colleague refer to you when they hear / see / feel the need of their conversation partners and market your service / product to them?

Fourth – close the deal: transmit emotion, overcome objections and fears by faith in your product / service and the ability to really solve the problem of your future customer. Be able to do this both online and in-person.

I know this about myself and strongly believe that strong personal and social capabilities arise from combining both web & social networking, which are essential to really touch people and connect with them.

http://www.th-insight.com

Networking Your Way To Millions

DANIEL SCHWARTZ

In this chapter I will share three major lessons with stories from my life here in Thailand that I believe have universal applicability.

When I arrived in Thailand full time in 2005, I decided I had to go to Networking functions to get integrated into the business community. I found a group called Networking for Success (NFS) meeting every Thursday morning for breakfast at 7am! I would religiously go there every Thursday, leaving home before 6am because it was part of my routine: the thing that I did every Thursday morning. Make networking a habit, find the groups that fit your skills and your interests and show up. You will be amazed at the results.

Here are three key lessons learned from my networking experience:

1. 90% of your success is showing up
2. Believe that someone is at that event with a check made out to you for $1 million
3. Seize Critical Moments ... be in the right place and the right time and then take action

Let's dive a bit deeper into these 3 lessons learned.

90% of Success is SHOWING UP!

Getting out of the house/office and showing up is hard for many people. What should you say or do? Many other things compete for your time. It may be a bit uncomfortable, but guess what, you will get better at it as you go to the events. Just think of it this way, what is the worst thing that could happen to you? Show up, pay a bit of money and get yourself a nice dinner/drinks, not a bad worst case outcome. And just meeting one person that you can eventually do business with, what would that mean to you?

As an example, my friend decided to launch a new networking group in town called Bangkok Young Professionals. Now I wasn't young but I was in Bangkok and a professional so two out of three wasn't bad. I went to the launch to support my friend, and through some other friends who came to do the same thing I ended up getting a connection to a potential business partner. A few months later this new partner and I sold the first aviation systems for video intelligence in the Thai market. All because I decided to show up.

Believe that whenever you show up to a networking event that someone will be there with a $1 million dollar check with your name on it.

This big idea specifically will help you with your mindset and motivation to get out there and network. Many people are afraid to network, they show up to the event, get their food and drink and then stand in the corner playing with their phone. Get over that fast, go in with the mindset that there is someone in that room who is holding a million dollar check with your name on it! If you knew that to be true, would you show up and try to connect with as many people as you could to find the one holding that check?

I had launched a joint venture with a partner in hybrid marketing targeting the pharmaceutical industry. I attended my weekly networking meeting ... and guess who showed up, a director of a pharmaceutical company (who had never attended a meeting before!). We met, discussed things briefly, and then agreed to meet again to speak in detail. That one meeting led to us quickly signing a contract. This illustrates the real power of networking and understanding that there will eventually be someone there **who really does have a check with your name on it** (okay, it wasn't a million dollars but you get the idea).

Seize Critical Moments ... when you are in the right place at the right time take ACTION!

In 2007 I was a member of an organization called the XL (Extraordinary Lives) Results Foundation, and I learned something quite important from the Founder and Chairman. He taught us that we come upon times in our lives that he called Critical Moments, places where fortunes are made or lost ... you have to have Belief, Courage and then take ACTION ... and seize them.

Fast forward a few years: Bangkok was having terrible floods. I was training, selling and doing internet marketing projects locally in Thailand, but during this period the floods were absolutely horrible. We had to move out of our house and go away for a couple of weeks – I came back home early and luckily the floods hadn't hit our street, but I felt there were not going to be any business opportunities here in Thailand over the next few months as everyone recovered from the flooding, rebuilding their houses and their businesses.

So what should I do? I remembered I had an account on a freelancer platform that I had used to source web development, so as I sat at my desk I wondered … maybe I should go see if there were any business planning projects that people needed completed. I figured these projects would pay reasonably well and I could do them from Thailand applying my experience in marketing, business development and management into helping others achieve their dreams. So I logged in and started to look, and a posting jumped out at me saying: "Come work for a Software Company managing Fortune 1000 Accounts and a team of inside sales people. You can work from anywhere!"

Now looking back, this was clearly a critical moment! I saw this ad, seized that opportunity, changed my profile to be a freelancer and applied. I had my interview, did a testing assignment and on December 9, 2011 I started working as an inside sales representative. But that is only the beginning of the story. I eventually grew this into a Vice President position that has allowed me to spend time with my family and travel the world. All because of that one critical moment when I saw that ad and hit the apply button (plus a bit of hard work too!)

I want to impress upon you that you MUST seize your critical moments and then take action! Meet someone new at an event, make sure you follow it up, it may lead to that next big contract or a new job or even your partner in life! See a job advertisement that stretches your skills and looks great? Go for it, if you don't, the answer will always be no, how about taking a shot at yes?

I believe you get the picture from my 3 stories and examples: show up and build your network, find that person with the million-dollar check, seize your critical moments and then take massive action.

www.danschwartzlive.com

Part Two

SKILLS, LESSONS, AND TACTICS

Section One: All About Sales

Will Work For Relationships

LIZ GRAMM

Many things happened in 1985; three of my favorite movies, *The Goonies*, *The Breakfast Club* and *Back to the Future* were released. VH-1 debuted on television and the Rock and Roll Hall of Fame was established. Future heavyweight boxing champion Mike Tyson knocked out Hector Mercedes in round one of his first pro fight. Madonna was ripping up the charts and tornadoes were tearing up Middle America. Microsoft Windows 1.0 was released and my personal debut happened that summer in Denver, Colorado.

I was a chatty kid, always assuming everyone was a friend who wanted to hear me talk. My grandfather would turn down his hearing aids while I'd follow him around, babbling on without reprieve. As early as three years old, I was striking up conversations with strangers at restaurants, proudly proclaiming that my dad worked in "Okanahama." It was clear early on that this product of the 80's was all about meeting people and creating relationships.

When I was five years old, my family relocated to a remote area in the Colorado Rocky Mountains. 18 miles from the closest town, I can still remember my excitement when we received an AOL dial up disk in the mail, promising 100's of free hours of internet access. I'd put the disk into the computer and wait for the dial up screaming to do its thing and shortly thereafter, I was finding people, learning about the world and building online communities in interest chatrooms. I loved the joke forums and regularly shared my ideas for new humorous answering machine greetings.

My love for connectivity and relationship building (in person and online) only grew. In an earlier chapter of my sales career, I was selling education to individuals who worked directly with the 65+ age group. We focused on ethical and effective business within the senior market. My colleagues were always poking fun at my enthusiasm for connecting to my clients and prospects over LinkedIn. I didn't mind that they thought it was funny, because I was meeting people who wanted to participate in the classes we offered and gain the subsequent certification. I was proud to show them how to branch off from just the phone and email sales approach.

As an eager young sales woman, I was anxious to find every prospect and close every deal I could as fast as possible only to move onto the next. Of course, in my naiveté, I assumed everyone who fit the profile of "prospect" wanted to hear about my service offering. One very memorable connection happened by chance; as most of them do. I had written a tutorial for our members on how to build their business and visibility using LinkedIn; I posted it on a couple of senior care forums and received a response from an Elder Care Advisor in San Jose, California.

He reached out to ask me a couple of LinkedIn specific questions and in my haste to close another sale, I attempted to pivot to my product. He said he was not interested in the class and implied that he could take the test without the course; he was quite versed in his field. Reluctantly, I put in the time to provide him answers to his LinkedIn questions. To my surprise, a month later, he called me. "Liz, I think I can help you get all of the students you need to hold an event in Silicon Valley, I also have a connection with a conference center manager at a hotel right by the airport. Let's put together a class!"

Due to his referrals and coordination efforts, my (now) friend, Skip, helped me coordinate and fill one of the biggest and most profitable classes we held while I was with the society. Subsequently, Skip was responsible for dozens of enrollments in the years following and still consults with the Society of Certified Senior Advisors to this day. He has earned a recognition award for work in his field and continues to support the mission of the education & certification to train ethical and effective senior business leaders. Many times I have been reminded of the importance of building meaningful relationships and adding value to these relationships even before a clear opportunity is established, but never so glaringly as my experience of working with Skip.

Most everyone I know in sales has heard of the WIFM radio station. Sales managers remind teams to remember this each time they are talking to a prospect to keep them on the track of selling instead of simply telling about their product. The whole pitch is centered on the prospect's ultimate question "what is in it for me?"

If you focus on what is in it for your prospect/client, you position yourself as the go-to, a resource, an esteemed colleague, connector and service provider. There is significant worth to a salesperson and entrepreneur in asking oneself "what is in it for them?" Rather than focusing on the close, the commissions and the bragging rights, the most fruitful opportunities have come from offering solutions to *their problem* before a clear sales opportunity presents itself.

While having huge professional impact in my sales years, focusing on what is in it for others has come full circle from professional to personal. About eight years ago, I introduced two former colleagues who I knew would hit it off. One day, after their first year of their marriage, I received a phone call, "Liz, I know you are ready for your next opportunity. What do you get for a girl who gave you the world?" He answered his own question "I think I have the perfect role for you." They are now happily married, raising two children and because of this introduction, I landed in an opportunity in sales for a company with a strong mission and the most excellent product offerings in their class.

My lesson was to stop pivoting directly to my product and the ultimate close. Ask yourself during every interaction, "what's in it for **them**" and put aside the immediacy of a sale for the value you can provide that individual by offering your expertise. If you do this during the courting stage of each relationship, you will easily uncover areas of opportunity that have the potential to pay off handsomely for you **and** the client/prospect. The self-worth that comes from offering a zero-reciprocation value to professional and personal relationships will be infinitely more rewarding than a fleeting paycheck.

Become The Company Rainmaker

AARON SCHNEIDER

Why listen to me? My name is Aaron Schneider, I have been a top salesperson at both Fortune 500 companies and startups for the past 20 years. I have won multiple sales awards and helped to train other salespeople to become top producers. I have also created a network of referral sources where many of my sales come from warm leads. And during all of that, I've learned that the sales rep with the most good prospects in deeper stages of the sales cycle is usually a top performer. In other words, if you are a fishing for lobsters, having 100 traps in good locations is better than 10 traps in good locations.

A rainmaker is a salesperson who always has a deep pipeline of deals, is always finding ways to generate revenue for the company, and is also helping clients and business partners generate more revenue as well. Here are some simple steps to double your commissions and be a rainmaker for your company.

Step 1 – Create bigger target lists, write up phone scripts, and write email introductions (no more than 6 sentences). To create a target list, use sources such as Hoovers (an online lead-generation tool), Linkedin, trade publications, and Google search. Practice leaving 30 second voicemails which quickly explain the value proposition. Identify the top salespeople at your company and shadow them. Ask the top salespeople for their introductory emails and presentations.

Step 2 – Make the phone dials and follow up once every 2 weeks via both email and phone. Don't rely on emails to start conversations. Call the CEO/COO/CMO and work your way down. Making calls at 4pm has higher response rates than 10AM. Wednesday/Thursday are the best call days for higher response rates. 80% of sales to larger prospects are made on the 5th to 12th call (persistence pays off). For prospects who never return a call, think outside the box and find other creative ways to contact them.

Step 3 – Warm leads are always better than cold calls. To create a referral network, identify companies that sell products/services to the same companies that you sell to. I then call the salespeople from these companies directly and discuss putting together a special offer that can help them close more sales and help me generate warm leads. For example, buy a Ferrari and get a free lunch on a yacht. Via networking, I have uncovered leads for other divisions of my company and helped to generate deals for others. This is another way to become a rainmaker. By being a rainmaker and helping others achieve their goals, this makes you a good teammate and makes you irreplaceable. Build your referral network at trade shows. Connect with other salespeople on Linkedin, buy them a beer, compare notes, or collaborate on a joint event for sales prospects. The other advantage to knowing people in your industry is that companies are always looking for top salespeople and the best sales jobs often get filled by people who have an inside track.

Step 4 – Be a consultant who helps your clients solves problems and gives clients a return on their investment. Listen more. Talk less. Lose the PowerPoint. Don't be a pushy salesperson. Respond to emails from prospects quickly. Ask prospects about themselves and their families. By asking open ended questions (not yes or no questions) and listening to the responses, you can often help to identify the problem and then start working on potential solutions. It is also critical that you are directly engaging all the decision makers. For example, if I have a good call with a merchant, my second call with prospects is a technical call to figure out technical obstacles. Once you start solving problems for clients and get agreement to move forward from all the major decision makers, many sales prospects will be the one to ask you to send them an agreement. Also, people like to buy from people they enjoy interacting with. Don't spend time complaining to a potential client about your problems. When a prospect asks a question, get answers quickly. This shows them that you are making them a priority and looking to help them. (as we all know, good/responsive customer service can be hard to find these days).

Step 5 – Get to a No as Fast as Possible. Time is money. If you want to make 6 figure commissions, then you need to avoid wasting time with prospects who are browsers (not buyers). I am fine if a customer tells me they have no budget for this year or their IT team is tied up for the next 9 months. Getting to a no quickly enables me to move on to the next sales prospect. I move on and put them on my sales drip campaign where I periodically reach out to them. Tell prospects it is okay if the timing is not right. Trust your gut. For the prospects who ask for an agreement, make sure to agree on timing and next steps before the agreement gets signed. A contract is just a sheet of paper. To turn a contract into revenue, there needs to be a game plan around next steps/timing.

Step 6 – Be laser focused. Checking Instagram costs you money. If you are new to sales, be prepared to grind before you earn bigger commission checks. Top salespeople have higher earnings and better work/life balance than most doctors or lawyers. If you are at 150% of goal by December 1st, then that is the time to relax and take a long vacation. Outsource and avoid internal logjams. Hire someone to clean the pool/mow the lawn. Avoid missing important family events. Avoid internal meetings when possible. Tell your manager you are booked on sales calls. Avoid travelling for smaller deals (if an account can be closed over Skype, then avoid spending 2 days in airports). If you have solved a problem, then meeting in person won't be a deal killer. Be able to handle numerous roles. If a client asks a technical question, then be prepared to answer most technical questions. Know details on your competitors' product offering. Be a social media proponent for your company. Ask current clients for referrals. Focus extra energy on your biggest accounts and sell them additional services.

I have been blessed to enjoy 20 years of success in sales and I hope these tips will help you double your commissions, enjoy more work/life balance, and become a rainmaker.

https://www.linkedin.com/in/aaronschneider01

Entering The Conversation In Your Prospect's Head

REGINA PARTAIN BERGMAN

Whether you agree that we are exposed to 500 advertisements a day or 5000, the result is still the same – we are inundated with marketing messages.

In this world of inundation, and with the speed of our lives ever increasing, it is very hard for any company, especially a smaller firm, to rise above the noise and clutter of those ever-increasing messages.

Many people have what I call "marketing burnout." If your prospective client is burned out on marketing messages, feeling that no one has the solutions to his problems, what can you do to get his/her attention?

Transient attention, a relatively new term for many of us, is a short-term response to a stimulus that temporarily attracts/distracts attention. Although there is disagreement on the exact amount of human transient attention span; many believe it may be as short as 8 seconds.

If your prospect only has an attention span of 8 seconds, what can you do to get that attention?

The answer lies in understanding the conversation that is occurring in your prospect's head. Basically, there are two elements of that conversation relative to your product:

1. I have a problem for which I need a solution.
2. I don't have this solution and don't know where to find it.

Now, if you want to capture your prospect's attention, your marketing message needs to address these two items. How do you do that?

Using the 4 elements of the Conversion Equation, you can rise above the noise of the other marketers vying for the attention of your prospect:

- *Interrupt*
- *Engage*
- *Educate*
- *Offer*

In order to interrupt the conversation going on in your prospect's head, the first thing you must do is demonstrate that you understand their problem. Your headline should address the pain of their problem. When you are successful in doing that, you have bought a couple of additional seconds of their time.

Now, in order to keep them engaged, you must address a solution to their problem, which you will recall is the second element to the conversation going on in their head.

Third, you need to provide some valuable education, or content that brings them closer to making their buying decision.

And, finally, you must provide an offer that has no-to-low risk for them.

Let's see what that looks like in practice.

Step 1: An interrupting headline might read something like this: *Are you sick and tired of* _____? (whatever the pain is that your product eliminates).

Take a moment and think about your ideal client. What pain or problem do they have that your product solves. Remember, the first part of the conversation in their head is "I have a problem for which I need a solution."

Now, write an interrupting headline for your ideal client. You want to rise above the noise of other marketing messages. As you do this, remember that you do not want to try to be all things to all people. You want to narrow down, or niche, your audience. If you have several products or services, you want to home in on the one problem or pain that will catch their attention. You can create several of these campaigns to meet the various pain points of your ideal client.

Step 2: The second part of the conversation is that they need a solution that they don't have. How does your product or service provide a solution to their pain? If you are not able to help them see very quickly that you have a solution, they will simply move on. You only have a couple of seconds to engage them.

Take a few moments now to think about your solution, then write an engaging sub-headline for your ideal client.

Step 3: Now that you have your interrupting headline and your engaging sub-headline, it is time to educate them.

The tool needed for this is not your website. Websites do a good job of telling people about you, or your company, or your services, but don't generally get people to take action. All of the information you are about to provide is useless if the prospect doesn't take action. So the tool you need here is the squeeze page.

A squeeze page is a type of website designed to get your prospect to take one action, and one action only. The prospect will enter their name, usually first name only, and their email address in order to receive your free information with the solution to their pain.

Once they complete this information and click on the "submit" button, they will receive your free, valuable content that helps them on their journey to finding a solution to their problem.

Step 4: It is important to know that at any given moment, only 1% to 4% of your ideal clients are actually ready to make a purchase. The other 96% to 99% are still gathering information to help them make that decision. When you provide free, valuable content, in advance of their purchase, you elevate your position in their mind. You are, in effect, tying them to you so that when they are ready to make a purchase, you are uppermost in their mind as the person to buy from.

This valuable content is your "offer." It needs to be low-to-no risk. They are not yet ready to pick up the phone and have a conversation with you. They don't want to be "sold". They are still gathering information. When they accept your free offer of education, they are in effect agreeing to receive other free information from you. You now add them to your email list and send them more information (also known as a drip campaign) as well as offers for your products. Continuing to provide education will set you apart from your competition, making purchasing from you an easy choice when they are ready to purchase.

Michael Corleone Was Wrong

JAY MUDRICK

Wow. Bold statement. A person could wind up "sleeping with the fishes" for saying that. But I'll stand by it – Michael Corleone was wrong. (For anyone who's not a Godfather fan, I'm referring to the quote "It's not personal, Sonny. It's strictly business." Fans may recall that after Michael said that, things quickly went downhill for Sollozzo and McCluskey.)

But I still say he was wrong. That's because the line between personal and business and relationships is a pretty fuzzy one. The less commoditized your business, the truer that statement. If you deal person to person (vs. a pure commodity sale), you're still focused on product or service differentiation. And if you're trying to differentiate your product or service, integrity, reliability and candor are critical elements of building personal trust within a business relationship. If a prospect doesn't feel a personal rapport with you, how can you expect them to take your word on less tangible product features or performance criteria?

While on the subject of integrity, reliability, and candor, there are an awful lot of salespeople out there who will tell you they use a "consultative sales process." Some will call it "solutions-based selling". In either case, it is *intended* to mean that the salesperson spends time with the customer to understand the problem they are trying to solve and recommends a solution designed to address that specific issue. Far too often it has come to *actually* mean "I want to understand your needs but only so that I can sell you on my particular solution" or "I want to sell you something while feigning interest in learning about your business." That raises the question of what a consultative sale process really means if everyone claims they're doing it. Or if they're using it to steer you to their particular solution, not the best solution for your particular needs.

In my field of fleet equipment leasing and services, no one provider does everything well. Some companies are better dealing with clients who need vehicle service whereas some are better at the pure "funding" or order fulfillment elements of the transaction. Some are more effective at offering particular lease structures than others. Thus, a truly consultative sales process suggests that providers should sometimes say "I'm not the best choice for what you really need. I think you should consider speaking with my competitors X, Y, and Z." That doesn't happen very often.

The astute salesperson needs to adjust their view on how to build rapport with their client and perform a true needs assessment. Inquire and investigate deeply long before you try to inform. Understand the customer's true needs. Not just pain points that you can refer back to in an e-mail or proposal or the time worn "What Keeps You Up at Night?" And if you're not the best solution for their particular need, be a big enough person to admit it. You'll save yourself time, energy, and disappointment. You'll be able to find more opportunities with a dramatically higher close rate because you're focused on situations where your solution really is the right one. And you'll turn the prospect into a friend who will trust you above all else, respect your opinion and professionalism, will see you as a source of valuable industry insight, and won't hesitate to recommend you to their peers or to come back to you when their needs do change.

Turning to the client side, how can you sort through all of the different salespeople with a "consultative sales process?" There are a few ways. First, get educated. Yes, listen to the sales people but work hard to separate the reality from the sales pitch. Research prospective suppliers – not just on their website but through trade associations and industry groups, peers, and online reviews. Undertake an objective assessment of what you're really looking for in a vendor, which may be very different from your competitors or peers need. Ask for references. Understand what each company offers and decide which is best for your unique situation.

Another way to develop realistic expectations separate from the sales pitch is to deal with an independent advisor. Someone who is not a product or service vendor but someone who can align their interests with yours, and someone whose only vested interest in the transaction is to get the best solution for you. Once again, check with peers and industry trade associations. Search the web. Spend time on LinkedIn looking for industry experts. If need be, solicit expert input from a professional knowledge sharing firm like GLG or Coleman Research Group. The key is to make yourself an educated consumer, to see beyond the fluff, and to ensure that you understand the solution that you're really getting, not just opting for the one the salesperson wants to put you into.

Back to my original premise – Michael Corleone was wrong. It IS personal and it IS business. Trust is necessary. It's a critical part of what one party sells and another one buys. Ignore that at your own peril. Or else you could wind up like Sollozzo and McCluskey – "Sleeping with the fishes."

jaymudrick.com

A "Good" Sales Rep

SARAH MILLER

The journey to become a good sales rep takes many different shapes and forms for each of us. I have known many different salespeople in my career and we all have different styles, personalities and strategies. I know there is not just one special or particular personality which is the magic ticket to being a good sales rep. In fact, with the stigma around sales in general, I'm not sure at the early stages of my career, I wanted to be a good salesman. It was almost a dirty word.

In the interview for my first sales position, when the hiring manager asked if I had sales experience, I said no. I thought, "this is not going well." He then asked if I had ever waited tables. I was currently working two jobs and one was as a waitress at a certain popular Australian themed restaurant. We talked about the fact that as a waitress I had a goal in sales to hit each evening, plus how I was earning tips. I was actually in sales and did not even realize it! I was selling a dining experience and hoping for return business in my section, since it was always the best to have regulars who wanted to sit with you. He told me I had a good personality for sales and hired me for a junior inside sales position. That is where my journey as a sales rep began.

Half the battle was getting over my fear of stumbling and failing. I learned quickly the more calls you make the better your chances of connecting with a prospect are – but you better be ready for when they take that call or let you into their office. I learned most things we do in sales is repetition, learning from your mistakes will make you better the next time around, and if you keep tackling your call lists and talk to people in your industry, you will learn to be an expert. Your customers will help build you into one.

Anyone who has ever worked with me knows I believe wholeheartedly that cold calling is not optional. When I lived in San Diego, George "King" Stahlman was a bail bondsman that advertised on bus stop benches around PB (Pacific Beach). They said, "It's better to know me and not need me than to need me and not know me." I would chant that internally before my cold call sessions.

He passed away in 2009 but that quote will live on in my mind forever. Maybe I did not connect with a prospect that day but I left a voicemail. I would follow up with an email. Maybe they did not need me today but now they knew me and if an issue popped up, they would give me a call.

Success for salespeople is measured each month and starts over and over again. A colleague and I often joke they must not be sitting around thinking about us, the way we sit around thinking and waiting for them to sign the deal. It is a numbers game and you have to have enough in your pipeline that you are not selling desperately because no one wants to buy something if you pester them to death. You will only do that if you do not have enough in your pipeline.

I am successful because I am an advocate for the customer and my company. I want the best for both of us. Sales to me is learning what problem you can solve and "why" they need your solution. Why choose you over a competitor? How you can help them reach their business goals? You do want to make sure you are targeting a prospect that would actually use your product so knowing your market and buyer are key. Just because they are not interested now does not mean they won't need you in the future but you have to learn when to walk away as well.

We do all "sell" even when we don't recognize it. So don't sell yourself short, there is a successful salesperson in all of us – even you!

People Buy From People They Like

JESSICA STEDMAN

When I first embarked on my career within the corrugated industry as a Trainee Account Manager, my line manager advised me, *"people buy from people they like."* For something that seems initially such a simple and obvious statement, it has continued to be consistent theme within my career development, that I keep coming back to and realizing the power of its meaning.

Within this industry, I have always worked within sales based roles and I love the people element of my job. I value the relationships, the conversation and the insight you gain from building, nurturing and developing relationships. A constant struggle seems to exist between combining the skills of selling with the importance of understanding the relationships you have built and the motivations of the people buying from you. From within a corporate environment, this people aspect of business seems to be an undervalued and rarely understood aspect of business.

Discussing sales roles can generally provoke mixed emotions within people; from either personal experience or in a business capacity, from bad to good, most people have experienced sales in some form. You can find sales people everywhere, from car sales to selling cardboard boxes, selling to the general public or in a Business to Business capacity. The sales role covers such a large array of business segments, resulting in the tendency to be stereotypically viewed as a job that's easy to fall into or is a good "backup." With the takeover of online media platforms increasing the general awareness of competitor activity, customers are more savvy. They know what they want, the modern sales role can no longer rely on "the gift of the gab" or general likability independently, nor can it be successful without operating a toolkit of specific skills. Furthermore, where I have seen sales operate best, have been where people have utilized and adapted this toolkit alongside their relationships, adapting their approach depending on the situation and circumstances unfolding in front of them. When you are lucky enough to experience sales done well, it's an incredibly exciting experience. Its these moments you can appreciate the artform of great communication and the importance of a good relationship.

It sometimes seems sales representative are never working for the same side. When working internally, we are the face of the customer; when working externally, we are the face of the business. In both circumstances, we utilize different relationship-based skillsets, understanding that the people we are dealing with have their own compliances to follow. We learn to rely on the relationships we build to support us. With a focus on B2B, it's been these relationships based on these understandings that have offered the real opportunities in my roles. Learning to understand the people we work alongside, the processes they face and the difficulties within their own process, is an absolutely invaluable tool. I would imagine this could be classed as "likability" as you build rapport based on shared understandings.

Utilizing this knowledge and developing methods to encourage a shared view and a "win-win" mentality has the potential to nurture and develop fantastic relationships by encouraging trust in practice. Discovering this information is a skill alone; asking questions in a way that builds trust is a fine balance. Half of the battle in sales is understanding what makes our customer tick and evaluating how and what we can do to resolve their issues. In many instances, almost ironically, opportunities to offer real financial value have come from having this deeper understanding of the customer's environment, rather than focusing too heavily on the sale of the product alone.

Understanding the larger impact of what we sell and how we can utilize this in conjunction with the relationships we build, is essential to understanding great sales. While price matters, in my experience it's never been the main driving force in closing a deal. I have been lucky enough to work with multinational customers that have chosen to move large contracts due to a proven offer, an understanding of shared value and a source of reliability in the relationship I had built with them. Some customers over time have approached us through word-of-mouth, some from a sheer dislike of working with the competitors, some have chosen to move supply based on demonstrating reliability or offering a solution when others had let them down. Where I have found real successes historically, have been where I have taken time to understand the ethics at a core of a business. Understanding how I could add value to a process that perhaps didn't always work brilliantly, encouraged movement in a relationship where the customer would have likely stuck to what they were used to, had I not utilized the relationship to become a "friend" to their role. Understanding the delicacies of a customer's daily grind, of their process and how we could use our products in a way that adapts to them, meant that we could truly target our response.

Learning to value the intricacies of people, and constantly looking to reflect and adapt skills so they are tailored and targeted, can help to encourage a valued approach to sales. They can encourage common values, shared vision, and a likeness of practice as well as each other, which can dramatically alter the outcome of a sale. Having the ability to ask questions and tailor communications are essential skills required to enable a good salesperson to close a deal and ultimately move from an unsustainable, transactional relationship, to one of value adding. Encouraging this requirement, recognizes the value of character and personality in business and they are for me the most enjoyable, surprising and rewarding parts to my daily working life.

Ultimately I believe learning to develop a consultative approach, offering valued solutions based on the needs of the customer, appreciate and value the nuances of individuals in ways that corporate conglomerates sometimes struggle to handle. People certainly do buy from people they like … and that's where the real power lies.

Jessstedman@aol.com

Consistency Is The Key

CHARLES C. BROADHURST

Sales people are wired to be optimistic; it's one of things that make us successful. It is an absolute necessity to have a positive outlook in a business where rejections are so prominent. However, there is a flip side that all great salespeople possess; I have personally referred to it as realism, pessimism, jaded, or my favorites that encompasses the whole mentality which are "Realistic Optimism" or "Cautiously Optimistic."

Just like pro athletes and performers must have the absolute most confidence in their ability to deliver and succeed at the highest levels, so do sales professionals. But what happens when we get blinded by our own ego or buy-into the hype of how great we are? Many times it leads to a very hard fall from the level that we once attained.

As I gained more and more success early in my sales career and in the early stages of my professional life, I carried that confidence to everything I did in and out of the office. My ego seemed to grow as my bank account and client list did. I started to think that I was the best and somehow all the hard work and preparation that I had put in made me entitled to great success now and for the foreseeable future. Don't get me wrong ... I DO believe hard work and preparation lead to great success, but consistent and continued success takes more.

So I rode my wave of success and got every ounce out of my hard work and preparation, that by now was all but a distant memory. Funny thing how Hard work + Preparation= Success in a relative amount of time. We get out what we put in ... simple concept.

Here is what I realized: Initially I invested (put in) so much hard work and preparation that my success (got out) lasted a long time, which is great if you remember the formula and reinvest. However I changed the formula to Really Hard work + Preparation + I am Awesome = Entitled Success Forever!

It obviously doesn't work that way, as I found out the hard way. So the sales dried up, so did the bank account and at this point my dog was eating better than me, really. I was literally subsisting on canned tuna. I was scrounging change from one of those huge novelty beer bottles that I had luckily filled almost to the brim over the years, to buy bulk canned tuna (I found out latter that apparently the mercury is not good for you) and fill my gas tank to get to and from work. So I had a choice, really not a tough one: win or lose, quit or preserve, fail or succeed, cake or death, you get the idea. Not really much of a decision. So I truly was humbled, I checked what was left of my ego, and got to work.

This is the important part; how? Did someone say sell more stuff? Yes, but how? Having a plan was my first key. I didn't focus on just the results. I worked backwards from my success to the beginning and found the process that I went through to get to the desired result. Key number two, I documented it and made it a process that I could replicate and ways to check it along the way so that I would not stray to far off the plan.

One of the hardest things about success is that for most it is fleeting. Even when you hit the goal or win the championship, or get the big bonus, the moment is there and gone. It can be truly exhausting, which is why true greatness is reserved for very few in any endeavor.

Some of the best examples of the consistent mentality that it takes to be great come from sports. Michael Jordan, Tom Brady, even coaches like Nick Saban and Pat Riley, for example all of these people have reached the pinnacle of success in their profession multiple times and that's the thing that really separates them. The ability to remain consistent when you have achieved greatness is arguably the most difficult thing to do in any profession.

If you listen to the interviews with great players and coaches after big wins or championships they all sound very similar. "We'll enjoy this one, then back to work". Nick Saban has actually gone from the site of a National Championship win to a recruiting visit the next day! Michael Jordan has done his post game work out after scoring 50 points in a game. The examples go on and on.

I was once told that the Journey that leads to a goal is the actual reward, not the attainment of the goal itself. Taking pride, enjoyment and reward from the challenge of reaching for greatness is the key to consistently achieving it.

It takes a workman like mentality and humbleness to constantly carry out a plan day to day. It's especially hard, when you're winning!

In sales that consistency comes in the form of our daily plan and output or sales report numbers not the total sales figures that look so great on the leaderboard. As Mike Krzyzewski puts it whether win or lose the next game is always 0-0.

Every day in sales the focus of our day has to be in the consistency of our output. By focusing on the little things we can assure ourselves the sum of our efforts will lead to ultimate success in any goal we strive for.

Sales Transformations: No Guts, No Glory!

MIKE KUNKLE

What is sales transformation? There's no standard definition, but generally it's a performance improvement methodology aimed at guiding a sales force through the necessary changes to dramatically improve results. Of all the approaches to improve performance, full-scale sales transformation is the most effective. Unfortunately, I don't see it often enough.

I've spent considerable time thinking about why so many business leaders aim for incremental sales improvements rather than sales transformations. I want to share lessons I've learned, address the fears that hold us back, and give you a path forward to breakthrough sales results.

Current State Challenges

You've probably heard the statistics that are shared by research analysts, such as these data points from CSO Insights' *2016 Sales Enablement Optimization Study*:

- 61% of new salespeople take at least 7 months to ramp up
- 43% of sales reps miss quota annually
- 25.5% of forecast opportunities end in "No Decision"

According to AON, sales turnover is at a 5-year high. The cost of replacing sales reps and managers is significant.

These problems plague many companies and are costly. So why don't more organizations attempt major sales transformations?

Why We Fear Sales Transformation

Part of the reason we avoid sales transformations is complexity. There are so many factors to consider, so many levers to align, and so much complexity to manage, that most leaders don't know where to start or what to do. The complexity is enough to make a hard-driving sales leader focus on their comfort zone areas, and spur their sales force to push harder, faster, and longer … rather than scientifically tune-up the machine.

Sales leaders are under intense pressure to "make the number" and turn over every 18-24 months, on average. Most are not familiar with, nor experts in, sales transformations. This is why we tinker safely and settle for a 5-10% performance improvement – rather than overhauling to blow the doors off.

Some Lessons Learned

With over 22 years leading sales performance initiatives, I've learned a few lessons:

- Aligned, systemic approaches get far better results than random, individual projects.
- Fear holds us back from taking big action to produce big results. Under duress, people revert to their comfort zones.
- A "Plan C" that's brilliantly executed beats a "Plan A" that's bumbled.
- Performance is a function of the person and the environment (thank you, Kurt Lewin).
- If you put a good performer in a bad system, the system wins almost every time (thank you, Geary Rummler).
- No guts, no glory! If you want a different result, you need to do something differently. The bigger the action, the bigger the commitment, the bigger the risk … the bigger the reward.
- Risks can be reduced and results enhanced, by using proven-effective methods that got results for others.

I want to share a logical, systematic approach that I've seen overcome the challenges faced by sales organizations. This structured approach reduces complexity and can be absorbed and implemented in phases, while getting results along the way. I've seen this approach radically transform sales results in multiple companies, industries, and situations. These methods have worked for me, I've seen them work for others, and I know they'll work for you.

The solution to our current sales problems and the vehicle for transforming your sales results is a **Systems Approach to Sales**.

A Systems Approach to Sales Force Transformation

There are many systems in the Sales Performance Ecosystem. To reduce complexity, I'll focus on just four. I call them "The Four Sales Systems."

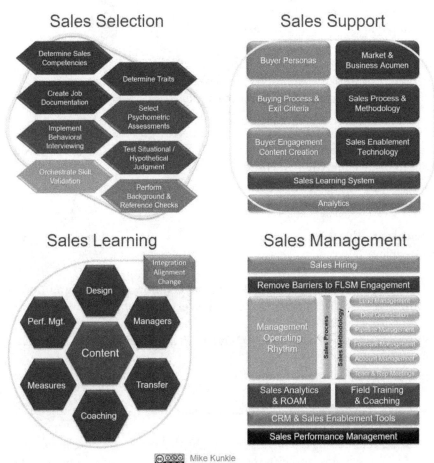

Why these systems? These are the 20 percent of the systems that will produce 80 percent of your results. If you start with these and ensure they're aligned and working, you can radically improve sales performance while reducing complexity.

Sales Selection System

Having the right people in the right roles is the first step toward better sales performance. The steps to hiring more effectively include:

- Determine sales competencies
- Determine success traits
- Create job documentation
- Implement psychometrics assessments
- Implement behavioral interviewing
- Test candidate's situational judgment with hypothetical questions
- Orchestrate skill validations using role plays and simulations)
- Perform background & reference checks

This foundation will help you not only hire better, go-forward, but allows you to assess the current sales force and use what you learn to coach and develop them to behave more like top producers.

Sales Support System

The goal with this system is to support the sales team in selling as effectively as possible.

- Ensure that reps understand their buyers, how they buy, and how to uncover what's important to them at every stage of their buyer's journey and provide it.
- Create content that will help buyers with their evaluation and buying decision.
- Use sales enablement tools to create efficiency and support effective selling behaviors.
- Use a buyer-friendly, consultative, solution-focused, outcome-driven sales methodology.
- Train reps to engage buyers in valuable business conversations and to create real value and differentiation, through business acumen and an understanding of how their products/services solve buyer problems.
- Use analytics to track training, content, sales behavior, and outcomes and provide feedback to your sellers, to help them improve.

Sales Learning System

- Ensure your training content will get results if it's used.
- Design great learning with plenty of skill practice and feedback.
- Engage managers so they know what is being taught.
- Find ways to sustain knowledge gained and help them apply it with buyers.
- Help managers prepare to coach their reps to mastery.
- Measure for success to see how reps are doing after training, and manage their performance.
- Help sales managers know how to lead & manage change with their teams.

Sales Management System

Frontline sales managers are a force multiplier for change and sales success. You should start by removing barriers so managers can spend time with their sales teams. Then, managers must be trained and prepared effectively to:

- Use the Sales Selection System and master hiring.
- Implement a proven-effective Management Operating Rhythm.
- Master your sales process and sales methodology.
- Conduct team and rep meetings effectively.
- Master sales analytics to know where to focus efforts to get the greatest return.
- Develop field training and sales coaching skills.
- Master your CRM and Sales Enablement Tools.
- Master Sales Performance Management.

Results

Here are some results that companies have achieved by implementing one or more of the systems:

- Achieved a $398MM accretive revenue increase in one year from final project completion.
- Increased sales 600% annually while decreasing operating expenses by 21%.
- Increased sales results 28.7% over previous year.

- Increased performance of new hires, so that sales reps with 120 days on the job outperformed a control group of reps with 5 years with the company.
- Increased sales per rep by 47% in 9 months.
- Improved average profitability per rep by 11% in only 4 months.

Conclusion

I hope you've found the rationale for tackling sales transformation persuasive and the introduction to the systems logical, if brief. If you want to get off the sales insanity treadmill, there is plenty of additional reading available and many sales consulting firms who can assist you, as needed. Whichever systems you implement, I wish you the greatest of success.

http://www.mikekunkle.com/connect/

Utilizing The Power Of The Emotional Brain To Boost Your Business

SHARON AIZEN

Ever since I was a little girl I was fascinated about life and what it has to offer. I was defined as a very emotional child and found that the effect our feelings have on our behavior really interests me.

As an employee I've seen managers with different styles of management, Companies that drive their employees in different ways. And the most fascinating thing is that the strongest most successful businesses were the ones that were able to tie a strong connection between their workers and the brand/vision while appealing to the emotional brain! Different styles of force and intimidation never seem to work. The employees are demoralized and not very cooperative. While brands with a strong story behind them that triggers certain emotions were able to unite all their employees under one big "family."

The appeal to the emotional brain was always a strong component in result oriented thinking. In fact, we know today that the emotional brain is behind every measurable outcome we have, both in professional and personal aspects. *The Emotional Brain* by Josef E. LeDoux and Martin L Rossman reveals parts of the brain connected to our feelings. The emotional brain is located beneath the cognitive brain. They found that our feelings affect the way we think in a very strong coherent manner which projects on our actions and results in our everyday lives

The importance of the emotional brain in business is vital to get to good results. In the following example we'll see how much the emotional brain is a key component when it comes to creating results in a creative way:

The year is 1920. The tobacco industries realized they have a problem. Only men are consuming their product, while it's considered taboo for women to smoke in public. Any woman caught violating this rule got arrested. They went to Edward Bernays, a pioneer of modern propaganda, in order to find a creative solution and get women to consume cigarettes on a regular basis.

What Edward did was very creative and revolutionary: He staged a parade in 1929 called "The Easter parade in NY City" showing models holding lit Lucky Strike Cigarettes labeled as "Torches of Freedom" walking down 5th avenue – representing strong independent women. Around a year after the event, smoking percentages around men and women were pretty much even. This "stick of poison" was suddenly a symbol of freedom, a symbol of a woman going against everything that is socially accepted and doing it with style. He tied a strong connection between the product and a certain feeling he artificially created – in this case – a Strong independent American woman. The great success in this matter was due to connecting this strong need of women to feel free and equal to men to the physical act of holding a cigarette, changing their image in a matter of seconds to a free strong independent woman.

Coca-Cola has a similar example: the language they use in order to get to their audience is emotional rather than Just seeing it as a product. Coca-Cola realized that if the focus will be on the product, they might be in trouble.

In the movie *Liar Liar* – a comedy where Jim Carrey was not allowed to tell a lie – Carrey was trying to sell Coca-Cola through the phone: "You want to buy a black colored beverage with lots of sugar in it, and other materials that are not supposed to get to the human body, but hey, it's very tasty! Wanna buy?" Clearly that was not going to work in real life. So Coca-Cola decided to trigger the emotional brain with their "Coca-Cola – Taste of Life" ad campaign. Positive feelings immediately pop up and Coke continues to sell.

Brands and businesses that were able to tie a strong emotion to their product/ brand have made millions. Those examples applied on cigarettes & Coca-Cola (which are not exactly a symbol for health, to say the least) show us the true potential of the emotional brain in business. Now imagine: What can you do with your business?

Recently I was hired as a consultant for a major luxurious cosmetic brand. The sales team were struggling to sell the brand due to fierce competition, high prices, and the fact they didn't have an emotional connection to the brand. I was determined to make them sell more.

It was clear to me that I need to form a connection between the emotional brain and the sales crew, and getting them to understand that people buy out of emotion. I knew that in order to get the clients to connect to the product emotionally, the sales team must project those certain emotions onto the potential buyer.

I wanted to do something that would trigger their emotional brain. My way of doing that was to create an experience that will trigger all their senses. I neutralized their sight by tying them with an eye ribbon same color as the cologne they needed to sell. I triggered their sense of smell by the cologne I sprayed on the eye ribbons. The sense of hearing was triggered by guided imagery I did – wanting to lead them their emotional side – to picture the man that uses this cologne, and the way he talks to them, flirts with them. How does he sound? What does he look like? Sense of taste was triggered when I gave them a piece of candy with similar tastes to the fragrance of the cologne – vanilla, mint, licorice. Sense of touch was triggered when they felt the shape of the bottle blindfolded.

That training session was one they didn't forget. The sales of the cologne skyrocketed since they were connected to their emotional brain, and that alone had a major influence on sales. The same principal I follow today, while mentoring organizations/businesses owners/individuals that are interested in improving their results.

In your business – check:

- Are you connected to the emotional vision your business have?
- Do you a have a target strong enough that motivates you forward?
- Do you have strong network in and out of the organization that has the power to increase productivity?
- Are your clients emotionally connected to the brand/company/product?
- What emotions drive the purchase of your product, and how can you connect with them?

Remember: **in order to have a successful business you have to make friends with the emotional brain.**

www.sharonaizen.com

How To Make Millions by Using Event-Driven Sales And Marketing

GREG O'DONNELL

The great challenge that most entrepreneurs and salespeople have is that of timing. We always seem to be too early or too late. When early we are told that now is not quite the right time, and by being late we are told that a decision has just been made to work with a competitor.

With a thirty-year career in sales I now have the advantage of seeing that timing and more importantly a sense of opportunistic timing can go a significant distance in changing the number of sales that one can make. In addition to more sales, better timing leads to a more connected response and rapport with your prospect, simply due to the fact that you have made contact at a more opportune time. The big challenge though is that we never seem to achieve this optimal timing on a regular recurring basis.

There is a solution to being there at the right time, being there when the client wants to talk about what you offer, being there when there is a real need for your product or service. The solution is "Event-Driven Sales & Marketing." To be clear we are not talking about an event as in a conference or party. The "event" we are talking about is a corporate or personal announcement that your client prospect makes to the world. They may make this by way of a press release, a news article, social media etc. The point I am making is that an important event has taken place at your prospects enterprise or in their personal life i.e. a promotion, change of company, firing, etc., and the company may now be open to new products or services. You now have an opportunity to introduce your offering.

This highly opportunistic approach is what will set you apart from other sales people that simply contact a prospect when the prospect truly does not have a need for what they are selling, and feel they are too early or too late. We want you to be there at the right time more often than being there at the wrong time. When you utilize this approach to sales and marketing you will appear as a sales person who has a unique sense of timing, a sense of when to approach a prospect with an idea or when to talk with a prospect about a solution that you offer to solve what is likely to be a current or future pain.

Now some of you have been sold a story line that being "opportunistic" is a bad thing. I beg you to remove and banish this thought from your mind. Every person in business is opportunistic. That is the whole point of a business to take advantage of what the marketplace wants, to deliver products or services at the right time, the right price, the right solution to the right people. As an entrepreneur or salesperson we must be opportunistic in order to survive and prosper.

Event-Driven Sales & Marketing can have its challenges though, as there are way too many means with which you can gather information about prospects and their announcements, their senior level corporate changes, financings, expansions, downsizings, mergers etc. A great sales person will expend a significant amount of energy though to try and stay on top of these events. They will read newswire services, social media, newspapers, industry trade articles and more. So I do want you to understand that this approach to marketing and sales is going to require a significant amount of work on your part. There is not a simple and easy path to this approach. You will be required to gather the information on a daily basis, cross reference it against your database. You will need to piece together the data and take action.

The good news is that this will separate you from most of the crowd that simply does not want to do the work. (There are software solutions that do make this significantly easier to accomplish, but they will not eliminate the work, only streamline it.) When you start with this approach it will seem like you are the crazy one and all the others are the smart folks, but when you start to see the results and the confidence you will have when you make cold calls the world will change for you and you will want to keep this approach as a secret. You will know that you have through your hard work found an approach that works.

Event-Driven Sales and Marketing truly can make you millions of dollars. This approach to sales and marketing will make you the money you have always wanted to earn and produce the results for your firm that you have been striving to achieve. And you'll always be that salesperson who is right on time.

www.LeadSmarty.com

Section Two: Management and Culture

Managing Without Leverage

GRANT NADELL

I was once a first-time manager, maybe like you are now or have been before. At the time, the software company I worked for was skyrocketing. People were lining up for jobs and managers held a great deal of leverage over their employees.

Do you know what I mean by leverage? It is like a currency that sums up which side, if any, holds the power in a given negotiation or dispute. When many qualified candidates wait outside the door to a company eager to replace an employee, the management holds leverage. When few qualified candidates are available, and the company desperately needs the staff and is willing to pay for them, the candidate and employees hold leverage.

Leverage can be a tricky thing though, right? If leverage is like currency, leverage is essentially power and power corrupts. So we see examples of companies all the time abusing that leverage, by taking from their employees right to the point of suffering. Fortunately, this particular company was good to their employees and everyone made out quite well.

But what happens when the reverse is true? The reverse, is when a company with little to no leverage tries to take from their employees. It happens all the time, as crazy as that may seem. How you may ask, it's a story for another book, but it has a lot to do with a 'Veil of Fear' that is cast over employees by their companies. A great example of corporate Stockholm Syndrome, if you ask me. I just so happened to arrive at a company that was attempting to act without leverage just a couple years later.

I had obtained my first director job for a small system integrator that I had worked closely with while at both my former employers, both Enterprise Software companies. This management job was far different than the Enterprise Software management jobs I had held. This management position had absolutely zero leverage with its sales employees. In fact, the employees had leverage on me, the company, and the executives.

To provide some context, this system integrator was only driving $12M in sales revenue per year when I was hired, and that great small team grew it to $18M over the next 12 months that I was there. That revenue was almost evenly produced by three account executives, seeing as we ran at around 25% overall margins, the loss of a single account executive meant closing the doors to the company the next day. It would be impossible to stay in business with that large a loss given that small a scale, PERIOD.

Well, the owners wanted me to make reductions in the overall cost structure of the organization by reducing the compensation of the sales team. Furthermore, I was tasked with getting the sales team to start forecasting in the CRM system. Because of leverage, getting employees to forecast at a large software company is easy work, but here at this small company, I had to find another mechanism for achieving those goals. No one at this company was going to do anything that they didn't see as in their best interest and it was uncomfortable to say the least. I like to think it took some courage and insight to determine how to succeed because it meant humbling myself. It was a significant challenge to be in a position of authority without any leverage. I began to realize that authority has two parts.

In my view, YES, in order to have authority the company has to entitle you with the authority to act on its behalf. But while many people think it ends there, I don't think it does. Anyone that has been told they are a manager, boss, captain, or chief without having credibly earned that authority in the eyes of the employees, team, or unit is fooling themselves. The employee must in all instances, except perhaps slavery, has to subjugate themselves in order for authority to function.

In all free societies, it becomes a function of the employee to decide whether or not to subordinate themselves to the manager. The employee doesn't have to subordinate themselves. Sure, they may be terminated for not doing so and consistently holding that threat over people's heads is a form of the 'Veil of Fear' I mentioned above. Ultimately, it is still the employee's choice.

This realization of the relationship created between employee and manager allowed me to see a path forward. I looked at examples of where someone led a group without leverage. Examples where groups of people were following their leader without being forced at great risk to their own security. Jesus was one example. Another was the military squad leader. Which is when I assembled these pertinent tenants for leading without leverage.

- Lead by example
  - Be willing to do the crappy stuff
  - Do the admin work
  - Roll up your sleeves
  - Get into the real meat of the work
- Be of service
- Remove the obstacles
- Give praise
- Be transparent
- Find ways to provide tangible value

This altruistic behavior, which focuses the energy and efforts of the manager and team on the greater good; drives loyalty, obedience, favor, respect, and appreciation. And really what more can you want?

What I haven't mentioned yet is the results this change in management style yielded from employees' perceptions of working for me. So let me tell you two quick stories that show you how employees have responded to the before and after.

A couple years ago I ran into one of the members of that first sales team that I managed, at the larger company, and he introduced me to his fiancée. He said, "this is the guy that threatened to kill my first born if I didn't hit my quota." Wow, was I taken back. There is absolutely no truth to that statement, he was making a joke, but there is obviously a reason he thought it was funny.

That was then and this is now.

A couple weeks ago, a company interested in hiring me contacted one of my recent employees (at the smaller company) about what type of manager I was and she replied, "he is a fantastic mentor and leader, someone that listens, provides great strategic and tactical advice, removes obstacles, and is willing to roll up their sleeves and chip in to get the win."

So which approach do you think was better? The one where I had the leverage, or the one where my account executives had it and I needed to manage them without it? In my mind, there's no contest. Leverage is overrated.

Two Key Factors In Business And Personal Success

JENNIFER LEAKE

I was sixteen when I got my first official job in our neighborhood drug store. Over forty years later, it is still one of my favorite jobs. Predominantly young (high school and college) workers knew exactly what was expected of them because we were given training and clear direction. I still remember one of the owner's rules – the phone MUST be answered by the third ring. No one was responsible for this – we were ALL responsible for making this happen. After the second ring, you'd see people running from all around to get to the closest phone before the third ring finished. Today, many years later, when I hear a phone start to ring, I still get nervous after that second ring!

The work environment was fun, we believed our bosses cared about us and we loved being there. So much so that we'd stop by to visit even if we weren't on the schedule. And if we had a wave of customers, we'd jump on a register to help out anyway. We hadn't punched a time clock. We weren't being paid. No one asked us to do it. We just did it because we were a team.

I thought that was what work was all about. You loved your job, cared about the others you worked with, knew what your job was, were trained to do it well, and had a boss that cared about you as a person. I've been lucky that many of my jobs were like that first job years ago. But one that was not still stands out to me many years later.

After successfully moving up the ranks in pharmaceutical sales and management, the company decided I should be promoted into a senior position designed to give me more experience in finance and operations. Now, I am well suited for anything that involves sales, customer service and building relationships. I thrive with a boss who gives clear expectations and trusts my abilities and talent to make it happen without hovering over my shoulder. After years of a good "job fit" and the resulting success, I found myself in a completely different situation. I was now involved in data, accounting and numbers. To make matter worse, I worked for a bully boss who micro-managed, set constantly changing expectations and goals, and publicly attacked me in meetings.

As the situation continued, I spiraled downward in motivation and work satisfaction. Going to work became such a challenge that I started carpooling with a co-worker to get me out the door each day. After 18 months in this poor "job fit" position, I could no longer bring myself to be motivated enough to go to work. Despite having 3 children in college, I sadly resigned. This 110% committed employee had employee engagement drained out of me.

It was a personal loss to leave a company I had dedicated myself to for almost 10 years. The company lost the talent, knowledge and experience they had spent years developing. That experience led to my passionate commitment to master two key things I believe are critical in business – Job Fit and Employee Engagement.

Why are these so important?

Job fit means the right people are in the right job, the right company culture and match the leadership style of the boss they report to. Your most expensive business problem is employees who are not engaged. Engaged employees come to work with initiative, a desire to solve problems and to contribute in a positive way. Disengaged employees more often sabotage and add to workplace drama. This positive or negative attitude spills over to affect their personal life too.

What lessons can be learned from this?

- Most people don't love the job they're in. Being in a job that you enjoy and are energized to give your best is far better than being in one where you are miserable and de-motivated. This is true for the both the employee and the company.
- No one enters into a job expecting or wanting to fail – but many do. This happens when a manager:
  - Fails to consider job fit when they hire or promote and a talented and capable person is put into the wrong job.
  - Manages and motivates employees the same way rather than understanding and knowing how to get the most out of each employee.

– Learns leadership through trial and error rather than seek training in things like Emotional Intelligence or Leadership skills.

Successful and profitable businesses need to strive to have their employees:

- **love what they do** – because they are in the right job, know what's expected of them, and have the resources and training
- **enjoy who they work with** – because they feel part of a strong team; and
- **respect who they work for** – because they believe in the company, what it stands for, who they work for and who runs it.

Individual success leads to company profits and success – and the opposite is also true. It is a costly business mistake when employees are unmotivated and underperform. You have a competitive advantage when they are motivated and excel at their job. The decision to devote attention, effort and investment in job fit and employee engagement results in bottom line ROI and both personal and business success. It's the difference between your worst nightmare … or the best job you've ever had.

www.AssessmentPros.com

The Cost Of Creating Buy-In

MELODY RIDER

Influence over your team is vital to be able to create the change or improvements that businesses need to make to stay competitive. Yes, as leaders we have the right to give marching orders without asking for input from our employees. At times we just have to tell them what to do, when to do it, and how to do it. But we all have been on the receiving end of being told what to do and walked away thinking of how we could do what was asked better and feeling a little bitter that we were not asked our opinion.

To just tell people what to do without asking their opinion or letting them come up with a solution can break down employee's desire to do what is being asked. However, strong leaders work to gain employees ideas and opinions on current business issues. Leaders do this so they create an environment where employee opinions and ideas are shared to aid in the resolution process. When employees feel valued their loyalty grows and they have more ownership to the outcomes. The employee will gain excitement by seeing their ideas being put into practice and work harder to ensure the success. This process of an employee feeling heard, valued, their ideas being put into practice then creates their *"buy-in"* to the outcomes. It creates their ownership to ensuring what you as a leader needs to get done gets done. Their *"buy-in"* means you have insurance that your marching orders now become their idea so they have more desire for it to be a success.

In my experience, by gaining *"buy-in"* overall morale improves and creating change becomes a positive experience versus getting push back on giving orders that they might not believe in. Too often, change gives the notion that what was been done in the past was wrong, that the hard work in the past doesn't have worth, and employee may even think that it is their fault that they change is needed. It becomes personal and they may feel attacked or judged that the process they have done for some time is now not good enough. Change is hard unless you make it your employees' ideas.

Now – here is the hard part as a leader, how do you make the needed change their idea? As a leader you know what needs to be changed and even most days how to make the change happen. Some leaders even map out the entire change process and every step the employees need to make to create the change expected.

Change management does require a clear roadmap of how to make the change happened with checkpoints and clear expectations for employees. In this process of creating "buy-in" you can keep your roadmap, your check-points, and expectations – the difference is you are now going to allow for all of it to be your employees' ideas. Wait, what? Why would a leader who knows how to solve an issue, create the change, and have all the expectation for their employees need to ask input from their employees or gain any ideas from them? Sounds like a huge waste of time, right? Wrong. What I have experienced when creating "*buy-in*" with my team, they end up having more creative ideas and looking at things much differently than I do. Their roadmap has more inventive ideas and higher expectations for themselves.

It does take longer to prepare the communication that you will need to have with your employees. It will require you to create a long list of questions that will get your employees to come up with the ideas that will create the needed change within the boundaries you know exist through your prepared road map. You will need to look at all angles, all perspectives, and already have the anticipated answers to the questions. This allows for you to be over prepared for dialogue that will lead the team or individual employee. I have gone into a meeting not prepared when attempting to create "*buy-in*" and it went very wrong. Especially if you are doing this in a group setting and the brainstorming about how to create this needed change derails and the change conversation goes negative. In those moments I want to go back to just giving marching orders without even asking an opinion out of frustration, but the responsibility lies on the leader for guiding the brainstorming in the direction it is intended to go.

In the end creating "*buy-in*" is orchestrated through a lot of preparation in knowing how the team or individual employee will respond to the questions. Identifying the ideas that leads to the next question, to the next great idea and so on. It is great to challenge the group and provide "what ifs" so they are looking at the issues from all directions, not from a limited space. This helps them grow to understand the "why" the business change needs to take place. This is also important piece of gaining"*buy-in*," is allowing the employee to understand the "why" gives the deeper understanding of importance and possible urgency.

Not gaining *"buy-in"* could result in delay in outcomes, poor outcomes, negative attitude, or push back. Gaining *"buy-in,"* although time consuming in the preparation, has high pay off in the end. I have endured teams taking my directive and seemly do as they were told. In these moments I can reflect back and see lack of excitement and ownership to the outcomes. I have seen employee hide behind saying they didn't understand the directive, complain that is wasn't working, or said they were executing what was asked but didn't because they simply weren't bought in. If employees are bought in, they have skin in the game by contributing their ideas they are more likely to give more, care more, and want the desired result to be success. The ultimate success as a leader is that when the change process is a success the employees own the win!! They get to be proud of what they accomplished, they feel successful. When your team wins that is when a leader can look in the mirror and feel the sense of victory – which is priceless.

Teach And Learn Every Day

JAKE BROSS

Throughout your career, you will find very few successful people who will say they got to where they are through only their own efforts. Somewhere along the way, someone helped them along. Someone took a few more minutes than they had to, explained what they knew, and took on the role of a teacher.

Successful people teach and learn every day. It's your duty to pass this on to the next generation. Teach what you know to anyone who wants to learn. Learn from anyone around you, even those that don't make great teachers.

Twenty-five years ago, my first manager was difficult. I had no experience managing, but I knew I didn't agree with the way he managed his people. He was a highly skilled salesman in his own right, but over the years I worked with him, he never shared any of his skills with his team; he was too busy managing. I thought it was a waste of his talent, and a shame that he could have elevated his team, but chose not to. I often asked for his time, but he didn't see the value in coaching. He had a transactional mindset, only focused on the short term ... and most coaching takes longer than a single monthly P+L statement to cultivate. However, I learned how not to manage by watching him. I told myself if I ever had the chance, I would teach my team what I knew, and develop them to a higher level as a group. If you are aware, you can learn from even the worst managers, even if it's how not to lead.

Another lesson: sometimes mentors are who you make them. Many of us imagine the perfect mentor as an older, wiser, and kind soul who loves to teach. This is not always the case. Sometimes a mentor is assigned the role. This doesn't mean they know how to teach and coach for success. Fast forward 10 years, to another company and another manager. I had lunch one day with my boss's boss. He asked how things were going. And like many great leaders, he knew the answers to most of his questions before he asked them. I told him I was struggling with my boss. He questioned everything I did, slowed down my processes and often delayed our activity for the sake of asking questions. He asked me if I thought my boss had anything to offer me; if I thought he was a smart guy. I said, "Absolutely, he is sharp and more experienced than I am." He suggested I think hard about what my boss could do for me, what he could teach me. He said, "I don't need you to like him or be best friends. I need you to see value in your boss and then extract any and all knowledge from him. Use that knowledge to propel yourself forward in your career. Ask him to teach you what he knows."

By showing the humility to admit I don't know everything, I gained my boss's trust. I went to him and said, "when you have a few minutes, can you teach me about ...." He was glad to help. Whether or not it was because I acknowledged he was the boss or that he knew more than I did; it worked. He spent extra time in the mornings and the evenings showing me what he knew and it explained why he asked so many questions. Point is, I went from being a victim of a difficult boss, to a situation of learning and guidance that prepared me for my next role. Most importantly, I found my mentor because his boss took a few minutes to coach me on how to utilize my environment rather than deal with it. By identifying who had knowledge I needed, and simply asking him to show me what he knew, I saw the value in a team member I never knew was there. I built a solid working relationship in the process.

Now, you do owe it to the next generation to teach what you know, because someone did it for you. Here is a solid method to begin creating a culture of personal and professional growth. Start by making a chart of the prioritized business and sales functions in your operation. Who excels in each category, such as administrative systems, closing the sale, creating leads/networking, or technical? Assign these mentoring activities with prescriptive details and a calendar. Quite often the best of intentions fall aside to business functions if they are not detailed on a calendar with a report-out to leadership outlining the results and progress. It's also a good idea to have gates or checkpoints along the way. Assigning mentorship is a great way to develop your next leaders and acknowledge their abilities. This is where establishing the culture begins. Some of the best companies in the world have a goal to have 6% of their employees' time dedicated to growth and development.

Downstream in this process, your ultimate goal is to have a cross-trained team with bench strength. This protects your business against gaps left by attrition. This new culture you're creating provides a foundation built on coaching and development, and leads to a more cohesive team that represents your company better in front of the customer. Development programs keep your employees engaged in their careers and reduce turnover. If you're in an environment that doesn't currently drive employee development, you can still take a leadership role. The old mentality says "If I'm the only person in the building that knows how to do something, I'm more valuable." A better attitude says "I'm 10 times more valuable if I teach 10 people what I know. I'll lead the way, and show my value to the entire team."

Another way to drive this culture is quarterly reviews. Many companies hold annual reviews or merit discussions. Most managers don't coach through the year, and try to summarize an employee's year-long workload into a one-hour conversation. Quite often, we don't assign growth or capability targets, so we spend more time looking backward than forward. Quarterly reviews keep it at the forefront and let everyone know it's important. Over time, you create a culture of teaching and learning.

Leaders' Positive Psychology Tools For Healthy And Hopeful Motivation

LISA M. MILLER

After many years of research, teaching, service, and consulting as a professor of leadership and performance psychology in higher education, I learned psychological knowledge and skills that help leaders pursue hopes of perfection. Perfection refers to the motivation of improvement until reaching a state of flawlessness. These psychological tools help leaders create a culture of hopeful motivation for perfection, caring altruistic relationships, and healthy balanced wisdom. In the following chapter, leaders' positive psychology tools for healthy and hopeful motivation for perfection will be discussed from a practical and action-oriented perspective.

Culture of Hopeful Motivation for Perfection

A leadership mentality that emphasizes the importance of a positive culture with hopeful motivation for perfection establishes both a caring legacy along with structures and formal processes. Leadership studies about this topic occurred at the rivals of Ohio State University and the University of Michigan in the late 1940s and early 1950s. Ohio State researchers found that the two most important dimensions of leadership included structures of work and consideration of others. Michigan researchers found that effective leaders tended to be job centered and employee centered. Despite the classic rivalry of Ohio State and Michigan, both research teams arrived at similar conclusions. Positive relationships matter for hopeful motivation, and structured processes also matter when creating a leadership culture of perfection. Cultures with positive relationships when striving for perfection build a flourishing legacy of high achieving beloved leadership. These cultures of hopeful motivation for perfection help to build flourishing organizations where people have more positive emotions of happiness and more engagement with one another while pursuing meaningful achievements. Cultures with this type of flourishing positivity require positive psychology leadership skills, caring altruistic relationship building, and trusted collegiality with healthy balanced wisdom. The feelings of hopeful motivation within the culture impact critical leadership outcomes. Restructuring for perfection in processes and procedures may provide better task completion, but a long-term legacy of flourishing as a beloved leader of hopeful pathways needs investments in caring altruistic relationship development for motivation.

Caring Altruistic Relationships

When organizations start to measure engagement with the workplace, the importance of caring, altruistic relationships becomes more apparent. Measurement of whether leaders foster engagement and a sense of community provides a message that people matter in our organizations. Engagement cannot be left to chance without structures to support altruistic care and concern for one another. Altruism refers to the ultimate motivation to improve the wellbeing of others. Vision statements, discussions, and personal approaches are signs that indicate whether a true commitment to community building and altruism exists. A leader must be chosen who values personal secure attachment and altruistic trust to provide a mission, inspiration, and transformations that transcend egotistical self-focused benefits. Without this personal, secure, and altruistically caring engagement, people may focus less on meaningful work and more on earning a paycheck. Altruistically caring leaders remain visible and interactional with others in the organization and in the community. This leadership altruism and engagement must seep into every level of an organization with every person in the organization.

Healthy Balanced Wisdom

When we find ourselves unprepared and unequipped to balance our required tasks for perfection, much stress and disappointment surface in our mentality, resulting in vulnerability to anxiety, burnout, depression, and suicidal ideation. Healthy leadership requires preparing and equipping our team with healthy ways of coping and designing a balanced life. A wisdom must be present for understanding our perfect balance of life goals that include both caring relationships and high accomplishments. Balance sometimes requires us to push ourselves to the limits to find appropriate and healthy boundaries that we must set and maintain for ourselves. Without a proper level of experienced wisdom, too much may be added to our ambitious schedule without the positive psychology tools to succeed in our most important endeavors. Wisdom also provides us with knowing we cannot achieve everything with a high level of expertise. If a leader decides to scatter the focus too broadly and does not listen to the needs of the team, the necessary depth of valuable expertise may be lost and high anxiety may occur that damages the hopeful motivational culture of the organization. Self-set passion and self-set expertise provides a lucrative self-motivated asset to organizations with lower anxiety provoking leadership. Society needs and craves experts, but experts also need healthy self-set boundaries for coping and flourishing. Due to our limited lifetime, wisdom indicates that we cannot be an expert on everything and still maintain a healthy full life with family, friends, exercise, and spirituality. Valuable wise expertise requires a detailed and deep scholarly research agenda with much reading, discussion, and observation on a significantly important topic to humanity. Therefore, we must wisely choose our own expertise to harmonize with the balance and passion of our lives.

Concluding Action Steps

Investments in leaders' positive psychology tools take time, practice, and measurement in order to provide benefits. Each tool in this chapter addressed the need of leaders to invest in interpersonal skills balanced with task completion structures for healthy and hopeful motivation toward perfection. Leaders invest day by day in their long-term legacy through these action steps:

1. **Strategically Plan Virtuous Living:** Effective structures for daily life include pre-determined time blocks for important engagement with others and investments in strategically planning virtues of the perfect balance in mind, body, spirit, emotions, relationships, career pursuits, personal finances, and healthy environments.
2. **Schedule Individual Life Balance Meetings:** Leaders talk with their team members and use tools to chart each team member's level of life balance as they strive to reach audacious goals together.
3. **Provide Ways of Coping Assessments:** Leaders become beloved and altruistic not by their completed tasks alone but rather by their investment tools in building long term positive relationships through caring and helping team members cope with striving for perfection.
4. **Track Hour by Hour Improvements:** An effective balance in leadership utilizes both high relationship quality and high project management

structures with tools of detailed hour by hour time studies, schedules, and daily improvement tracking toward perfection.

5. **Maintain an Observation Journal:** The hardships with work-life balance in leadership could be monitored and continuously improved through tools of wise observational journaling of both facilitators and barriers to positive relationships and task completion.

The investments in positive psychology tools for healthy and hopeful motivation for perfection help avoid mental and physical barriers while also helping to facilitate the wise and steady journey of a beloved altruistic leadership legacy.

This chapter is dedicated to my children, Christian and Hope, as they help lead our future generation.

http://www.theschoolofpositivepsychologyeducation.org/

Keep Things Simple And Listen To Your Customers

RUDOLPH "RUDY" ANTONINI

Flashback to 2003, fresh off the dot-com bubble. Some online businesses were flourishing, others were dropping like flies. It was an exciting time to be part of an internet startup company, especially one that was really taking off. This was my first corporate job out of college and like most 23-year-olds I had no idea what I wanted to do. So I decided to go work for a bank. An online bank actually. Online you say, like the internet? "What the heck is an internet bank?" "Do you really exist?". "Where are your branches?" (Those were typical questions I fielded day-in-day-out as a call center agent.)

The truth is I loved every minute of it. I enjoyed connecting with customers, problem solving through issues, helping them understand who and what we were, and what our organization stood for. Our mission was simple and it made us different than anyone else. Being part of a mission-led business made it super easy to stand behind, commit, and wake charged each morning to help Americans simplify their finances and save for the future. The challenge with a mission-led company is that it's easy to steer off-course, especially in the banking world. You're aware of most big banks today, incredibly complex systems cobbled together through countless integrations, creating twenty of the same products with inconsistent experiences because they can't get out of their own way. Well, we were in fact truly different and it was all due to culture-driven leadership. And you had to be all-in, all the time. We kept things simple and we were obsessed over customer experiences. There was one individual that taught me the value of keeping things simple very early on, our CEO.

Now, he didn't know that he was teaching me anything at the time. His desk was conveniently located on the call center floor out of the way, but close enough that he could eavesdrop on customer conversation (phone calls) whenever he wanted. After a while I started to pick up on his patterns. He'd sit there in the early AM, drinking his coffee and pretending to read email. All the while he was listening in on the business that he and many others had built from the ground up. He made it a point to be there at his desk, almost like clockwork, on Fridays around 8:30am right before what I later found out was the weekly Product and Marketing meeting. This was a standing-room-only meeting made up mostly by product, marketing, and engineering leadership. The brains of the organization and the folks that were building and designing new features and our latest digital experiences. This is where most of the magic happened, the really great ideas.

It wasn't until a few years later that I found out what really happened in those meetings. Lots of heated debate, lots of arguing, lots of opinions, but all over the customer experience, how to make it better, and with all good intentions. And after having an hour or more of customer listening and feedback our CEO would have more than enough ammo to spark up some heated debate in the meeting that followed.

There's one story in particular that stands out and I still remember to this day each and every time I began a new initiative or project. CEO to team: "I just spent the last 20 minutes listening to one of our employees try and explain the account opening process to a Customer. 20 MINUTES ... did you hear me? If we can't explain how things work in less than a minute or two than we've failed. We need to tear it down, re-build it." It was this type of mentality that fueled our employees and leadership team, kept our Customers coming back for more, and what would eventually become the largest savings bank and number one direct bank in the United States.

For anyone out there about to construct, create, or design something (anything) remember to keep it simple and ask yourself if you can explain it in less than a minute or two. If you can't do it than how the heck is anyone else going to? (And while you're at it, don't forget to listen to your customers.)

Breaking Into The Boys' Club

CASSANDRA WESCH

Many of us share the same motivations, but what separates us is how we turn motivation into a relentless pursuit to achieve our dreams, no matter the obstacles.

After college, when I was 24, the city I loved so much began to feel small. So, I moved from one beach town to another, San Diego to Miami Beach. I had no job, no friends, no family in Miami Beach, and no idea what my next move was going to be. I just knew there had to be a beach.

For a while I took odd marketing jobs and account executive positions for little pay. Then finally an opportunity came along working at an early-stage e-commerce startup. It was less than 2 years in business, and as time went on, I went from team member to VP of Marketing and later an equity partner.

Fast forward to when I was 32, and we sold our startup to the world's largest retailer of sports licensed merchandise, valued at $3 billion at the time. The fruits of my labor paid off, literally. Post-acquisition I remained with the acquiring company for 3 years to spearhead the marketing for a new division. Today, I'm a self-made entrepreneur with multiple business ventures, but I pride my work in helping online brands establish a digital footprint.

What is my point? The point is that as easily as I wrote this, the exact opposite is true of the journey. At times the struggle was incredibly intense. I was a minority, a female working in a male-dominated industry of sports and technology, and in a highly-coveted position on the executive team.

As the only woman in the room, I had to walk a fine line between exerting masculine leadership and maintaining femininity. I want to make it clear I am not victimizing "femaleness." I do not wish to be a part of the "archetypal woman entrepreneur." Through my experience and professional development, I had many micro-moments accumulate over the years that simply taught me how to be successful in a male-dominated industry.

Sports and technology industries are notorious for having predominantly male senior management, and there is a stark gender imbalance. But even so, I gained a seat at the table with a lot of hard work and people skills.

Having a strong personality and applying a masculine leadership style was expected of me. I had to speak up in meetings and present ideas with conviction, but do so without talking louder or becoming aggressive. There can be a lot of egos in the "boardroom," especially when the company President decides to drop in. I've witnessed colleagues trying to one-up each other and talk over one another. I learned very quickly to never try to be the smartest person in the room. No one likes a show off. Instead, I offered suggestions as a better way to do things, rather than the right way to do things. This worked really well. When I had the floor, it was mine. Everyone listened to what I had to say, and there was no undermining or dismissive attitudes.

It was also important that I always present a positive attitude and build trusting relationships. If you bring good energy and vibes into the workplace, people will naturally enjoy working with you. I sparked up conversations with every person in the company, no matter if it was the intern or the President. This relationship building brought me huge professional benefits in that people were able to help me do my job efficiently. I was able to leverage my relationships to prioritize my marketing initiatives. For example, my tech tickets were implemented ahead of other departments, irrelevant of resources, timeline, difficulty, or red tape. Ultimately, I was able to spearhead marketing campaigns quicker, drive sales, and boost my department numbers by truly understanding the "it's all who you know" rhetoric.

Being social is an extension of presenting a positive attitude and building strategic relationships. Grabbing a brewski after work or making lunch plans was essential for my career advancement. I would attend work functions, going away parties, happy hours, you name it. After that, the trust was in the bag. Certain projects called for certain people and I was always called in.

I had to be knowledgeable. Being in an industry dominated by men for decades, I felt I had to try even harder to prove my abilities, and it was important I was a valuable member of the team. I was constantly growing, improving and evolving in my profession and staying on top of industry trends and innovation. I made it a point to educate my team on what I was learning from the front lines of marketing and technology. This did not go unnoticed. I was bringing advantageous information to my superiors where they were in the dark. I kept our business ahead of our competitors by beta testing cutting-edge strategies and technologies.

I also learned to tap into my strengths. Women are typically good at empathizing, multi-tasking and understanding people. I used this to my advantage and excelled in areas where others could not. I was known to take challenged and diverse teams and make them strong and successful by simply being empathetic. The Darwinian world of corporate climbing can include empathy despite what others say; it's definitely a strength, not a weakness.

Lastly, I always conducted myself professionally. Being dependable, reliable, honest, and keeping my word garnered recognition and respect. If you can stand out as a solid person with a great reputation then you can influence people's view of you in a good way, and hopefully influence that promotion you've been eyeing.

Maneuvering the boys' club has its advantages and can bring higher levels of success. Join the club.

www.upwardcommerce.com

The Power of Dialogue

THERESA ASHBY

Write them up, fire them or ignore them. That was the "expert" advice I received in response to how I should handle underperforming employees. However, the advice did not sit well with me. It was disrespectful to the employee and absolutely did not serve the organization. So with resistance from others, I took the path less traveled. I decided instead to engage in thoughtful and honest dialogue with my employees.

Let me tell you a story about Henry, a company director. Henry was well organized, meticulous, and watched the budget like a hawk. Henry also had an ego that often got in the way of making balanced decisions. He also could enforce the rigidity of rules to the extreme, blinding himself to the bigger picture. For example, he refused to purchase a $250 printer for an employee who routinely traversed a 50-acre campus to pick up work orders, rather than have another printer. Let's see ... $250 dollars, versus walking across campus 15 times a day, multiplied by his hourly rate ... see my point?

I coached Henry and provide resources for him, which helped him improve to an extent. He engaged in the conversation, he worked hard to change and become a better leader; nonetheless, he continued to lack the ability to influence his team and his ego was always lurking just under the surface.

It was a Friday afternoon when I invited Henry to the conference room. I never have these conversations in my office, preferring neutral ground. I purposely sat so we faced each other with no table in between. I started the dialogue, "How is your family?" "Did you enjoy your vacation?" I then asked, "How are you doing with your relationships with your employees and your critical projects?" He answered appropriately.

I transitioned into "How are some of the relationship issues going?" "Are you working on repairing them?" "Do you see yourself improving as a leader?" I got the typical answers: yes and yes. Yet I knew he was still struggling with managing his employees. I then moved to the one question no one expects,

"Are you enjoying your role as a leader?" I could tell he was shocked. He was searching the sky for answers. I said, "I don't want the right answer, I want the truth."

His face flushed and he became visibly nervous. "Look," I said, "I am on your side, what's going on? Talk to me about the pressure and what you really want." We simmered in uncomfortable silence. With a cracking voice, he said, "I know I am not doing a good job and it is causing problems at work and at home." And as fast as he said it, he realized he had just dropped his armor and then retracted the information with "but I can handle it." He and I continued to talk about the potential perils of leadership and the power of being able to admit we don't have it all together. We talked a lot about having a balanced ego and how purposefully setting ego aside can open up transparency and elicit trust from his staff.

I communicated to him that I saw us having two options. I explained how much I appreciated all of his work and how I saw the effort he was investing towards self-improvement. I informed him that despite this effort, I did not see him being successful in his current role. I told him he had an opportunity to stay in his current role, but that disciplinary measures would likely escalate to an eventual termination. I let him sit with this for a minute.

I then presented him with another opportunity that would lend more to his current skill set. I was very clear, if he took on this new position, in the future, with coaching, he may be able to work his way back into a leadership role. He was hurt. He was concerned about his reputation and the communication with his staff, which I indicated we would manage together with a positive spin. I suggested he go home and talk it over with his wife, consider the financial implications, and do earnest soul-searching. He and I had a dialogue about how he might approach the conversation with his wife.

It was a sleepless weekend for me – I am sure it was worse for Henry. He knew if he stepped down it would mean a significant cut in pay and no bonus, but for him, it was about saving face in front of his wife and colleagues. I never wanted to hurt the "nice" guy and I never underestimated his feelings and concerns. But again, as a leader, one must balance what is right for the organization and the person.

Henry chose to step down, and we worked closely to transition him into his new role with dignity. The only thing people knew was that I asked him to take on another role. I explained I needed someone to straighten out a separate set of issues, which was the total truth and I knew he could do it. Months later, Henry came into my office and said "Thank you." He went on to say, "I feel less pressure, I feel like I am successful in my new role and best of all, I am much happier at home and I have gone back to school, which has been my dream for years."

In the end, this story had a positive outcome. Sometimes it is about moving away from what everyone is telling you to do and doing the "right" thing for the employee. Before you want to just fire your next underperforming employee, have a dialogue and see what is really going on. It is hard for both parties and it takes time, but in the end, if we choose to be leaders, it is our responsibility to lead people carefully and respectfully, helping them clear the path that is right for them.

www.dynamconsulting.com

Self-Development In The Workplace

RYAN M. MCDOUGALD

Our work is a major component of our time. Statistically speaking, it consumes approximately one third of our lifespans (homemakers waaay more)."Captain Obvious" is telling me that Work is a BIG part of our daily routine. Still – one basic question remains? ... Awareness in the workplace – What does THAT mean?

I work in the Greater Los Angeles area, where it is a cultural melting pot, and if culture is what you are after, there is plenty of different cultures around, but ... I am not sure, how many of these cultures are intimately infused within the corporate cultures of the companies of today? I suspect not many ... so how do we get there?

Self-development should be a part of each employee's training plan. It should be included as part of the annual appraisal process, maybe this single component is **weighted 25%** and is based on personal development progression. And it does not matter what role you play within the organization (household) ... you could be the weakest link in the chain (temporarily), but personal growth and development programs/strategies MUST be a primary focal point within any progressive company's vision.

Regardless of your profession ... Most people have the same ***wonderful hangover*** after going to a live Speaking Engagement, that was impactful. Let us say you went to an awesome Tony Robbins conference, or a week-long 360 workshop to discover what type of personality you are ... How did you feel that same evening? Or the next morning? Maybe even throughout that entire first week? ... You felt AWESOME, POWERFUL, PASSIONATE, right? And you have always ask yourself this question "WHY can't I be like this all the time?"

I believe the solution is in making personal development an integral part *of* the new job requirements. When you are interviewing an applicant, **I want to see this resume requirement: how much personal development**

have you had, how many workshops have you been to, how many speakers have you watched? Let us talk about them, and what did you learn about yourself in the process, have you reflected back on the old you versus the present you, and what is the plan and strategy for personal development for the future? These questions may lead to profound insight as a new form of behavioral interview data.

Maybe there is need for a new role to emerge, a PR Coach of sorts within the corporation that has someone focusing on Social Investments in the local community, but also serves in a new *coach-like role*, primarily focused on improving employee morale, etc., leading by example, being polite, kind, hold doors open, give way to others, etc.

Suggestions for companies to use in promoting personal development in the workplace may include:

- A profound "quote of the day" on the lobby TV, or a daily morning business affirmation that is spread via email companywide each morning. Involve the employees in the selection process.
- When meeting a new employee that is from outside the US, the **easiest way for them to assimilate** and at same time celebrate their cultural differences, is **getting them involved with social investments within their new local communities**. Nothing connects you better to your surroundings, than being of service.
- Weekly TED Talk sharing should be a part of the plan, five-year plan on living strategically within the organization.
- Successful companies have at their core an understanding, and culture, of giving back to others, realizing that philanthropy is the responsibility of everyone, that it's everyone's job to help our fellow man/woman in need.

I currently work with so many awesome people from diverse backgrounds, sometimes on work visas, leaving close family and friends at home, young, single, new to the company/country ... BUT with a shared common goal and purpose: to support the organization, to align with corporate social responsibility campaigns outside the company.

The only additional required step/solution here is simply to involve their employees more INSIDE that same strategy, getting employees into action.

Section Three: Well-Rounded Skill Sets

How To Become the B.I.C.

PATRICIA SUFLITA WILSON

Some of the most defining and memorable moments we have as a leader come as a bit of a surprise and in the face of adversity.

I've always been a believer of setting a good example by doing. I implement "all hands on deck" projects where everyone is on the same team. Regular job: Accountant? Not today, we've got signs to make. Someone has a computer component not working? Yup, that would be me crawling on the floor to troubleshoot.

I feel when you join in and lead the way by embracing tasks that clearly are not your area – it sets an example and speaks volumes. No job carried out by a member of your team should be beneath you. I know you are an important leader and all, but let's face it, we are all interim leaders.

Some years ago, I created a food and wine event that has become a spectacular annual event. It now generates upwards of $1,000,000 and is attended by close to 1,000 guests, vendors and volunteers. This is definitely an "all hands on deck" event. Some critical staff still came to the office but were "on call" should we fall behind and need help setting up.

I still vividly remember the year our caterer chose a fancy metal chair for our guests. It looked so good. And the rental price was right. The downside? We had to unload the chairs and set them up themselves. As it turns out? Metal chairs are rather heavy. I carried two at a time. And made lots and lots of trips. This part of set up occurs the day before the event, so I hoped the night of I might be recovered a bit. That might normally be true, but carrying heavy metal chairs apparently causes bruises on your arms. Which I didn't notice until I was dressed for the event (sleeveless dress) and had several guests grab my arms and ask me what the hell happened.

Another year, we are setting up for the event (thankfully, no metal chairs!) and I'm carrying cases of wine. I think on average the event between auctions, tasting and dinner is somewhere near 100 cases of wine. While I do enjoy drinking wine, carrying it by the case can wear you out. Obviously on set up days, wearing comfortable shoes and clothing was critical.

As such, I was dressed down and didn't look very CEO-like.

I was helping set up in another area of the venue, and I made it back to the main room. This room is cavernous. The size of a football field. I entered at the far end, but could hear a "situation." It was a male voice, one I didn't recognize and I couldn't make out what he was saying yet, but his volume, tone and body language told me everything I needed to know. As I got closer, I can discern he was literally chewing out our incredible and positive Events Director. The closer I get, the more I'm able to make out in his anger. He's obviously a vendor. Not that it matters, but technically, he works for her! She is trying to make the most of it and resolve his issue – but clearly he prefers to dwell on it and seems to almost relish demeaning her.

The entire time I'm beelining to go to the area of conflict (clear on the other side of room) he never looks up. He just glares at her while being verbally abusive. He is apparently upset she didn't know to order some piece of equipment he needs. He is using profanity (the body language is crazy!) and she is nodding and trying to be understanding. And the dozens of people in the room? Yup. All eyes glued to this confrontation.

I think she would have done just fine resolving the conflict, but by the time I am in close proximity, something in me drives everything that happened next. You should know I don't look for conflict, rather I am solutions focused. So, I take my conflict averse self, all 5'12" of me (no, that's not a typo – somehow it seems shorter than saying I am 6'0" tall) and I step into his space. He finally, yet almost robotically, he finally moves his gaze (aka hateful glance) from the Events Director to me.

I ask, "How can I help you?"

He gives me a once over and says with disdain, "And who the hell are you?"

There are dozens of people in the room. At this point, you could have heard a pin drop. All the vendors have stopped working and all eyes are glued on us.

My response to who I am? Words I don't think I had EVER uttered before. It was completely spontaneous. I introduced myself and held my hand out. "I'm Patricia, the CEO."

Insert long awkward pause as he glares at me, but he says nothing. And then out of nowhere, I add "I am the bitch in charge!"

There it was.

His gaze no longer focused on me. He suddenly became aware all eyes were on him. And you could hear his team choking back laughter. I had called his bluff and was prepared to fire him on the spot – even if it meant panic and possibly putting us way behind in setup. But I also knew this attitude and abuse have no place in the workforce.

I earned more respect in that moment than I could have ever imagined. I backed up my team and let them know they don't ever have to tolerate verbal abuse. And I do think the element of surprise (the underdressed woman CEO) had some shock value that actually worked in my favor.

In that moment? Without prompting, I earned the nickname B.I.C. It is now a term of endearment that I am proud to behold.

I hope you find your inner B.I.C.

When the moment is right, you need to be prepared to defend your team. It might be symbolic at the moment. But it truly is critical in building a loyal, cohesive team. Sometimes the most obvious conflicts can present an opportunity for a leader to demonstrate extraordinary leadership. Even if you are woefully underdressed.

Psthinkbig.com

Financial Empowerment: Don't Forget Your Accounting!

MARI RAMIREZ

As a certified public accountant, I provide accounting, bookkeeping and tax services to businesses and individuals. I've seen many people come and go in the twelve years I've been in this field. That's not surprising. What's surprising is the number of businesses I see fail in that field. Even in the best economy, accounting is just as susceptible to failure as everything else.

Starting your own business takes a certain type of person, and of course it calls for passion and dedication. Businesses started by people who are passionate and have put much into starting this one endeavor fail even when the product is amazing, the marketing is on point, and the business plan sounds great in theory. Failures do not occur in just one type of industry – and I usually start seeing signs in the accounting early on in the journey.

From month to month, are revenues growing? Are expenses consistent compared to revenue? Some of these simple questions can help understand how your business is doing and where it's going. Businesses that I've seen fail vary from startups with lots of investor money or they've been started by people who have no money, putting in everything they have. Passion for the work you've chosen and dedication to your business is essential, but you cannot build success on these elements alone.

Although there are plenty of outside reasons why businesses might fail, one of the biggest ones is planning and budgeting. For those who received investor money, this is of the utmost importance as money will go just as easily as it came. To build a successful business, simple financial education in planning and budgeting is a key component. You don't have to be an accountant to do this. Here are a few tips for easy budgeting while still focusing on what you do best.

1. Know your monthly burn. Monthly burn is the amount of cash you are spending monthly regardless of how much revenue you are making. This includes salaries, rent, overhead, and other expenses that make up your month. When you know this number, keep track of it. Know your average monthly burn rate. Do a quick spreadsheet and at the end of each month, add up your monthly burn rate. Is your monthly revenue keeping up with it?

2. Know your gross profit margin. This tells you how well your company is doing. The higher the number, the better. For some, this is the hardest thing to do. This ratio calculates the percentage of sales that exceed cost of goods sold. Be aware that your inventory can affect that amount of profit in unexpected ways. If inventory is involved, make a habit of doing inventory on a regular basis. This could be monthly or quarterly, but without it, you will not be able to trust your gross profit margin. Those inventory costs can make or break the profit margin, so keep track of them. This profit margin is important; if it is too low, then your costs may be too high or your pricing is too low. It's always important to find out what a normal profit margin is in your industry and if you are falling short of industry averages, there might be a reason why: spoilage, theft, giveaways, cost or pricing models.

If your business is a service, this will be easier to figure out. You can also find averages online but I find if you just make friends with others in your industry, you'd be surprised at how much you can learn from each other.

3. Know your cash on hand always. It's great to look at financial statements consistently but knowing your cash keeps a constant reminder of what your business has on hand. Too many get out of the habit of looking at their cash while only relying on their net income. Net income is the bottom line number, that includes your sales, costs, expenses, depreciation and interest over a certain point of time. The net income number will NOT include assets bought, loans received or paid, credit card liabilities, etc. So, net income will most likely NOT equal cash. The balance sheet, on the other hand, includes the cash balance as of a certain date. While both are important, knowing your cash on hand will help with future budgets and help you make sure you don't run out of money before more comes in.

4. Goals, goals, goals. Have a financial goal this year. Have a cash goal in the bank by end of year. Have a payroll expense goal. Have a sales goal for the month. Those goals are BUDGETS. If you want to succeed at that goal, what are you going to do to make it happen and how will it help you create the budget for the year? Keep track of your budget and goals and see where you are falling behind. How far from our sales goal are we this month? What can we do to get to our goal? It doesn't have to be complicated – just that the conversation is happening and ongoing. Although there are so many different apps for financial goals (Mint.com has a small business budgeting app or QuickBooks online has budgeting abilities), you can easily create a budget on excel for every goal you have. You can have one row with January through December in each tab, how many clicks do you want to have each month? What does those clicks represent in customers? What is the sales goal for that month? Entrepreneurs that are creating these goals and budgets in ways where they see the shortfalls, more often than not find themselves reevaluating what they are doing and creating ways to make their goals and budgets become a reality.

While these all seem like simple things, they are important to DO on a regular basis. Create a time/day each week to update these things and see where you are. See how this changes your plans, your marketing, your future. I had a client that kept having huge costs to only find out their fulfillment was shorting their inventory. Without looking at those costs and budgeting, they would have never seen this anomaly and would have lost thousands of dollars. They were able to find it, fix and even get money back. Without that regular check, it would have been hard to know. I also had another client who kept having huge inventory adjustments. As we looked further, we found shipping agents were keeping the items to sell for themselves. It's not always easy to find fraud, but looking at the numbers tells a story and you can find where that story leads to.

If you love Excel, use that to keep track. If you love notebooks, have a GOAL and budget notebook. Do what you can to make sure you are looking at it. These simple things in hand with a value and passion for your business can mean a more profitable and sustainable business. I've seen those that have shut down their business just to start another one – and then, JACKPOT. It takes time and practice and taking some time to see the numbers and understand what they mean to you and your business. That small amount of time can make a world of a difference for your business.

www.maricpa.com

Surprising Leadership Traits: Lessons From The CEO Suite And Boardroom

PATRICIA LENKOV

Leadership books, research and theories abound. A quick look at Amazon shows 191,739 books that have something to do with leadership.

Strong and effective leaders create companies and improve countries. They solve problems and are counted upon by those that they lead. The role is often complex and can definitely be challenging. Hence the perpetual study of leaders and the attempt to unravel their constitution.

As an Executive Recruiter focused on the C-suite (CEOs, CFOs, CMOs, etc.) and the corporate boardroom for the past twenty years, I have had the great privilege of working and interacting with many senior leaders. I have interviewed them, counseled them and had them as my clients. As a result, I have come to realize that the most successful of these individuals share certain traits and characteristics. Some of these are counter-intuitive and surprising, some are less so. Here they are:

Perhaps most surprising in what I have experienced with the many leaders I have crossed paths with is how approachable they really are. That is not to say they will spend time with anyone for any reason but for those that have a purpose or reason to connect with them will find a receptive and courteous individual amongst the best leaders out there. If you really think about it, leadership by definition involves other people and the guidance and oversight of them. Therefore, qualities such as congeniality are actually inherent in the role and necessary in order to rise to the top of whatever organization or agency one is involved in.

Another prevalent and perhaps surprising leadership trait is how personable and engaging leaders tend to be. They are interested in others and ask good questions. We often don't get to see this side of those leaders that we don't know well. In public an executive or other chieftain may appear serious and even intimidating. But the best leaders know when to be reserved and they also have to be a master of being likeable. Failing this, their ability to impact and influence those around them is compromised.

First-rate leadership also includes a good dose of humility. There was a time in the not too distant past that CEOs who behaved as and considered themselves "Masters of the Universe" were admired and revered. Today, not so much. There is a new era of corporate leadership that entails the humble CEO. Examples who make the news are Tony Hsieh of Zappos, Mary Barra of General Motors and Satya Nadella of Microsoft. Humble CEOs listen well and seek feedback. They are self-aware and less autocratic than their predecessors. They know what they don't know and are not afraid to admit it and seek support and expertise to complement their own.

There is an interesting inverse relationship between leadership and needing to prove oneself. That is, the more senior the leader, the less they need to prove themselves. Correspondent to this is enormous freedom. Freedom from competition as well as the sharp elbows that some of us display as we work our way to the top. Leaders who are comfortable and accustomed to their role don't need these traits.

Lest you think that leadership is all about temperament and style, it is important to note that the best leaders are also laser focused on their goals and they know how to make decisions and execute accordingly. They can be visionary and inspiring and most have integrity. They are accountable, dependable and typically quite intelligent. But all of this you knew. It is the other traits and characteristics mentioned above that can help provide insight and a more nuanced understanding of leadership for those seeking to move in this direction or simply bask in the shadow of someone else.

www.agilityexecutivesearch.com

Reacting To Situations Rationally

MARK ORLINSKY

One of the most important lessons I have learned both in my career and life is to react rationally rather than emotionally to situations. Many times we say and do things we wouldn't have, had we taken the time to reflect on our reaction and consider the ramifications that our words or actions will have. Unfortunately, once we have done it we can't get that moment back no matter how much we wished we could.

In both our personal and work lives we will have to work with others. While doing so we all undoubtedly are put in situations which may greatly frustrate or upset us. Instinctively we want to respond but doing so immediately may interfere with how we choose our words or actions and the effects of that may be very damaging.

I learned the value of this early in my career. It was my first "real" job working a large consulting firm home office. I was ambitious and worked long hours (at no overtime) and frequently offered recommendations on how to improve the services we offered our clients. I had begun working there as a college intern and transitioned into a full-time position. I asked for and was given the opportunity to work on projects and tasks well beyond my "level" in the company.

At the end of my first year I was proud of my accomplishments and looked forward to my annual review. I was most anxious to hear how much of a pay increase I would be receiving. The meeting did not go as I had planned. Despite the long hours, team play and recommendations which expanded our services and increased revenue, I was awarded a 3% raise which amounted to about $10/week. I was furious as my expectations were much higher. I hastily reacted and expressed my disappointment immediately and was told "this was a rough year and even though my manager had requested more, this was what the company authorized."

This made me angrier and I decided to approach the partner who oversaw our department. This is someone who I had the opportunity to work with throughout the year and when I knocked on his door and approached him about giving me a minute to discuss something, he readily agreed. I proceeded to close his office door and sat down at the chair across from his desk. He listened quietly as I ranted about all the accomplishments I had made during the course of the year and how I didn't think it was fair that I was given such a modest pay increase.

After giving me the opportunity to finish, he leaned forward and told me that I got what my manager had recommended and that I should never barge into his office again to have a discussion like this. I could see the anger in his face as I apologized and quietly left his office with no resolution to my issue and embarrassment over my behavior. In particular, being a young man who recently has graduated from college, I showed my immaturity and lack of understanding about the proper way to handle situations in a corporate environment.

In about 20-30 minutes I had reacted emotionally to a situation and destroyed my future in a company I had worked for as both and interim and full time employee for four years. It's been a long time, but I believe I was a rising star in the organization and could have had a tremendous future in the industry we served. Unfortunately my actions sealed my fate and I had no choice to move on from the company.

Looking back I think of what "could" have been and how my life likely would have taken a completely different path. I regularly share this story with young ambitious people that I meet. I now have a son who has the ambition and drive that I had at that point in my life and remind him of my story. I encourage him that if he is in a stressful situation at work, to take time and consider how his words or actions will affect his near and long term future. I encourage him to step aside, take a deep breath and even call me if he needs to vent or discuss how he should react to the situation.

We all have different triggers, personalities and emotions. It is important that we are conscious of these traits and develop individual ways to handle these situations when they arise. In my case, today when faced with challenging situations that stir my emotions, I have developed tools that allow me to release my frustrations elsewhere not to the antagonist until I have thought things through thoroughly. First I take a deep breath, gather my emotions and wait until my frustration subsides to a manageable level. If I still not capable of reacting rationally at that point I either begin writing an email or letter that I have no intention of sending or reach out to a friend or loved one and vent. Once I have regained my composure and analyzed the best way to react, I do so.

It is truly remarkable how a few seconds of words or reaction can have such an impact on our lives both personally and professionally. So next time you are pushed to a point where you are about to do say of do something you may later regret, think about the ramifications. I encourage you to develop an individual process to control your emotions at the moment and respond after careful thought.

Proof That Practicing Empathy In Your Business and Life Really Works

SHINJINI DAS

Empathy is such a loaded word and honestly one whose meaning was lost on me until very recently. The large majority of us directs a big focus on ourselves and a small focus on everybody else, because we think we know ourselves best, and find this way quite simply to be easier. As entrepreneurs, business leaders, and people who ultimately want to live lives of meaningful fulfillment, we must in fact pause our frantic fast-paced days and tune into others to learn about their intuitions, mindsets, beliefs, and joys.

Over the past year, public speaking has enabled me to truly dive into the minds, hearts, and souls of my audiences with unusual depth, depth which has opened my eyes as well as my heart to welcome human empathy. When we are in a mindset to receive not simply give consistently, the universe gives to us what we need to do and act upon. Perhaps we find that we are no longer in charge, but that the universe has a flow to point us in the right direction. Admittedly, I have always been more of a talker than a listener, but ever since I began consciously understanding before speaking, I have noticed a transformative shift in the success of both my business and personal relationships. Instead of glossing over the intricate social, mental, and physical differences which in many ways define us, I explicitly called out what differentiates us and emphasized what unites us in my recent keynote. Recognizing that our differences mean that we do not experience success, career, rejection, relationships, or failure the same way enabled me to build a meaningful relationship with my audience, who respected my efforts to not cluster everyone's experiences in a generalization. Expressing vulnerability by choosing to listen and empathize before speaking is powerful.

As a result of practicing deep empathy, my business relationships became far deeper as clients sensed my ability to walk in their shoes and give them acutely personalized advice which exceeded their expectations. This happened because I tuned into their struggles, problems, pitfalls, and created specific, as opposed to standardized, solutions to address these areas. In addition, my personal relationships also became significantly more intimate as I began understanding people on a deeply visceral level by skipping the small talk and jumping headfirst into the big talk.

All considered, everyone just wants to feel loved, validated, admired, respected, heard, appreciated, and worthy. If we are not validating people in our business and life, we are not fulfilling our duties as human beings. Please understand that empathy is the cornerstone of success in business, and this is something no one ever told me, but something I have had to figure out on my own. So, I want you to know first. When you first choose to tune into humanity and truly listen to people as individuals not as members of a group, personalize your interactions to fulfill their needs via your business and via your personal presence. I have come to fall in love with people, humanity, the world, and have begun to think about business problems and life from a much deeper intellectual level this past year.

What is perplexing to me is why empathy is not formally taught as a cornerstone of business success. No one told me that developing empathy would be a critical business skill. The reality is that a person or business will have great difficulty succeeding without deeply listening and engaging with core audiences to learn about their needs. To succeed, we must practice self-reflection in order to fully understand ourselves before reflecting on others' needs to deeply understand their perspectives. Deep and daily reflection is very key.

I highly recommend integrating deep empathy into your business and life. If you too want to live a full life bursting with joy, meaning, and passion, practice listening deeply before speaking with the understanding that deep perspectives build rapport with people and brand you as a truly-world class business leader as well as human being.

Empathy is important, and without building empathy, we fail as businesses, people, and humanity at large – it is our responsibility to practice empathy, kindness, respect, integrity, and morality in our day-to-day business transactions but also embody these qualities in our daily lives. Build your empathy by recognizing that you have a duty to learn about others to best serve them in this world.

The More You Learn, The More You Earn

JEREMY MEYER

Learning from others and teaching yourself are great fundamental skills that will help slingshot your growth in any area. I tell myself, "If I'm not embarrassed at how little I knew last year, I'm not pushing myself enough." As a software engineer and entrepreneur, I find great results from learning as much as possible from as many sources as possible. I try to take ideas from many fields and apply them to my own work, making useful connections between different topics.

There are several types of learning:

- (Experience) Learning from your own successes and failures
- (Knowledge) New ideas; information from books or talks, etc.
- (Advice) Specific information from people who are familiar with your personal experience
- (Skills) Honing your abilities through practice

The most fundamental learning trait is to critique your own experiences, especially your mistakes. For that, the key is to honestly assess yourself, which requires self-awareness. Meditation is one proven way to increase your self-awareness. It doesn't have to be a lot. I have experienced an increased feeling of self-awareness from just a few minutes each morning. The same way you notice a thought or a breath during meditation, you can build a habit of noticing your mistakes throughout your day.

At first, noticing and acknowledging your mistakes may overwhelm you a bit. This is good. You will make tons of mistakes every day. Relax, forgive yourself, and let the mistake go. But also make a note to yourself about what you learned. If you think you made a mistake, but are having trouble thinking of a takeaway, ask for advice from a trusted friend or mentor. Personal coaching is very valuable in this regard. If you reflect on each mistake, let negative feelings pass, and identify lessons learned, you will greatly accelerate your growth.

Secondly, learn new information. There are a ton of sources these days, including talks and conferences, online informational videos, and full-blown interactive courses. And of course, the good old standby, books. I recommend Goodreads for tracking books and finding recommendations, especially if you have lots of friends who read. I'm always discovering new ideas and finding inspiration by reading books. I listen to a lot of audiobooks, which are great to listen to while doing chores, commuting to work, or whatever else. There are also a ton of great informational and instructional videos on YouTube. I challenge you to set your own goal of reading at least one great book each month. Even if you aren't a reader, try watching a TED talk, attending a conference, or enrolling in a training program. Above all, apply what you learn by taking simple actions in your daily life.

The third form of learning is to seek advice and feedback, from mentors as well as peers. For any difficult or important life decision, you should seek advice from mentors you trust. Especially if you feel like making a decision on your own, I urge you to find one person you trust and get their honest opinion. Friends and advisors can help us see our blind spots. In fact, our blind spots can be such a blocker to our personal growth, that one of the most powerful things you can do is ask a few trusted friends the following questions: "I trust your opinion and would like to ask for your honest and direct feedback. I promise to take any feedback well and not to get defensive. What are my top 3 areas of growth? What are the top few things you think are holding me back the most? What is my biggest challenge or blocker when dealing with people? What do you think is holding me back most from achieving my goals?" For bosses and coworkers, "What is holding me back most in my work?" If you ask 5 people these questions and record their responses, I guarantee you will learn things about yourself you didn't know. Even if you think a response is skewed, off base, or just plain wrong, accept the fact that this person genuinely gets this impression from you. Taking feedback without getting defensive and resolving to improve, even in light of your own doubt, is one of the best ways to grow.

Finally, you should always be practicing and improving your skills. Scott Adams, creator of the Dilbert comics, recommends taking a systems approach rather than just setting goals. If you set a goal, you can either achieve the goal, or you can fall short and keep trying. Taking a systems approach means setting yourself up to learn and improve incrementally. This is especially helpful when you don't achieve a specific goal you've set for yourself. Focus on the nitty gritty actions that will help you practice, develop, and hone your skills. Additionally, a goal, such as "Make 100k in revenue," could quite possibly be a limiting underestimate or a demotivating overestimate. Instead, focus on the skills you (or your team) will need to hone to result in increased revenue. Make sure your skills are always improving as a result of working on a project, rather than after it's completed. You are your most valuable asset. Increasing your knowledge, skills, and experience over time is more valuable than achieving any particular goal.

The world is becoming more complex and fast-paced every year, requiring extreme flexibility, adaptation, and resiliency. To succeed, you will need to know the latest techniques, state of the industry, competitors, and developments. Being an avid learner helps set you up to be and do all these things. In light of this, your best strategy for taking on new challenges and changing environments is to learn from your mistakes; absorb and apply new ideas from many sources; seek advice and honest feedback from peers and mentors; and hone your skills.

Always Give Them Hope

AMANDA FLEISCHUT

Imagine this. You have been suffering from lower back pain for months; in reality it's actually been years. You have pain radiating from your lower back down the back of your leg to the foot. It used to be an intermittent pain, a nuisance more than anything. You could live with it. However, all those long hours you've put in at work are starting to make this pain constant. You work a labor intense job coming up on your 20th anniversary. Long hours coupled with sitting for over half the day doesn't help one bit, the other half of the day is spent lifting heavy material and boxes. And yes, this work is more intense then all of your training and double-sessions during your high school soccer days. You finally muster up the nerve to ignore your inner "Suck it up" attitude and finally go to your doctor for some help.

To make a long story short, it takes you three months of doctor visits, physical therapy, and fighting with your insurance company for a Magnetic Resonance Imaging (MRI) to finally get in with an Orthopedic Spine specialist. You had been seeing their Physician Assistant (PA) who has been taking you through all conservative treatment options prior to you having to see the surgeon for a possible surgical recommendation. So here you are, the patient, just having gone through three painful months of physical therapy and all types of medication with no pain relief in sight. The Physician Assistant offered you the idea of epidural steroid injections into your back but after finding out they were long needles that were going into your back you decided to decline that offer for now, due to your fear of needles. The spine surgeon comes in, looks at your MRI only to explain to you in detail that surgery is not going to help relieve your pain. "There is nothing surgically that can be done for you."

And before you can blink, the surgeon has left the room. You're left sitting in the office feeling alone, hopeless and aggravated with the waste of the past five hours, the half day of work you again couldn't afford to take off, the hour of pain it took you to drive to the office, two hours in the waiting room and another hour just to be seen and told "there is nothing surgical that can be done for you." Most of all you feel hopeless – if not surgery, then what?

I am a Physician Assistant and I've observed dozens, if not hundreds, of situations like the one I just described. The doctor gives the patient a correct diagnosis or analysis, but forgets or doesn't bother to give them what they really need: hope.

Hope could have been given to this patient in the above example in many ways. Hope that something else can be done for them. Hope that there are other options. Hope that they are not alone in this. Hope that we understand their frustrations and encouragement not to give up. And hope to not give in to the frustration of time and, ironically, allow more time for healing.

Now, I'm not telling any medical professional to lie to a patient nor give false hope, nor am I saying to advise surgery even though a surgeon with years of experience may not think surgical intervention is the best option for the patient. But giving hope doesn't mean lying or making bad recommendations. Hope can exist and be shared even in difficult and painful moments.

This holds true for most aspects of business. Building hope between you and clients means building trust. How do your customers, patients, colleagues etc. believe in you or your proposed idea? Without trust how do you implement strategic ideas within your workforce?

We are all human and the remembrance of always giving hope to those around us, in both the medical and business fields, can often become obscured. For example, in the medical field it may be forgotten in our rush to see patients in a quick manner or ignored after a frustrating interaction with another patient just prior. Or in a business example, let's say you are a startup company building investors and you need to go into your team meeting to break it to the team that you just lost your major investor. It is very easy to lose your own hope in what you are trying to achieve that you forget to implement it into those around you. So instead of throwing in the towel and giving up you need to remember that there is hope still, that you, as a team leader know that it is going to be an uphill battle but with hope you'll make it through together and come out on top.

We are all going to go down paths in which we feel our own hope is lost. But learning to hold onto hope even in these tough moments is key to our everyday business practices. For example, when I feel I have lost all hope and am frustrated my patient has not gotten better, after it feels as though we have exhausted all possible options for treatment, I try to remember why I am here. Why I am a PA. Not because I have to, not because it is my job and I will get fired if I don't, not because of the money; but because I love what I do. I remember all those success stories, all those patients I have helped. I remind myself that I am here for a reason, that I am a support link and provider to those who are in need. People lean and rely on me because I help them, this gives me back the hope, the confidence, I need to then effectuate back into my patients themselves when I have those moments of lost hope. Hope installs optimism; optimism is a key to success for any business.

Now let's take the above patient's experience a different direction with the mindset of giving him hope. You're sitting there frustrated just moments after the spine surgeon told you there's nothing surgically to be done that can help you. Instead of getting up and leaving the surgeon starts to talk to you about different treatment options other than surgery. The PA walks back and proceeds to explain to you that epidural steroid injections may significantly help take away some of your pain. The PA understands you are deathly afraid of needles but explains to you how many other patients in your situation have tried them with significant relief. There have even been cases where the injections had resolved patients' pain completely, lasting years before another flare up occurred. You could not be happier or more relieved to hear there are other options for you. You get a prescription to see a pain management doctor for lower back epidural steroid injections and are told to return one week after your first epidural for reevaluation.

Four weeks pass by and you are back in the office after your first epidural steroid injection. The PA and surgeon come into the room and you are smiling from ear to ear. They ask with some hesitancy, "So, how are you feeling after the injection." Your response: "I couldn't be happier, I'm amazed, I feel 80% better than when I first saw you."

Thanks to the surgeon and PA giving the patient hope, that patient (you!) is still a frequent visitor to our office to see us for monthly updates. Not because the patient is in pain anymore but because we instilled a trust for them in us. Why? Because we gave them hope.

A big part of giving hope lies in treating the patient/client/customer as if they are valuable, worth talking to, worthy of your time and that their comfort and security are a top priority for you. So this way, even if there is nothing you can do for them, they still feel as though you care about their needs.

In our field, as medical professionals, giving our patient hope is what brought that patient back to us. It did not send them running to another orthopedic group never to return, but rather it brought them back to our office and our business. I have seen this with a number of our patients throughout our orthopedic practice as a whole. Hope is what keeps our business thriving. Hope is what brings our patients and customers back to us. Always give them hope.

Digital or Physical?

TODD MEDEMA

These days, if you want to make a product, you have a lot of different options. Should your product be physical, such as a bike or board game? A digital website or an app? Or a physical product with a digital component, such as a smartwatch or Internet-enabled light bulb, which is becoming increasingly common?

There are significant pros and cons to each type of product. But before we dive deeper into each type, let me explain why I'm even talking about this topic. I'm a Carnegie Mellon alumnus with a B.S. in Technology, Entrepreneurship and Design. My experiences include crowdfunding a physical + digital roleplaying game and founding an investor-backed advertising software startup. In other words, I'm a tech nerd, inventor, builder, tinkerer and gadget freak who always seems to end up with too much time on my hands. So when I talk about the pros and cons of digital vs. physical products, I'm not just speaking from experience – I'm sharing stuff I love talking about to begin with.

Anyway. Let's compare some of the main factors between these two product types.

First, **how much will it cost to develop and maintain?** Will it require a large upfront investment? Will it be expensive to maintain, slowly bankrupting your company?

Physical products are slow to launch, but are low maintenance. Your first manufacturing batch will be the hardest, requiring multiple rounds of iteration to design for manufacturing, but additional batches will be easier since you've already designed for manufacturing. Unless you mess up a batch ... in which case you'll be on the hook for managing (and paying for) returns.

Digital products require the least effort to launch, but can be a headache to maintain. Continuous updates mean you can launch quickly and iterate later, but, because consumers expect regular updates, your work is never done. Plus, software is constantly changing. Every OS update breaks old apps, which will either obsolete your software or cost money to fix. If you go this route, consider making a web-based application to support the most platforms at the least expense.

Digital + physical is the most effort by far. Not only do you have to create both digital and physical products before you can deliver to customers, you have maintain a digital product that's tied to a fixed physical version. Just check out a physical + digital Kickstarter like the Lockitron (which delivered 3 years behind schedule) to understand the extraordinary headache these types of products can be.

Next, **how will your product make money?**

Physical products can only be monetized when you sell the item – but you can get creative. For example, physical expansion packs or new content (e.g. Magic: The Gathering, OXO), or monthly subscriptions to receive new objects (e.g. Dollar Shave Club, Loot Crate), to name a few.

Digital products are most successful with ongoing revenue streams, such as through in-app purchases, subscriptions and marketplaces. While software used to sell for a fixed price, this was terrible for software companies, who had to pay to support customers who hadn't paid anything in years.

- In-app purchases allow users to get started with your product for free (which will save you marketing dollars) and then purchase affordable pieces of functionality (or virtual rewards, or to hide ads) once you've earned their trust. This is especially common with mobile apps because app stores handle the micro-payments, reducing friction for consumers.
- Subscriptions are a powerful revenue source for products that provide recurring value, such as productivity and creativity software. For example, Adobe Creative Cloud. What used to cost thousands of dollars is now $50/mo, making it accessible to many new users, including art students and small businesses (many of whom previously pirated it).
- Marketplaces enable your users to create and sell their own paid content. This is the end-game for most digital business models because it's scalable and defendable. Once you have a large enough user base, your users can create far more content than you can, and large amounts of

content is more defendable than a specific technology (which is reverse-engineerable). For example, the Android app store: Google only has to maintain the app store software, yet they get a 30% cut of the billions of dollars in app purchases each year.

Digital + physical is especially interesting. Since you're selling a physical object, you might think to charge once (e.g Amazon Echo). However, as we've discussed, digital products mean ongoing maintenance and infrastructure costs. Search "Pebble Smartwatch closure" if you want to see how charging only once can bankrupt a digital + physical company. To keep cash flow strong, consider using a digital revenue model (marketplaces, subscriptions or in-app purchases). If your product is especially expensive, you can use these models to subsidize the upfront cost.

Finally, let's talk **feedback and product design**.

Feedback for **physical** products will take more time and effort because users will need physical access to the product, either in person or by mail. Changes in physical products are also easier to make earlier in the process (before designing for manufacturing). Finally, because of the large, slow and expensive nature of manufacturing runs, you want to make absolutely sure your design is as polished as possible before manufacturing. In order to succeed, you must pursue feedback early and plan on a longer product development cycle. Don't be afraid to delay manufacturing if you find an improvement opportunity. If you have enough orders, you can manufacture a small batch first, ship them to users, and wait for their feedback to tweak the design one last time.

Feedback for **digital** products is faster and easier (especially if you add a prominent "send feedback" button to your software, which you should). You can also monitor detailed analytics with tools like Google Analytics. But, large amounts of user feedback does not mean it's useful. Instead, you'll have to find the signal in the noise, politely ignoring most feedback so that you can find – and fix – the most valuable. And although analytics are a powerful tool, numbers only tell you what's happening, not why. Your daily active users might drop, but it's still up to you to figure out why.

To make a quality **digital + physical** product, you'll have to employ both strategies, working hard for feedback early on and setting up analytics and feedback frameworks post-launch. But, you don't have to limit yourself to doing one at a time. For example, you can let early adopter users try your software before the physical product arrives.

Though there are many more complexities to developing products, this should help you decide which type of product is best for your personal resources and goals. Once you've made your decision, find and reach out to people who've made your category of product before. Bring a notebook, ask lots of questions and learn from their mistakes. And whatever product type(s) you choose, remember to keep creating.

ToddMedema.com

Effective Storytelling Through Video

DANIELLE GOMEZ

When you think of storytelling, what do you think about?

You probably think of families grouped with friends in a circle, telling stories; roasting marshmallows and perhaps singing Kumbaya. A good storyteller is always respected and welcomed in that situation, telling heroic or impactful stories and often reaching a position of respect and power.

During my most recent trip to Venice, Italy I became fascinated with a different kind of storyteller – a specific one, in fact: Marco Polo. Most people think of him as the great explorer today, but he actually got more famous as a storyteller – such a persuasive storyteller that he was able to build rapport with one of the most influential leaders of Southeast Asia, Genghis Khan, the founder and Great Khan of the Mongol Empire.

In 1298, Marco was captured in a battle between Venice and its rival city-state Genoa and it was during his imprisonment that he met a romance author and fellow prisoner, Rustichello of Pisa, with whom Polo shared his stories with about distant lands, exotic cultures and wealth.

What many people do not realize is that Rustichello of Pisa wrote *The Travels of Marco Polo* based off of the stories Marco shared – not Marco himself. However, his stories still impacted millions of people around the world. I'm convinced if Marco Polo would have had access to a video camera and the Internet during his time, perhaps he would have been a huge YouTube star.

If you are watching videos online, you will notice that stories connect and define our humanity.

And this is the same thing in business and life. When we share our stories on podcasts, on stages or videos, we can increase our authority in the marketplace. Have you ever seen a Youtuber rise off the charts? Or an online nobody who at first couldn't afford to pay his utility bill leverage videos to explode business revenue?

The power of video is strong but, the power of storytelling is stronger. Human-to-human connections rise above all of the noise and as a byproduct bring in new prospects. People want to work with people they like and trust – and stories help build those bridges.

For example: here's something you didn't know about me. Before running a business, I was working as an Operations Manager with a company that I had been at for eight years. I had stable pay and benefits but, I was completely burnt out. I didn't want to be an Operations Manager; it fell into my lap after college.

You see, I went to school for Biology, not Business. So, when the opportunity was presented to me, I declined at first. I thought that wasn't the plan to complete college and work with the same company that is irrelevant to my field?

And then I thought about it ...

I was dead broke ...

My car had broken down ...

I had thousands of dollars in student loan debt ...

And I decided to jump right in. And I'm glad I did.

From that decision, I learned a lot about running a business from accounting, human resources, sales, marketing, people development, payroll, law, raising money for charity and more. And from that experience, I was able to apply it to running a business.

Sometimes when we think we aren't cut out for one path – we are. It opens our eyes to a world of possibilities.

That was a story about me (it happens to be true). I could have simply said that I studied biology and then went into operations, but you wouldn't remember that or care about it – according to a Stanford study, stories are remembered up to 22x more than facts alone.

Effective storytelling through video builds awareness, it builds credibility, but more importantly, it builds rapport with the right people.

And when you leverage videos, you can scale your story to the masses.

Yes, video isn't for everyone, but the sad thing is that a lot of people who could do really well with it never even try. If you're interested but video seems scary to you, you have a choice.

You can stay in your turtle shell meaning your comfort zone by not utilizing (or at least trying) video. Saying things like …

"I'm too scared to do video."

"My mouth gets dry."

"I hate the way I look on camera."

Or you can break out and sing "I'm Like A Bird" by Nelly Furtado and allow your message to fly out to the masses.

The decision is yours.

Part Three

THE JOURNEY OF BUSINESS

Section One:
Point A To Point Business

The Evolved And Evolving Business Owner

JOHN WAYNE ZIMMERMAN

Three years ago, I was in a predicament. I had reached all of the goals I had ever wanted in business. I was working a corporate job, making over six figures, and I had a ton of perks. I had built a house in Chicago that had all of the American dream features (white picket fence, 3-car garage, and all the things I thought I needed).

However, I was commuting 15 hours a week, I worked in a cubicle, and I felt stuck after doing the same thing for 14 years. I was empty inside. I felt like something was missing. That is when I chose to become an entrepreneur.

Several months later, I discovered that being an entrepreneur was hard work. I had created a job for myself by sticking to the same kind of activities that I did in corporate. I was doing the same tasks for a lot more clients. I was making more money, but I was spending even more time working. Something was still wrong. I thought entrepreneurship was supposed to feel like freedom.

A friend of mine suggested I do some personal development work. I trusted him so I jumped at the chance to learn more. I took a 9-month program learning about psychology, the art of listening, and how to really be with people in the world. It was profound. I discovered who I was and who I wanted to become. I saw a new stage of consciousness emerging in the business owner, a profound shift that opens radical possibilities for the future of business.

The world is no longer fixed in only top-down authority, dogma driven, bottom line management views. We are called to discover our true self and go on a journey to find our unique potential and identify our gifts to the world. The once fabled notion that we can become anything we want to is now an acceptable fact. People are starting to resist doing what they think they are supposed to and are instead listening to their inner compass and going where they feel most alive.

Following that program and that inner compass, I set out on a plan to really create my life. I was going to sell everything I had and move my family to California.

And so I did it. I sold almost everything I had – the dream home I had built, the sports car, the motorcycles, almost all of my worldly possessions ... and I found a tiny cottage to rent in Carmel-by-the-Sea, California.

When I first visited Carmel, I felt like I was meant to be there. I felt like I was in a fairytale land where I could use my imagination to create anything I wanted. I felt empowered. I felt at home for the first time in my life.

My business changed when I moved to California. I figured out that in order to make consistent money, I needed to get bigger clients that would sign year-long contracts. That way income would be consistent monthly. The thing was ... there were all kinds of red tape and committee meetings, and it took forever to accomplish any work. It was like I was working in corporate again. Part of the broken culture from those businesses found their way back into my life and I was fed up with them.

I decided that who I really wanted to work with were other entrepreneurs. And even more specific, I wanted to work with authors, speakers and coaches.

And so I did. I rebranded my business, went to a lot of conferences and marketed my services to this new niche. It felt amazing. I felt like I was on top of the world because I was working with people that I could easily relate to. I knew exactly what they wanted and I could help them. I was now living in my dream town and working with people I was aligned with. The only downside of this new path was that I was making less money. And I really struggled with my own ego wanting me to go back to working with larger clients and get paid more and feel like I was worth more.

Most people are driven from ego. It runs our lives. The fears, ambitions and desires from ego are what is in the background and running most everyone's world. When we learn to start listening to our own voices, we start to follow the path we were meant to go on. This is business evolution – people are learning to tame their egos. They are learning to trust themselves and others and that is changing the way businesses are beginning to operate.

Two years later, I decided that I was done with my business partner. We were no longer aligned as a team. I wanted to really grow the business – the amount of clients and revenue. I wanted to work a lot more hours, bring in more staff and build a big agency. He wanted the opposite. So I had to ask myself a lot of questions. Closing down a business takes a lot of work. And how in the world was I going to manage the business on my own. I did some soul searching and it all went back into alignment.

Where we are going is shifting from external factors to an internal compass in decision making in business.

Asking questions like:

- Does this feel like the right decision?
- Am I in alignment with my true self?
- Am I being of service to others and fulfilling real needs?

I was ready to make more money and I was ready to do it in a different way. It just so happened at this point in my life I was working with a dozen coaches. I loved their business model. They made phone calls and charged thousands of dollars per call. I decided that I was going to become a coach.

And so I did. I closed down my marketing company. I rebranded myself again and I became a marketing coach. I went to a lot of conferences and marketed my services. And again, it felt amazing. I felt like I was on top of the world. I got to know exactly what my clients wanted and I could help them.

And that brings me up to now. Will my inner compass direct me down a new path in a few more years? It's possible – and if it does, I'll be ready to listen to it.

It's time for you and your business to evolve from the inside out. Ask yourself questions like:

- What is it I want to accomplish right now?
- How would it make me feel if I had that in 6 months?
- If I had that, would I be fulfilled?

There is a lot of pain and emptiness in today's everyday life. We are conditioned for achievement, success and recognition when we are running our companies. However, everyone has deeper longings, hopes, dreams and aspirations.

Go out and find someone that has done what you want and talk to them. Learn from them. And take actions to create your reality. It will change every so often, and that's okay.

http://www.iamjohnwayne.com

The Path From Unconscious Incompetence To Unconscious Competence

CHRISTINE DURA

Anything we learn, any skill set we acquire, begins from a point of unconscious incompetence. Once we realize that we had not known something we move towards conscious incompetence, then conscious competence, as we strive towards the final stage of learning of unconscious competence. This process is known as the Conscious Competence Ladder and was developed by Noel Burch in the early 1970's. The ladder is important because with every piece of knowledge you gain, and skill you hone to proficiency, you create a toolbox that allows you to continuously improve by building on your successes.

My journey towards unconscious competence began in September of 1991. It was at my first job in "corporate America." I was in sales where I was earning the princely sum of $16,200 a year. Six months into the job I was summoned to a meeting with my sales manager. Across the desk, her steely eyes glared into mine, as she slid in front of me a notice to "improve my sales conversions or I would be terminated." We spoke briefly and she said my performance was suffering due to a below average sales conversion ratio. Dumbfounded, I asked "What's a sales conversion?" Seemingly miffed, she pulled out a printed excel file and a red pen and circled where I was and where I stacked up with my peers across our three-state region. I ranked last. Very simply, I was not closing enough sales in relation to the number of sales calls I was making. Not knowing what to say, I thanked her as she left and spent the remainder of the afternoon studying the blood bath of red ink in front of me.

Although it certainly did not feel like it at the time, in hindsight, I realized that moment provided me with one of the greatest gifts of my career. I was given a piece of information that allowed me to move from unconscious incompetence to conscious incompetence, where I could then work toward conscious competence. I decided I would prove to her, and myself, that I would not be beaten. I was determined to exceed every benchmark set by every other sales representative on that list. And that I did ... Within three months, my conversion rate was the highest in my local office. Within 9 months, I was ranked the number one salesperson in my three-state region. Soon after I was promoted and relocated to Atlanta where I was tasked with leading a sales team for startup office. Not long after, I was the number one performer over 1000's of reps across the United States.

In a continual effort to better myself set out to earn my Master's Degree in Adult Education Theory at the University of Georgia. In this program, I discovered the Conscious Competence Ladder and how it worked in learning new skills:

- Unconscious incompetence – when you're doing something wrong and you don't know you're doing it wrong
- Conscious incompetence – when you're doing something wrong but you know you're doing it wrong
- Conscious competence – when you're doing something right but you have to consciously focus on doing it the right way
- Unconscious competence – when you're doing something right and you don't even have to think about it

When learning something new, most of the skill-based tasks we do we do poorly and we don't even think about it. Our default state is #1: unconscious incompetence. When I first started my sales job, I was blissfully ignorant. I had a complete lack of knowledge and skills in a specific area, and had no clue. My confidence far exceeded my abilities. My manager pointed out where I was making mistakes. Step by step she showed me how each engagement in the sales process impacted the net results of my sales performance – from initial contact to application to face to face meeting to close.

I immediately became hyper-aware of every step of the process and recognized that even the slightest improvement at each conversion point would increase the end result – more sales. There were so many new things to work on improving, I couldn't keep it all in my head at once. I had to make one little adjustment at a time until it felt natural – like building blocks of a house. That's what it means to be conscious of your incompetence. This is the most frustrating stage of learning any new skill – because you're painfully aware of the gap between where your abilities are and where you'd like them to be. It's also where people often give up. It's disheartening to realize you're doing something poorly and yet trying so hard but still can't get it right.

Yet eventually you wake up and realize you have crossed to chasm to the third level which is conscious competence. Getting here often takes a while, as you steadily learn about the new area, either through experience or more formal learning. This process can go in fits and starts as you learn, forget, plateau and start anew. The more complex the new area and the less talent you have for it, the longer this will take. For me I refused to fail and through my own sheer persistence and grit, my conversions started to go up and eventually my sales did too. It wasn't easy because I still had to focus on every little detail because it was all still new.

Finally, I got to the place where I didn't have to think about every little thing I was doing. I was using my new skills effortlessly and you performing tasks without conscious effort and suddenly felt completely confident of my own success. I had finally arrived! I had become unconsciously competent – and my numbers proved it. I felt blissful again!

Why not embrace and apply the Conscious Competence Ladder theory to every aspect of life? First, you can use it to understand the flurry of emotions you'll experience during the learning process of anything new. This helps you stay motivated when times get tough. It also helps you manage your expectations of success so you don't burn out trying to achieve too much, too soon. For example, during the consciously incompetent phase, you can reassure yourself that, while learning this skill is difficult and frustrating right now, things will improve in the future. When you're unconsciously skilled, the model reminds you to take time to value the skills that you've gained, and to be patient with yourself and others.

As uncomfortable as it is knowing what you don't know, it's the only way to grow and evolve. By understanding the Conscious Competence Ladder, and how to use it to continue to gain success, you too will be able to create entrepreneurial opportunities for yourself and others that culminate in personal satisfaction and financial independence.

https://www.linkedin.com/in/christinedura/

Failure In The Field Of Dreams

DARYL CROCKETT

Most of you have seen the 1989 film *Field of Dreams*, starring Kevin Costner. The movie is about an Iowa farmer who builds a baseball diamond in his corn fields after hearing voices prompting him to do so. The most enduring quote from the film is "If you build it, he will come."

It's a great movie. I loved it! However, many people have adopted this fictional feel-good film's famous quote as a guide to launching a business. And this can spell ruin for entrepreneurs trying to successfully bring their products and services to market.

Here's the honest truth from a seasoned serial entrepreneur who has dreamed big and risked it all – only to find out that what we built was *not* what the market wanted.

In 2009, I filed a patent for a modifiable children's shoe which allowed kids to decorate their shoes with interchangeable covers and then attach and arrange cute little collectible gizmos on their shoes. It was called ShuGizmos®. This was the jingle: *It's a shoe with a kit, you create designs with it. ShuGizmo, so cool! ShuGizmo!*

We drew up designs, showed them to all our friends and family. Then, based on overwhelmingly positive feedback, we embarked on the long and expensive process of manufacturing our shoes overseas. We built a website, an online marketplace complete with shopping cart, and all of the materials necessary to show off the products to customers. We even recorded our jingle. This was a huge outlay of money, time, emotion and energy.

I remember the day when we got the notice that our shoe container had landed at the airport in Boston and was going through customs. We rejoiced, we celebrated – finally the hardest part was behind us! The shoes were beautiful, high quality – these were the "next big thing!" – everyone said so. We had built a great product – so they will come, right?

Well, not exactly. Selling the shoes proved to be much harder than we expected. While we had hired experienced shoe industry people on our design staff, we never really had showed the shoes to any stores and retailers. The market was changing quickly, and there was an 18-month window while we were waiting for our products to be shipped in. We had a big cash investment and we were not about to discuss anything with anyone during that waiting time because we feared that someone would produce a competitive product.

The shoes proved to be a flop, pun intended! But the gizmos – well, people just loved those gizmos and the things they could do with them. Things we had never imagined. At an industry event, a lady came over to our booth, pondered the shoes (for a few seconds) and then started asking us all sorts of questions about our gizmos and if we could build a big motivational leader board for her bank so that she could track and reward behaviors of her employees in a fun way using our gizmos.

We had serious conversations with a children's educational game developer group about using our gizmos as badges that could be snail-mailed to their online players when they completed certain milestones and achievements. We had a teen drug and alcohol abuse center inquire about designing special gizmos to use as motivational tools for their clients. The final insult to our shoe concept was a connection from Parents Magazine. She bluntly told us – love the gizmos, but lose the shoes!

So after two long years of sluggish online shoe sales, sweltering summer days at fairs and festivals and many "come see us later when you have some more sales" shop keeper conversations, our company was finished. We had run out of time and energy even for the gizmos. Our funds, our enthusiasm and the patience of our spouses had evaporated, and we trudged off to other opportunities while 900 pairs of beautiful shoes stacked floor-to-ceiling gathered dust in my spare bedroom.

While I was not successful with ShuGizmo, I was able to quickly rebound and channel that product development and patent-writing experience into the field of software which has been very fruitful for me. It is clear that failures are opportunities for doing *even better* in the future. So I want to share what I learned from my experience in the Field of Dreams.

These are the myths of the "Build It and They Will Come" model of business:

1. **We shouldn't share and socialize our idea because someone might steal it**. If idea stealing was such an issue, Kickstarter wouldn't be the success that it is. Be prudent, but socialize your concepts!
2. **Friends and Family are a good sounding board for your ideas and designs**. They love you, they believe in you. They want to say what makes you happy. But most friends and family are really bad sources of honest and helpful feedback.
3. **Everything needs to be perfect and complete for your big launch.** Absolutely not! Do the least amount of work to share your MVP (minimum viable product).

So what's is the better way to design and launch a product or service?

Dream big, build small, test-tweak-test, build bigger, *then* launch

The real magic is in the test-tweak-test cycles. These re-design activities should be based on FEEDBACK FROM REAL CUSTOMERS. This advice applies to all businesses whether you are building a product or a service.

In my case, we had a few pair of sample shoes in my hands at the very beginning of my journey. We could have easily showcased the shoes in a simple website and eBay store to test the "stickiness" of our product design. We would have found out fast and early that our beautiful shoes were flops – long before we had to wire funds to China for manufacturing. Even though our egos would have been bruised, we would have had a lot of money in the bank to do a successful pivot to gizmo glory! Instead, we sat, sadly defeated in our empty field of dreams.

Enjoy Your Struggles And Never Stop

ALEX KAPRALOV

We all have an idea of what we want out of life. Some of us want to attain financial freedom,

and some want to be admired for their looks or to be famous, while others would simply like to live care-free. We all have an ideal vision of the person that we'd like to be, and the life we'd like to live. It's easy to imagine and fall in love with that endpoint.

Unfortunately, many of us don't really imagine or think of the process required to reach these end results or what we are willing to give up in pursuit of them.

Most people who desire financial freedom never imagine themselves working 70 hours a week, nor they envision themselves being continuously sleep-deprived to dedicate themselves to a project. It's easy for us to focus on how great the end result will be, while putting little thought into what it takes to get there.

Behind every success there is an equally important struggle. As we plan for our successes, it's also just as important to plan for our struggles. Without them, there is no financial freedom, no perfect looks, nor fame or care-free life.

But how do you choose or plan for your struggles?

The trick is to pursue the things in life you are most passionate and skilled at. Ask yourself, "Does your passion or hobby offer value to others?" If not, figure out how your passion can solve other people's problems. If you don't have a passion, find one and then figure out how it can solve other people's problems. Easy, right? Then put all your focus, energy and time into what you enjoy the most and start enjoying the struggle. Keep going until you do it better or differently than anyone else out there. Eventually you will turn your hobby or passion into a profitable business.

Then your success will all depend on how much struggle you will invest into it. It's as simple as that. If you're planning on being successful, you can expect to face adversity. However, if you are able to pursue your passion or hobby, the struggle will be much less painful.

Let me give you an example from my life.

In my college days I was very passionate about good-looking websites. I didn't know anything about coding, but I was curious about the site creation process which led me to learning a new skill.

I knew there was a demand for it, but at that point I enjoyed the process so much that I spent days and nights "struggling" and building one site after another. From entertainment sites to ecommerce sites, I just kept going as I enjoyed every single minute of it.

Building effective and visually appealing websites became a lifetime passion for me. I was even recognized by and featured in Forbes. As exciting as that sounds, for me the joy didn't come from the recognition, it came from the process. All those sleepless nights, early mornings and overnight coding sessions didn't seem painful to me. I was just passionately doing what I love to do and enjoy the most. And when I realized I was able to turn my passions into businesses and make a living by monetizing all those sites, I enjoyed the "struggle" even more.

Today I run a worldwide digital advertising company that connects websites' owners to advertisers. I understand and appreciate the struggles of website owners because I was once one of them and I put all my efforts and passion into building innovative solutions to help them become more successful in a crowded online marketplace.

The struggle never truly ends, but if your "struggle" is your passion you can overcome almost anything.

PixFuture.com

Adapting To The Chaos Of Startup

ROBERT DEVON CHRISTENSON

"Chaos ... is actually balance at a different pace!"
—*Robert Devon Christenson*

It's not until after things happen that we realize the impact our decisions have on us.

I'm going to share my journey of not only starting and operating a business but the life lessons and knowledge that will open the next opportunity coming my way. For me starting a business isn't about the money at all. It has been more about the process and the journey. For me it was coming to a major decision to move away from an amazing place to live with a great group of people around me to begin the journey.

Part of the decision process for me was finding and understanding where my true abilities were. What I already knew is that every day the environment I was living in was pulling me in what felt like the opposite direction I should be going. How do I get on track and know I'm going the right direction? How do you find that place where you just know it's the right place? That moment we've all had in our lives, no doubt, no questions, no what if's ... with these thoughts going through my mind it reminded me of an idea my sister told me about 25 years ago. So I tried what I thought would be a very simple task and realized in the middle it's not as easy as it sounds.

The idea was to write out 100 things you want in life. I'll challenge you to do it yourself with no duplicates. Every time you tell yourself that's dumb, write it down anyway – you're gonna need them all! Through this process it became very clear what my purpose was and what I loved.

This move was not going to be for the short term, it was intended to be the "forever" move. I knew it was the best decision for me and my daughters and I knew what to do next. Then faced with the choice of building the business alone or with a business partner. I chose the business partner route and I found the perfect one. A man that would allow me to be me at all times and never questioned the vision I saw. In a funny way it's almost as if he was allowing me to lead but guiding me at the same time.

The future was on its way ... walking into an empty room to start a company, what now? I've always been good at the startup of a business, although to many people the startup is very chaotic. So many things need to be completed before you can do anything. This is where I've been most at peace and confident in every step to the future. So here's where I began.

In order to have a company people could understand and believe in was vital to success. Developing the story of our company to cement the vision for others to follow was the perfect starting place. Then we could name our idea and build around it. After that I spent countless hours developing a logo that truly meant something. Not just a logo to have a logo but a logo where every curve and color had meaning to it. Believe it or not the company is our logo, I was building every department of our company including the core vision all at the same time.

It was time to start selling, this was an interesting time on its own. Imagine going out to sell for the company you work for now. Now delete the history of the company, delete the staff, delete the processes in place and go from there. It was ok for me to not have all the answers but it was an absolute necessity for me to find a way through it. Find a way to believe that I was worth it and the only way they should go. I was very successful at selling our vision, so much so that the first 10 contracts I signed up all cancelled the next day. For all you sales professionals you know what that means. I sold them so hard it scared them away. Back to the drawing board I went!

Oh, the questions you ask yourself about how to change your presentation for others to believe. It wasn't until I realized it was my intention to sell them that was the problem. So the next 10 I signed didn't cancel and the only secret I can give you is I trusted in myself and what I've created to this point. I didn't' ask for the sale, and it seemed like the customers were even hungrier for the message I had to offer they asked me to sign them up. This starting process ultimately has become our primary focus as a company today.

Starting and operating a business are very different things and operate at a very different pace. Learning to transition from startup to operation after about 18 months was challenging for me. I have so much joy and excitement in the chaos of starting a business and creating something from scratch. So after it was moving along just fine staff was happy etc. What did I do? Well, I don't recommend it but hopefully it'll open your eyes if you're the same way. I would dig into different parts of the company and tweak it just so I could have something new to build. Yes, that's right, I was messing things up just so I had something to build again. Fighting the urge to adjust to the pace at which the business was operating at. It took remembering back to the beginning during those first sales that all cancelled. I was doing this to my company and my staff, it was time to trust what was created already and more importantly trust my staff.

I love the chaos of business startup, not knowing what's next but still knowing at the same time. It allows me to build build build and invent. Knowing that I am capable of hyper focus and being a hyper focused visionary and not only knowing what's being created but seeing it as it's happening is easy for me but, not so easy for those around me.

The magic started happening when a few years later and others started seeing my passion behind WHY we created this company and how different we are from the competition. My list of 100 was my map to finding my authentic self, it really is that simple and it has nothing to do with what's on the list but everything to do with the process of writing them out.

Now in the beginning of our 5th year in business, it's still a daily struggle for me to trust what's created and continue to look forward. I was able to recognize the need to continue building the future but, now I dig into our competition to understand their story and why they are what they are. I figure if I'm half as good at messing up my own company I might be able to clean up the industry a bit! Keep pushing and continue to find ways to see what can be with what is and never give up!

The Importance Of Patience In The Instant Gratification World

ELIZABETH DE ZULUETA

Today we want everything now. We send a text message to a friend and want a reply immediately. Our device usage has decreased the human attention span and studies are finding that technology use and sugar consumption cause the brain to release the same chemicals. We are literally getting a high from our devices, so we use them more often and require them to be faster and more powerful. We want faster speeds, higher bandwidths, more apps, and we want them now. This phenomenon is spreading to other parts of our lives, such as work and relationships.

We have all experienced the awe of hearing the story of a company that seems to have come out of nowhere and in record time became a billion-dollar company. This isn't just in the media or online, startup culture glorifies this fast-paced race to be the biggest "unicorn." The journey is supposed to be so incredible and unbelievably fast that they literally call these billion-dollar companies "unicorns."

But unicorns, like "overnight successes," don't exist. The most successful people know that it takes years of hard work, quietly fighting for every bit of exposure, to gain widespread recognition. We all fall prey to this instant success mentality, including me. I grew up with technology and throughout school, books and a laptop were the first two items on my school supplies list. I grew up with the internet, instant messenger, and cell phones. These technologies make things faster and more convenient, so obviously building a company should follow suit.

I always wanted to start a company so after I finished engineering school, I went straight into entrepreneurship. I was the young entrepreneur with the right skills, right experience, and right amount of passion. The problem was I didn't know what to build, what problem to solve, or who to help in the process. Regardless, I forged ahead. I had to, because at 24 years-old I was behind. Bill Gates was 20 when he founded Microsoft, Steve Jobs was 21 when he founded Apple, and Mark Zuckerberg was 19 when he launched Facebook. All three dropped out of college to start their companies, while I stayed, finished my Bachelor's degree, and then dedicated 2 more years to get a Master's. I graduated at 24 years-old and didn't know what to focus on, so I moved home to find clarity. I had ideas but nothing that excited me. I felt stuck, like I was taking a test with a ticking clock and had yet to learn the answers.

Then right before my 25th birthday, I dislocated my kneecap, landed in a wheelchair, and started the long process of relearning how to walk. My first day of physical therapy, my leg muscles were so atrophied that I couldn't lift my leg. This was a problem, I needed to get my company on its feet. So, I designed an outdoor robot, it was still rough but was something to move the company forward. After a few months, I was finally walking so I got back to work. Like with everything else I pushed myself. I needed to make up for lost time, the time that I spent getting a Master's, the time I spent thinking of a product, and the time I lost being injured. However, I pushed myself so hard that 5 days later I reinjured myself and was back in a wheelchair.

Now I was confronting the tough decision of putting my company on hold, concentrating on myself and getting better or risk never getting off my "injury hamster wheel." This was a hit to my pride. I thought that after a year or two my company would be making revenue. But the reality was, that a year after graduating I was putting my business on hold and planning to spend 6 months focusing on recovery. Once again I was losing time, putting me further behind. Nonetheless, I couldn't risk injuring myself again and landing on an operating table.

I slowly went through the process. It wasn't easy, in my therapist's own words "trying to bend my leg was like trying to bend a 2x4." My joint stiffness is a good metaphor for my frustration, not accomplishing anything I had planned was demoralizing. However, I trusted my therapists and become close with them and the other patients. I would cry, laugh, and swap stories during my appointments. My therapists didn't just help me recover, they became friends. The other patients and I would complain about the pain from our injuries and celebrate everyone's recovery successes. The other patients and I were always mentioning the frustration of no longer being able to do things on our own. This led me to an epiphany: the main reason I entered entrepreneurship was the ability to live life on my own terms, and many people due to illness or injury don't get that chance. I realized I wanted to help people live independently, regardless of physical limitation.

It was like a path clearing. I finally understood how these experiences were essential for me to reach my goals. Although I had felt like I was wasting time and would never get that time back, that year and half helped me find my way. I invented a robot to help people with mobility restrictions do household tasks independently, so that anyone can live life on their own terms. What sometimes feels like our biggest setback can become our greatest victory. In his 2005 commencement address, Steve Jobs recounts when he was fired from Apple and said it "was the best thing that could have ever happened ... It freed me to enter one of the most creative periods of my life." Setbacks, obstacles, challenges, etc., help us see life differently and give us opportunities we would never otherwise encounter.

Don't let the setbacks scare you or make you feel like you cannot achieve your goals. Because that setback might just be the key to reaching your dreams.

www.zulubots.com

A Second Opinion

TERRENCE CASH

I had been living in an affluent enclave of Long Island, New York since September 1987. The subdued section of high-end retail shops and tree-lined homes where I lived was mostly popularized by its elegant and stately golf courses, nestled on the coast of Long Island's South Shore, just one block away. It was here, that I then unexpectedly found myself summoned into the Vice Chairman's corner office at Dayton T. Brown Inc. As I listened dispassionately to the details of the company's current round of downsizing, I realized I was now the lead actor in the on-going documentary on the perils of wage slavery. Being abruptly laid-off from my $80,000 a year engineering management post after the merits of four years of exemplary work performances, was not just disheartening, it should have been criminal. Of course, the typical suspects here included hundreds of hours of unpaid overtime, over three hundred thousand business travel miles and my acquisition of over two million dollars of unexpected revenues for the firm, just 6 months before my forced exit. But it wasn't about the money. Well, it wasn't just about the money, but rather the spirit of ease and detachment with which an employer can suddenly, and with no warning, send a valued worker's world spinning into unreserved panic.

It was at this point in my life, in 1994, before the defense industry bubble burst and an illegal eviction occurred, that my fortunes and destiny would be rearranged to New York City. Ironically, I was considering carefully a New York Times Classified ad, for something that was up until that point in time, ridiculous altogether. Here I was, an entrepreneur who had launched a startup tech company, seriously considering a full-time day job in the computer industry, with the competition. The night before I had tried unsuccessfully to convince my then best friend Gerald Knowlden, that my sudden and urgent quest for employment was merely a matter of changing strategies. That is, for my dreams to be realized, I was going to need regular bi-weekly paychecks. "I'm not quitting and giving up on my entrepreneurial dreams after striving so hard the last four years. It's not in my DNA." I told him. This was more by way of admission than bragging, then explained that I was completely out of money, with bills in arrears and how poverty acquires romance only when escaped.

The response of my childhood friend was as humorous as it was unforgiving, "You are ruined my friend, and your return to wage slavery is a cruel and twisted joke that will never work for you. On the other hand, perhaps you should just run back to the cover of anonymity, stagnant wages and periodic layoffs. Maybe then you will finally realize that the only way most likely to produce financial freedom is having your own business." So after begrudgingly following his advice to stay the course with my languishing tech startup, I ended up winning a few dozen technology projects worth over two million dollars. But when I sat with him for dinner two years later in a small silver and gray booth at the White Plains Coach Diner, I couldn't even evoke the past.

As the ultimate testament to the resilience of the human spirit, the past, for better or worse, always loses to the future. And the power of this new reality, is that it only requires that you understand two basic truths. The first truth is that your success is largely based on the fact that everything you do in life, serves to create the future or relive the past. The second truth is that true freedom in life is measured mostly in the things that make you healthy, happy and rich. Thus, you can through this freedom gain an upward leap in opportunity, choice and control previously unthinkable.

But I did not always have access to these hidden truths and secret facts. Twenty-five years ago, I believed winning involved stacking job upon job like steps on a ladder. Wherein, each job's salary was higher than the previous one, until the path it created led inexorably to the way out of financial troubles. However, the truth is, that after almost a dozen years of demonstrated accomplishment back then, at a patchwork of employers, financial prosperity was still placed well beyond the rescue of a bi-weekly paycheck. In fact, if the world of work inadvertently does place someone on the road to financial freedom, it is almost certain that such a person is walking.

You see, this is regrettably due to the fact that the dynamic in the modern workplace has only grown worse over the years, mostly for the employed. In other words, the undeniable truth is that everyone is vulnerable to the financial and lifestyle terrors wrought by overzealous tax authorities, out-of-control employers and unproductive retirement plan investments. Consider first that the virtual disappearance of the American middle class over the past 30 years has followed a familiar but troubling trajectory. A trajectory which falsely suggested that society could keep its existing shape, only by remaining largely ignorant to the wealthy's little-known business model of assets, equity and entrepreneurship. As a result, everywhere today, we can see the consequence of this ugly, selfish and doomed fantasy. A fantasy that seems almost a parody of logic and fairness. One which consumes more than it saves, and saves more than it invests. One which also seems to promise employment without layoffs, government without taxes and wealth without production.

To put it another way, a clear but ominous shadow is cast over our perceived notions of winning at work when a majority of our income is spent in taxes and other deductions even before the first dollar is spent on household expenses, much less anything else.

Beware: The Unexpected IS Coming

KUJAATELE KWELI

The focus of this article is how to prepare for the unexpected even if you cannot, by definition, know what it is coming because, well ... *it is unexpected.*

The Amazing Opportunity

By way of background, in 2003, I was 52 and CEO of a group of businesses that had grown from a start-up in my garage 1995 to a group of companies bringing in $2.7 million in annual revenue. My primary company, Rising Star Telecommunications Inc., designed and built an international universally accessible debit card backed by gold that allowed our targeted customers to engage in international financial transactions without engaging in credit or usury. Usury is the illegal action or practice of lending money at unreasonably high rates of interest. This is prohibited in both the Old Testament and the Koran (the Islamic sacred book). This potentially creates a huge market niche and business opportunity. There are over 2 billion people around the world required by their faith to avoid usury, whenever and wherever possible. Additionally, there are 100s of millions of Christians and Jews who also subscribe to the need to avoid usury.

My clients were a consortium of 22 Arab nations who routinely paid for my company's services in cash, up front. In retrospect, developing the technology was easy, negotiating the politics was difficult and the competition (the banks) was, to put it mildly, fierce. Initially no bank we contacted wanted to work with us for fear it would threaten their credit business – the foundation of modern banking. Nevertheless, we got it done and were preparing to roll it out when the unexpected, beyond our imaging, happened.

The Unintended Consequence of The Patriot Act

Out of nowhere the horrific 9/11 attack took place. Until that terrible moment of man's inhuman cruelty to man, money had never a problem on this project. However, Congress quickly passed the Patriot Act. The killer provision in the Act seemed, at first glance, innocuous. It simply required that American companies doing international business "**know their customers**" and "**know**" that the source of their money was legitimate (for example; not drugs or from arming terrorists). This seemed straightforward enough, at first, and we were not worried since our client was the king of one of the United Arab Emirates and an established friend of America.

However, one day shortly after, I got a call from my bank informing me that my company had received $50,000 wire transfer from the King. This was not particularly unusual since I had received up to $1.2 million dollars from the King in the past. However, my bank informed me that because of the Patriot Act that they could not release the funds until I provided them with proof that I "knew my client" and the "source" of these funds. I told them what they already knew that the source was the King and the Central Bank. They explained they needed more personal and confidential information about my client, such as: information on his other business interest, activities, "real" private residents, itinerary, personal phone numbers, bank accounts balances and proof that his source of his funds were legitimate (not from arms, corruption, drugs or other criminal activity) or they would have to return the money and refuse to accept any more money for my company from the King.

It turned out that personal and confidential information for heads of state in that part of the Arab world are national secrets – even their phone numbers, itineraries and "real" addresses are secrets and revealing them is considered treason – a truly capital offense. When the King or any of his royal family or representative would travel to America they would never tell us the exact date. Or to put it another way the date they provided we knew would not be their actual date of travel – they would usually arrive ten day earlier or later. So I had no way of giving the bank the newly required information they were asking me for.

The Price of The Unexpected

As a result of my inability to provide the bank with the information they demanded, they return our money and refused to accept any more. In the end this was the kiss of death for many small international companies like mine doing business in that part of the world. I ended up selling my company's R&D, patents and assets to my client for $1 and moving on to other business ventures. The King on the other hand was not able find another U.S. company, even a major bank or financial institution, to partner with them in the development or deployment of the project.

Additional Lessons

Based on my experience let me share three additional cautionary strategies that I would strongly urge anyone considering international commerce to employ. They are:

1. **Think Positive and Prepare for a Crash** – This is not an either/or proposition. Build yourself a parachute and be prepared to use it before your business crashes. Always keep enough resources in reserve to survive and rise again;
2. **Diversify Your Product, Services, Market and Clients** – Almost every successful business begins by specializing in one thing with one client. However, every products or services, no matter how good it is, has a life cycle. It is wise to develop new products, services, markets and clients to protect your business from becoming obsolete and unexpected changes in laws, politics, technology, weather, geography or demographics. My rule of thumb is there is no product or service should be expected to last over 5 years. Today, computers alone double in speed and memory every 18 months.
3. **Prepare to Defend Your Assets Before They are Under Attack** – The more successfully you are the more vulnerable you are to changes in public policy, competition, hostile corporate takeovers, tax audits, FBI investigations and scams. If you wait to you are under assault you have often already lost.

Major Conclusion: Like Water is Wet and Rocks are Hard, the Unexpected is Coming.

Contrary to popular belief, it is the not the rich or strongest that survive. It is the quickest to adapt. Don't confuse product or customer loyalty for business acumen. There is always a competition between the priorities of the present and research development for the future. There is a tendency for what is important, but urgent (the right now) to win. The problem with this is that while the future never seems urgent, it is alway inevitable and when it comes it must be accommodated whether you are ready for it or not.

Successfully balancing these competing issues are critical to the survival of your business.

In short, never fall so in love or get so comfortable with your market, product, service or your client that you do not prepare to replace them.

TheKOOGEShow.com

Presidential Progress

PATRICK AHERN

I was standing in a hallway on Arcadia University's campus in Glenside, Pennsylvania. There was nothing special about it, in fact it was quite ordinary: white cinder block walls, clean porcelain floors, and fluorescent lighting. In fact, it was the setting itself that made the situation I was in even more surreal than it already was. Standing all around me was an eclectic gathering of people; men and women in dark suits and discerning glares kept their heads on a swivel; highly engaged staffers hustled to-and-fro. Echoing above the slightly hushed conversation came the rising crescendo of the voice of the President of the United States.

Okay, perhaps I should explain.

Over a year before, in the early spring of 2008, I was completely adrift. No really, I had no idea what was going on. I had graduated from high school nearly three years prior and during the intervening years I felt that I had accomplished very little. Oh sure, I had a few college credits under my belt and I had held down a job during that time (well, jobs). But for a guy who had charged into his college years with high aspirations and dreams of becoming a successful lawyer, 2008 was shaping up to be the year where I would have to face the raw reality that somewhere along the line I lost the thread. Life, I was learning, did not give a crap what my plans were. I was going to have to rethink my whole approach. My means to an end came in the form of a self-described "skinny guy with a funny sounding name:" Senator Barack Obama.

I had found myself enthralled with everything to do with Barack Obama the minute I first heard him speak at the now famous DNC Convention of 2004. It was a dark time to be a young person. My peers and I were coming of age during the era of 9/11, the Afghanistan War, the Iraq War, economic bubbles, vast inequality and injustice, and much more. Obama's speech came at a time when uncertainty, fear, and doubt were mainstays of the American Experience. When he spoke not of a Red America or Blue America but of the United States of America, I knew that there was finally something to be hopeful about again. And so, four years later, as I searched with increasing anxiety for some new path to take, I realized that it was time for me to throw myself into something new and that something new was Barack Obama's Campaign for Change. A new campaign office had recently opened nearby in advance of the May Primary so I drove over and immediately volunteered. I made thousands of calls that spring; knocked on hundreds of doors; registered dozens of voters and definitely changed a few hearts and minds through my zeal but what it did for me on the inside was incalculable. It set me on a new course.

On Primary Day, Obama got walloped but it did not matter. At that point, he had the nomination in the bag and for my part, I was thrilled to have been a part of history. But it was only the beginning. That night I hitched a ride downtown to the luxurious Waterworks in Philadelphia where the Obama Primary Day After-Party was taking place. The lawyer whom I had spent the day working with bought me a drink and asked what I would do next. I replied that I had no idea but that a friend in the campaign had suggested that I apply for the Obama Summer Fellowship Program which was essentially a prelude to the General Election campaign. He asked whether I was going to apply and I told him I honestly did not know. He looked at me and said: "You should do it. You'd be crazy not to."

I will never forget that conversation. I did end up applying and was accepted to the program which tasked us with building a campaign infrastructure in Pennsylvania. In August, I applied for a job with the campaign and was hired as one of the Field Organizers tasked with running field operations in Montgomery County. By Election Day, I had opened and funded three campaign offices, staffed them with thousands of volunteers, given many public speeches including one introducing Bruce Springsteen to 80,000 of my fellow Philadelphians, and organized events for Dr. Jill Biden, Hillary Clinton, Michelle Obama, and, of course, the Senator himself.

These series of events were how I found myself in that hallway in Glenside a few months later. A White House Staffer had called me a few days prior to ask if I would be interested in driving one of the vehicles in the Presidential Motorcade. I reported for duty a few days later, drove my vehicle to Willow Grove Air Force Base, watched as Air Force One landed on the tarmac right next to me, and observed with awe as President Obama bound off the plane and hopped into his limo. I was 22. I had no college degree or any formal experience but because I had dared to throw myself into the unknown the year before, I now found myself at the beginning of a thrilling career. I would go on to help run a Senate run-off campaign in Atlanta, a State House race and Judicial campaign in Montgomery County, and a congressional race in PA. Somewhere in there I also earned my BA in Political Science from Temple University.

At some point during the reading of this chapter you probably started asking yourself: "I thought this was a book about business." You are right, it is, and so is this story. During the campaign, I received some of most comprehensive corporate-style training I have ever experienced. I learned flexibility, adaptability, discipline, and perseverance. The campaign did not provide a single dollar for any of the offices I opened. Nor did it afford me the necessary equipment, staff, or budget I needed to achieve my goals. I had to find it myself so I did. It is the same in business. You have to be prepared to learn self-reliance but also be willing to yield to others to help you implement a plan. It was campaigns that taught me this but it was in business that I applied these lessons for myself.

Eventually, I took a break from politics and became part owner of a home remodeling company. During that time I also provided consultations to asset managers who were renovating houses and worked with property owners to enhance the profitability of their network of homes. Now, I run my own financial services practice for a Fortune 500 company. This may seem like a stretch to some but for a person who was once an uneducated twenty-one-year-old who leapt into an historic presidential campaign without looking. But the Obama Campaign set me on the unlikely path towards the entrepreneurial career I now find myself in. The lessons I learned nearly a decade ago showed me that trying something unfamiliar can be exactly the thing that leads to great transformation and eventual success. Recently, I heard someone say: "Doing the uncomfortable thing, the thing the other guy won't do, is what leads to success." If there is anything you should take away from this chapter, it is that. Take the leap. You won't regret it.

Section Two: The Journey Within

Find Your Big Why (And Lose Your Fear Along the Way)

GAIL MERCER-MACKAY

It was a moment I will never forget. The ringing of my home-office fax machine late one evening woke me from a deep slumber on my family room couch. *"Dear Mrs. MacKay – Your services are no longer required. Please return your laptop and cell phone at your earliest convenience ...."*

I had been axed. By fax. I had been *fax-axed*.

As a Senior VP running global sales and marketing for a fast-growing tech company, I thought I was indispensable. My company obviously thought otherwise.

The shock of being fired also rattled at my deepest insecurities. Four kids and a mortgage meant no early retirement. But more than that. I was terrified of being unemployed. Of being unemployable.

Fear. It had driven my decision-making for most of my life. I did all the "shoulds." I went to the right university and took the "safe" courses. English and business seemed like the smart thing to do. I secretly envied students in the journalism program but my well-intentioned family planted seeds of fear when I expressed my longing to be a writer. Writers had no safety net. A good business career (supported by my ability to type) meant I would never be out of a job.

I put in 60-80-hour work weeks. I travelled 30 weeks a year. I commuted 3 hours every day. I left home before the sun came up and often arrived back just in time to crawl into bed. Feelings of insecurity meant I needed to prove that I was willing to work harder than anyone else. I was on a treadmill but did not know how to get off. I was exhausted, miserable and felt like I was completely missing out on my life. Still, I was driven by fear.

The firing was a blessing in disguise, but I didn't see it that way at first. Because in spite of always playing it safe, my biggest fear had actually materialized. I was out of work and utterly terrified.

My instinct was to immediately look for another job. But I would simply be trading logos on a business card – back on the same old corporate treadmill. Nothing else would change. And so, as my gut churned, something inspired me to pause and take stock. I left home for two weeks and travelled through the southern United States. I did a complete digital detox. I walked, read, played golf and journaled. Every day.

The journaling helped me reconnect with myself. I was able to admit that I wanted more out of life. Something that brought me joy and a sense of purpose every day. Today I hear people refer to this as their "Big Why". At the time, for me, it was about finding, believing in, and realizing my life's purpose.

Lesson Number One: Trust yourself and your instincts. Deep down everyone knows the right thing to do in any situation. Allow your own inner self to guide you at every moment in life – both large and small.

Sound lofty? Yes, but even though I still felt fearful, I was no longer willing to make fear-based decisions. I was willing to risk everything to find my right place in this world.

During those two weeks of journaling, I came to the conclusion that I needed to be a writer. I didn't know what that would look like. I didn't know how it would feed me. But I knew it was what I was here on Earth to do.

Friends told me I would fail. I ignored them and took a giant step outside my comfort zone.

Lesson Number Two: Feeling fear is okay – in fact it is healthy to feel fear. Making fear-based decisions is not okay.

I took a large sum out of my savings – enough to live on for a year. It would be my safety net but if I failed? It would decimate my retirement fund. I decided not to worry about it, gave my fears another kick to the curb, and instead focused firmly on pursuing my passion.

I knew absolutely nothing about starting a writing business. And that showed up as I tried one idea and then another. Of course there were lots of hurdles – what to write, where to find clients, how much to charge – but I never once wavered in my determination to be successful.

And I was. Work came in slowly at first but today, ten years later, I have a staff of over twenty – freelance writers, editors, project managers, videographers, graphic designers and office support. Business continues to pour in, and we have a global client list that includes some of the top Fortune 500 companies around the world.

I guarantee our work. I tell my clients if they don't like our work, they don't have to pay for it. I am not afraid of going bankrupt with this guarantee. I have only had two clients take up that guarantee in ten years, and they were both so grateful that they continue to give us business today. They trust our integrity.

I am not afraid because I am guided by, and live in harmony with, my "Big Why".

Lesson Number Three: Live in harmony with your "Big Why" and understand how it fits in with the world around you. Make sure that your "Big Why" has integrity and helps others. (Especially if you decide to offer a money-back guarantee.)

I'd like to say that everything was perfect once I started my own business but that would be a lie. I had hurdles and roadblocks. I tried some things that failed miserably while others took off. I had an unexpected tax bill the first year that left me begging the bank for a line of credit. Two clients cancelled big contracts at the same time and I had to scramble for work to fill the void.

Fear would lick at me every time an obstacle arose, yet a growing faith and belief in myself was strengthening. I knew I was following my own "Big Why" and that knowledge kept me on course.

Lesson Number Four: Be curious. Every day we are faced with new competitors, new technologies, new market trends, new ways to do things. Don't be afraid of what is new; instead, embrace it and be curious. Learn how you can capitalize on trends to address potential new markets.

The business I am running today doesn't look anything like the one I thought I was going to be running when I started out ten years ago. But that is okay. I trust myself and am no longer ruled by fear.

I believe that no matter what our circumstances are, we are all born with talents and gifts that can flourish if we are willing to do the work to uncover those talents; and then let them shine, strengthen and grow. It is natural to feel fear – especially if we are going after a dream. Feel your fear and do it anyway. Others may try and dissuade you. But listen to your own inner voice.

You can go as far as you want when you trust yourself. Believe it. It is true.

Your "Big Why" has the power to lead you to places well beyond your imagination and your dreams. Because while you change the world for yourself, you will be changing the world for others. And that is the best reason I know for finding and following your own "Big Why."

www.mercermackay.com

Hold On To Your Integrity

MITCHELL JOHN CAMPAGNA

I grew up in a town of less than 50,000 people: Bismarck, North Dakota. In Bismarck, your word was everything. If you borrowed five dollars from a friend because you were short, you were good for it. I was honored to be chosen captain of the football team, by my fellow teammates, where I learned leading was a privilege. Little did I know, after college and moving to the much larger city of San Diego, California, that my beloved home town with my parents and friends, provided me all the integrity I would need in my business life.

Fast forward to my early professional years as an architect, when I thought everything was clicking and couldn't be better. I was making great money and working for the 10th largest developer in San Diego as their Director of Architecture, and I was still in my twenties! I had even joined the company's Cash Flow Division, that had a return of 18% on any cash I contributed. This seemed like a no-brainer to me. Heck, I even started to take money off credit cards that had a lower percentage rate, and place it in there as well.

This was going great for a couple of years. Besides getting my salary and bonuses, I was also getting a monthly check from my investments in the company. Then it stopped. I was still getting my salary, but the cash flow checks stopped coming. I was good friends with the firm's accountant and his office was right next to mine, so of course I started to hear about the financial instability of the company. He started telling me how the company was too spread out, basically robbing one project to fund another, so my small pittance was the last thing on their mind.

Here's where my integrity took over. This was a lot of money to me. I could not afford to lose my $40,000 principal, while still owing on the credit cards, paying rent, owning a rental and all my other bills. I started letting everyone in the company know that I was drawing a line in the sand. I was tired of being a pawn and being ignored, when they owed this money to me. Besides, I had something they wanted more: my architectural stamp. My license and stamp was their key to getting these multi-million dollar projects permitted and built, and hence, it controlled access to their investors' pocketbooks.

The timing was perfect. I had arranged to fly back home with my sister and my two young nephews, at a time when the company needed me to stamp and sign our largest building to date, a downtown high rise. This was worth millions to the company, and would release a flood of cash from their Japanese investors. Panic started to set in with the two Vice Presidents of the company, as they knew I would be gone for more than a week, so they started to pressure me into signing before I left. I told them that I wanted my original investment, plus the interest to date, before I would sign.

I was waiting at the airline terminal with my sister and nephews. Suddenly, my right-hand man in the company, Doug, came around the corner, like it was slow motion, carrying two sets of large blueprints, with a look of fear on his face. It reminded me of when I would catch a touchdown pass and how time would seem to slow down, as I took each stride. He said, *"Mitch, what are you doing? They're extremely upset. Do you know who you're messing with?"* I took the set of plans from him and said, *"Don't get involved, Doug. I'll take care of it."*

As soon as my plane landed, I told my mother to stop at FedEx on the way home. I shipped them back ... unsigned. As a result of this decision, I knew then that I would probably not keep my job. Heck, they were in such a panic that I even got a call from the Vice President while I wa at my friend's parents' house, back home! Still, I held my ground.

Monday morning, I walked into my office, the same as always, but this time I got a visit from our newest Vice President. *"Mitch, let's go for a ride."* Driving along, he started telling me how foolish he thought it was for me not to sign the plans, and how he didn't plan on staying with the company either. He said that we should band together to start our own company. To be honest, my small-town "integrity" radar kicked in when I had first met him. I concluded that he was as corrupt as the rest of the management. I said, *"Sorry, if you guys are not going to make me whole again, I will not sign the plans."* He then said that I have two choices, I could resign or be fired. In my mind, I was prepared for either scenario, but I wanted them to own this decision. *"You'll have to fire me."* I went back to the office, gathered my things and said goodbye to the President. He also couldn't believe I was carrying through with this.

The next year was tough since the real estate industry was imploding. As the months went on, my own implosion was coming at me. I was over $60,000 in debt, it was just ten days before my wedding, and I had just lost another job! I even had lawyers giving me advice to go bankrupt and start over. However, I went back to my integrity and thought, *"Wait a minute, even though it's Visa, MasterCard and other banks, I still borrowed the money and I'm responsible for paying it back."*

So, in order to survive, I worked jobs that I was tremendously overqualified for. I dug trenches, peddled magazines, and even sold Tupperware! I also wrote a "lesser" resume, as I wasn't getting anywhere as a licensed architect. I even worked under people, at a design firm, in a position that was four levels below my qualifications! But in the end, it was worth it. I could get up every morning, keep my integrity intact, and face myself in the mirror.

This took many years of grinding and saving to pay off the debt, but it gave me a return I could never buy, the integrity to be the businessman I am today. I have had a business for almost two decades, generated tens of millions of dollars in revenue, and have been faced with many decisions to "bend-the-rules" along the way. In every instance, we have operated with the honor and integrity that I was blessed with, in that small town, where your word was everything.

www.mitchellj.com

Trusting Your Inner Guidance

ANGELINA SAMADHI

I was on the phone with Albert Hughes, the Hollywood director that did *The Book of Eli* and other multi-million dollar films. He had just offered me my dream job.

I was to be his right-hand on an upcoming movie. The contracts were drafted, in my inbox, waiting to be signed.

I was sitting in my tiny bedroom, staring out the window, reflecting back to a few weeks prior when we visited Joel Silver at his home in Beverly Hills. I hadn't heard his name before but was briefed on the drive over. Apparently Joel was the producer of *The Matrix* series as well as many other prolific films.

When we arrived, I was in awe. I'd been in mansions before, but not like this. I was told it was a Frank Lloyd Wright original. There was a fountain in the middle of the living room, glass sculptures dangling from the ceiling and a private movie theater where we watched *The Maze Runner* with him and his family.

I was in.

Just a year and a half prior, I had sold the last of my belongings and took off to explore the world with my first DSLR camera and a backpack. I had just closed the doors on the agency I was running for the last 7 years and was ready to follow what I thought was my passion: film.

I gave up everything. I really thought this was what I wanted.

When Albert and I hung up the phone, I was instructed to review everything and send it back in a few days. Shortly after reading the script and the contracts though, something felt really off.

I found myself "excitedly" talking about the chance to work with actors like

Denzel Washington and other A-list celebrities but realized I actually didn't care. The more I learned about the film industry, the more turned off I became.

Everyone was expected to put in absurd hours with this underlying competitive "do whatever it takes to make it to the top" energy. It felt inhumane and exhausting.

Part of my reason for making such a drastic shift was to achieve more balance in my life, yet, this seemed to be at odds with the path I had chosen.

And there was this contract, awaiting my signature. I had already verbally agreed to take the job and move to London where I would live for a year, but I had also just finished traveling extensively and really did not want to move.

At this point, I had two choices: 1. proceed forward with the original plan and see what life had in store for me or 2. let it go and start all over *again*.

I was having a hard time distinguishing whether it was my fear of the unknown or if it was, in fact, my intuition warning me. Finally, I decided if it feels that bad in my body, void of excitement, I needed to trust it.

In the back of my mind, I was dreaming of finding my life partner and somehow knew London wasn't the place I was going to find him. After years of being completely career focused, this was the one thing I felt was missing from my life.

If anything, I knew I needed to spend less time focusing on my career and more time doing things I loved outside of work.

With each day that passed, the uncomfortable feelings inside my body increased. Finally, I had to make the call.

I asked Albert how many hours we'd be working per day, if I'd be able to get sufficient sleep and have time for balance. There was a long awkward silence on the phone. Then he came back and said, "If you're asking me about sleep, film is not for you."

I knew he was right, and I knew what that meant. It meant that I was going to have to give up everything I had worked towards over the last year and the story I'd been telling everyone; that I shut my company down to follow my passion which was film. I had invested everything I had.

But, still, I had to say no. I just knew it wasn't the right thing for me.

So there I was, in debt, with no money in the bank and had to figure out what to do next.

This was one of those moments where my ego and my intuition were not getting along very well. But it wasn't the first time I'd done something that seemed crazy either, like shutting down my agency during our best year ever.

I guess I've learned that listening to my intuition, no matter how scary or illogical it seems, always leads to something better. The universe responds well when we act with courage.

A branding contract popped up out of nowhere to support my transition while I planned my next steps. And about a month later, I was guided to the path of digital products.

Knowing the possibilities, I set the goal of creating a fully passive income business so I would have time for yoga and meditation, for a relationship and balance. And within a few months, it all started to come true.

I was able to create a 5-figure/mo. digital products business, meet my soulmate (who I've now married) and created the life of true freedom I'd always wanted.

The universe is programmed with supreme intelligence and knows exactly where to guide you but we have to be willing to listen and take action, even when it feels scary or unsafe.

Jim Carrey once shared that "So many of us choose our path as fear disguised as practicality." If we rely too much on logic, we miss the whole point of this life experience. We are here to play, to explore, to grow and expand.

We don't always know our purpose right away, sometimes it takes a bit of trial and error. As long as we don't get hung up on failure or other people's ideas of success, we can move forward with faith and confidence.

We are always being led. We always know what to do next.

Remember that and you're well on your way to everything you desire.

www.angelina-samadhi.com

Your Heart Will Get You There

AMY ZDUNOWSKI-ROEDER

While mentally reliving my unusual career journey here in my beloved New York City, I am overcome with gratitude and thankfulness over the obscure path that finally brought me to where my heart is happiest and where I truly belong.

It was 1996 in Bethlehem, Pennsylvania when I finished my four-year trek to earning a Degree in Music as an insecure, anxiety-ridden violin major, when I had my sights set on New York City. Since orchestra jobs were tough to come by, I decided I needed to enrich my knowledge of music into a money-making field such as Audio Engineering. This way I could have some sort of stable backup since for me, being accepted into a World-Class Orchestra seemed quite precarious and totally out of reach.

I enrolled in 1997 at the Institute of Audio Research in Greenwich Village as one of three girls at an audio school filled with impassioned metal heads, Hip Hop artists and even in my own class there was a member of one of my favorite 80's bands – The Psychedelic Furs. Musicians from all parts of the world surrounded me like a big warm musical hug and in turn I felt like part of a very unique team. It was such a year of great joy for me because I finally grasped firm knowledge of electronics, multi-track recording, audio splicing and knew what all of those little buttons did on a soundboard. I felt so full and excited, that upon graduation I landed my quintessentially perfect first job – an internship at the world-famous Juilliard School where I would be assigned to record classical artists and even enhance my own violin playing with lessons from willing teachers and students.

After I finished my internship, I landed an entry level job at Atlantic Records working in A&R. 1998 – what a great time for the music industry! People would send in cassette tapes and I would listen to them and sort them for my bosses. Music was blasted out of every office and it was a buzzy, perfect situation for a bright-eyed 23-year-old ex-musician. I worked at my day job down in A&R and then a few nights a week, I would be the second assistant to the President of the company who got most of his work done after-hours. I had beautiful conversations with Tori Amos on the phone, chatted with Sinead O'Connor, retrieved coffee for Fat Joe and joked with the Stone Temple Pilots. It was my dream job, but in truth I was starting to resent it since my salary was quite low and I was having trouble making ends meet despite my interactions with incredible musicians.

Fast forward to the year 2000, I landed a job at Sony Classical. I was so happy since I'd found a place where I could apply my long forgotten classical training. I loved working at Sony. It was a palace where Yo-Yo Ma or even Mel Brooks would say hello to me in passing. I met my husband there. Life was good until ... layoffs. Digital downloading had happened and it took over the entire music industry. I had to do something. I know my time was limited. I needed to LISTEN. What was my heart telling me? It was clearly telling me to find another job – even if it's one outside my comfort zone.

In 2004, a dear friend had mentioned that there was an Executive Assistant position open at a Real Estate company available. "Real Estate? What? I know zero about Real Estate?" I said to myself. "Can I type? Check. Can I answer the phone properly? Check. Do I need this? YES. Let's get outside of the comfort zone and TRY. YES TRY. What is there to lose? It's going to be your turns with the layoffs, Amy, so take the plunge. Do it Amy!" So I went one lunch break and had an interview with some remarkable gentlemen who I immediately wanted to be friends with and even better, work with on a daily basis. I got the job.

My first month was so incredibly awkward and difficult and every day I questioned my decision to embark on this strange new industry. As time progressed, slowly things improved. However, something was missing. I had felt a deep desire to be CREATIVE again. I longed to work with my hands. Being a violinist, I was singing through my hands to people's welcoming ears and I was yearning to do that again. Deep down I knew I wasn't TRULY happy at my current situation. My heart was telling me to be honest with myself.

The Real Estate market crash of 2008 happened and it was a very different place in my office. People were stressed. The market was affecting people's lives negatively. Things felt very gray. Every morning my poor husband would pat my back as I sat on the side of the bed sulking saying "do I really have to go in today" and he would give me such beautiful encouragement it would sustain me for at least the subway ride. I could feel a change in myself. I was less happy. I was less excited about life & a bit depressed. Until … I started working with my hands again. Secretly, on the side of my daily life, I was following my heart and cultivating a long-time hobby. It was a hobby that truly gave me life: MAKEUP. Any chance I could get, I would do makeup – in the bathroom of my job, out at bars with girlfriends, late nights at buddy's houses, parties, Sunday afternoons, you name it. I always had a makeup stash with me and was ready to use it.

One day finally, I faced myself in the mirror and decided to leave the Real Estate Industry. It was the most empowering move I had ever made and I decided to follow my dream. I went back to school and studied makeup. From Special Effects to Editorial & Fashion, I went head first into makeup. I loved every aspect of it. I took every job that came my way. I reached out to my contacts from Sony, Atlantic & real estate and made myself available for anything they needed. I worked tirelessly for years. I put up a website. I started booking celebrities. I made a name for myself. I was on TV. I started writing makeup tips for national magazines. I landed loyal clients. I expanded my business. I finally believed that this whole convoluted journey brought me where I am supposed to be. I LOVE MY JOB. My heart is happy.

The biggest lessons I learned from this whole entire, crazy life experience from start to end is: LISTEN to yourself. Be truthful and honest with yourself. Try everything. No life experience is wasted. Where you begin is not necessarily where you will end up, so trust your heart – it will get you there.

Change Is A Constant

VERA KOLESNIK

"It is not the strongest of the species that survives, nor the most intelligent that survives. It is the one that is most adaptable to change."
—*Charles Darwin*

We live in a time where 65% of the US population has a smartphone, while only 20 years ago less than 9% had a cellular connection. World population today is triple of what it used to be just 50 years ago. We are now testing a self-driving cars while only 130 years ago a car was just an invention. Our parents get older every day, we ourselves start getting wrinkles, losing hair, and taking longer to recover from a night out. 300 million cells in our body die every minute and our skin regenerates itself every 27 days.

If change is all around and inside us, why are we so surprised when we face it? Why are we so attached to reality as it is? Why are we caught off guard when co-workers leave, customers go to competitors, new strategy is rolled out and more complicated software is installed? If we go through change every day, why are we so attached to stability?

Did you know that 75% to 90% all doctor visits are stress-related? What is stress? According to Merriam-Webster dictionary: "one of bodily or mental tension resulting from factors that tend to *alter an existent equilibrium*." The biggest effect on our health and mental wellness is dealing with change.

I was first faced with the concept of change during a yoga class in a crowded NYC on a chilly spring morning. I became curious about a mantra often quoted in yoga: "the experienced practitioner is not seen through the depths of the postures but rather through the *transition between postures*." Think of yoga as a set of poses with a goal of not getting into the most advanced pose, but rather *developing ability to move through uncomfortable poses with ease*. Buddha himself contemplated change and found enlightenment in detaching from reality and therefore accepting constant evolution: "in life you cannot avoid loss, you cannot avoid

226

change, freedom and happiness is found in the flexibility and ease with which you go through change."

Right about now you might be thinking "how is this ancient concept relevant to the business world?" The biggest lesson for me was realized through the application of this ancient wisdom both at the office and in personal life and seeing transformation in my attitude and satisfaction and as a result – my performance.

I started applying this concept with my family & friends first by really accepting how they are and what they go through in life. I could finally accept my father's differences and his choice to leave my mother to be with someone else. Someone I loved at the time choosing I was not the right person for him, a scar that at the moment I thought could never heal.

I could not help but bring this wisdom to work and was able to navigate through transitions with more success than I could have if I was attached. That triggered multiple promotions and a team to manage. My mantra became "anticipate change, accept change, create change" because change will come and only if you have the right mindset you can turn it into your advantage. Since then I have switched industries, cities and lifestyles and now on top of running product & marketing for a company in the hospitality industry, I started teaching yoga and meditation and spreading wisdom that was once sprinkled on me to the fellow human beings.

So how does one develop tolerance towards to change? Recognizing the issue is the first step, the second step is continued practice. You need to learn the tools for immediate troubleshooting as well and long-term conditioning.

Immediate troubleshooting or Phase 1

When you feel overwhelmed, stressed, agitated or angry, instead of embracing these feelings and experiencing them – interrupt them. How do you interrupt them? Go back to basics, something that is the most essential to every living being – breathe. Let's do this 30 second exercise together:

Sit in a comfortable cross-legged position, spine is straight, close your eyes, place your hands on your knees, palms facing up. Take a deep breath in and imagine how your chest expands on each inhale and you become lighter and taller, on the exhale you become heavier and more grounded. Take another inhale (count to 5 on the inhale), hold your breath (count to 3) and exhale (count to 5 on your exhale). Notice how the air is cold on the inhale and warm and moist on the exhale. Notice if there are any physical sensations in your body – tingling, itching, if you feel tension … mentally release it. Repeat for at least 10 rounds or up to 1 hour.

You don't have to be seated to do this exercise, you can do it while waiting in a long line in a grocery store, on the crowded train, next to a screaming baby on the plane or sitting in traffic in your car (for this one we do not recommend closing your eyes, and for screaming baby we also recommend earplugs and potential change of seat … this exercise does have its limitations).

For best results practice this every morning before leaving your apartment, you can also set intention for the day and mentally say what you are grateful for.

Long-term structure development or Phase 2

Develop a practice that you do weekly. You can choose from yoga, meditation, breathing exercises, physical exercise, journaling, painting, reading, playing music or any other creative expression that you enjoy (anything but Housewives or Kardashian TV shows, let's say any TV and/or drinking). Commit to doing it weekly, at least a few times a week and at least for an hour each time. You will find this to be a great outlet and develop emotional stamina to start feeling more grounded.

The main purpose of all of these exercises is to realize how strong you really are and that you can weather any storm like an experienced sailor.

Enjoy the journey everyone!

The teacher in me bows to the teacher in you. Namaste.

kolesnik.vera@gmail.com

Dreaming Forward

MARIA GUERRERO

"If you can dream it, you can do it." —*Walt Disney*

I believe dreams brings the hope and strength to keep us moving forward. I also believe the dreamers are the ones who achieve and create the most beautiful things and the biggest impacts with their work. In my case I consider myself a dreamer because I am pursing the dream of a little girl, my own dream. It probably took me into one of the more rough and competitive industries, the fashion industry. But it's still a dream I've cherished all my life.

I was one of those people who was so enthusiastic about my career that I started doing internships before I went into college. I always was driven to learn more and more about the industry and how I could pursue my goal. Through my journey of learning experiences in different parts of the industry during college, I always felt something was missing. Having great internship opportunities where I dealt with different people and different personalities taught me about how the fashion industry is in reality.

Art school or more specifically fashion school does not show you much of what reality is in terms of the people you have to deal with. Sometimes when you work you will find people who are better than you, whom you might feel intimidated by, others will be lazy and you might feel empowered or better. But the trick is to not get influenced by the atmosphere of fear and surviving competition. It is always good to know that healthy competition is what makes us improve in our works A constant change in our process could get us in the path to fulfill our wishes. But I can say this now – I didn't know it then.

When I graduated from college I thought I would get a job as easy I got internships, and here is where everything started; as an intentional in the U.S. I was trying to get a job and also a correct immigration status. It was tough. When I graduated from my BFA, thinking getting a job was a very easy thing, I had no concrete plan for after college. Although I had a strong resume with six internships in different areas of the industry, it was not enough experience for an entry level position. I might say I got a little frustrated when I was going to interviews and being rejected or not elected with excuses like I was very young, that I did not have experience, I was not qualified because I was recently graduated, and being foreign was a strike against me. So I decided to stop applying for permanent entry level positions and I started working as a freelancer.

It worked, but it didn't work well. I learned that as a freelancer you are not secured in a company, it's a very tricky work label where you have to do your best to keep the job – but sometimes you give your best ideas and the company just does not have the way to sustain or afford your position, so you're out.

I did not give up, and I got an internship to keep my immigration status, I was working as freelancer at night time and working in catering and retail. I was very overwhelmed at the moment, and I felt like nothing was working the way I wanted for me.

So I took a moment to think what I wanted with my career, where I see myself and how I thought I could reach what my goal is; I talked with many different people like entrepreneurs, company owners, employees and people that actually have their own brands. And I decided I wanted to open my designer brand. I changed my whole life just by making this decision. My decision took me out of my comfort zone, moving out of the city I wanted to live in. Everything looked like it was falling apart, so I thought I took the wrong decision. When I moved back to my country, an island in the Caribbean, after living in New York for a couple years, it was a shock. This influence on me in the sense of I lost my focus and believes for a moment. I asked myself many times why I took the decision of moving out of a city in where fashion industry is so strong, how I would create a company, how I would be successful. The more I read about other people's experiences of opening their own brand the more scared I felt, and the more far I started seeing my dreams. It put me in a very weak position and I was about to give up my goal.

But why give up when things are getting harder? It is just proof to see how much you really want your goal. I was not a business person, I am just an artist, but I had my own dream. I was just looking for hope, so I had to decide whether I should try or If I would give up before to even started. I decided to keep on with my plan. It was very tough to make my mind understand how to plan a business. Also it was tough to understand that even when you are your boss, you need the help from others to create your product, so you actually keep working along with other people. So you have to be patient.

Patient is not the word I most like to hear, sometimes I still hesitate because I would like everything to be settle down but as starting up brand I have a long road to keep walking.

The best learning experience so far that I can share is that questioning yourself whether you want to be your own boss or an employee is the key question. By questioning yourself you can find the answers. And if the answer is to have your own company, you might know that first few month and years you will have to invest all your time and money in your project, and sometimes you can feel all your opportunities are far or the doors are closing. But don't hesitate, there is always another way to succeed. Passion and patience is all we need.

Section Three: The Pace of Life

Gardener To Gardener

JORDAN GRIFFEN

It's always seemed to me that you learn the most about your business when you're off the clock. I've heard about epiphanies happening at retreats, conferences, sporting events, and even parties but I'm hard-pressed to come up with an example that happened at the office. I guess it should come as no surprise then that my greatest breakthrough came far away from the workplace as I toiled away in a garden.

For as far back as I could remember, my grandfather had tended to a garden in his backyard. Every day, he would spend his time quietly working in the clay. Everything he did had a purpose. I never understood his infatuation with the garden until his health began to slip. As the cancer slowly took away his strength, he began to rely on me more and more for help. He'd sit in a lawn chair behind me, providing careful instructions and telling me stories as I worked. Each session was an opportunity for him to pass along a little wisdom, gardener to gardener. He preached the importance of developing consistent good habits and dedicating resources like water and nutrients to the plants that required those most. He insisted that the entire point of having a garden was to provide sustenance and would give away much of his harvest to friends, family, and those in need.

The man even gave meaning to the task of pulling weeds. Ask any gardener and they'll tell you if there was one task they could do without, it would be weeding. It's a thankless job. Dirt gets everywhere, you cut up your hands and knees, and after hours of being hunched over the plants it would hurt just to stand up straight. I hated it. My grandfather recognized it as one of the most important things a gardener can do. "You learn to live by pulling weeds," he would say. "You need to be able to kill the bad shoots so that the garden can grow. Don't let weeds steal your sunlight."

There's a lot to unpack in those three sentences. Thinking about your life as a garden is easy enough. It's that concept of weeding that makes it interesting. What exactly are the weeds in the first place? It differs person to person. No two garden plots are the same. Some struggle with crabgrass, some with dandelion, some with purslane. The commonality is that all three need to be pulled to ensure the garden continues to survive at the end of the day. Weeds can be bad habits that are holding us back. Perhaps the weeds are negative people in our circles than our extracting all our energy. Getting rid of the weeds can be difficult and downright uncomfortable, but ultimately we have so much to gain from their removal. Once they are gone, we find our lives to be so much more fulfilling.

This becomes even more important as our business and personal lives continue to overlap. Companies have become concerned with more than just sales and profits. Now, they have causes and missions that are undoubtedly tied to our own identities. In many ways, our businesses are just as much a living, breathing organism as a garden. Therefore, they need to be tended to as such. What practices need to be pruned? Are there employees that are stealing sunlight? Gardens and businesses require constant upkeep if they are to continue to grow and bear fruit.

This isn't to say that all weeds are bad. Sometimes, what seems like a problem at first can later appear to be part of a bigger solution. There is a time and place for everything. Many gardeners spend the majority of their time pulling clovers from the dirt during growing season because we don't want their roots competing with our crops. But what happens after growing season? A wise gardener may actually plant white clover over his garden plot in order to help prevent soil erosion and put nutrients back into the ground. It is not necessarily about what pops up in your garden, but how you use it. Maybe at your place of work you have an extremely competitive coworker. Hell, maybe that competitive coworker is you. If this contentious behavior interferes with the team dynamic and you are constantly trying to show you're better than the person working next to you, it could be a problem. On the other hand, if you redirect your competitive fire in a way that drives you to improve from yesterday and deliver a better product for your consumer it becomes an asset. In life, what stands in the way often becomes the way.

Remember, the true goal of a garden is to provide sustenance to those in need. Our businesses are designed to provide our customers solutions to their problems. When we keep that in mind, the unglamorous side of business becomes more rewarding. Diligent weeding goes a long way in providing the environment necessary for our businesses to grow tall and flourish.

www.linkedin.com/in/jordangriffen

Following A Passion

LIZET ZAYAS

For as long as I can remember I have always loved to sketch the beautiful form of the human body. The seeds of inspiration came from my mother who was a seamstress and a very talented sketcher. Every night I would ask her to make a drawing for me and I would learn by watching her. Through sketching I found joy knowing I was creating something beautiful with my hands. It was then that I knew my life was meant to be in the creative arts.

I started my career in graphic design, architecture and branding, and designed for Fortune 500 companies for 16 years. The structure of a corporate design environment taught me skills in many areas of design from fundamentals, to how to express my individuality visually. I became immensely passionate with creative work and loved to play with acrylics, chalk, experimenting with shapes, textures, patterns, colors, and fabrics. All these materials moved me artistically.

The idea of creating a unique fashion line started when I worked in the corporate world. I fell in love with the expression of a feminine dress with playful sophistication. The trendy and professional dress code at work was the perfect opportunity to nurture my desires to dress fashionably. Every day was a chance to carefully create the perfect outfit. The daily dress ensemble inspired co-workers who would tell me they loved the styles, and encouraged me to start a fashion label. At first I thought these were nice compliments and did not immediately consider it as possible.

Thoughts then turned to flourishing ideas, and quickly realized I could not find certain styles in the current market. I felt I had a marketable, feminine and stylish vision with potential to create products that customers would love. This triggered a desire for me to create my fashion line and with time the desire to create, branch out and express myself became more prominent and harder to ignore.

Two years later, I committed to enroll in a fashion school and immediately knew I had found my passion. From little girl sketches to creating patterns, and tangible products made sense. I was on a new journey to create something beautiful with my own hands. Combined with computer skills as a graphic designer was also applicable for fashion design, and my experience as a creative director, and project manager allowed me to transform fashion concepts into a reality. With my branding experience, I was able to develop and define my own brand, and through a family network of support, and the guidance of my mother as a seamstress allowed me to develop my own samples. I felt I had all the necessary tools to pursue it. Fashion school was put on hold to focus on product development, and for three years, on top of juggling a full time corporate job I prepared to launch a new fashion brand.

The entrepreneur life has allowed me to re-invent myself, and liberated my creativity. But in this journey the challenges and lessons have been tremendously rewarding. Many sacrifices had to be made in order to pursue this. It started with investing time, and money, but after a few years it felt my whole world had been turned upside down.

Now, I've learned to take it slow, and not rush to invest aggressively with inventory until a selling strategy is in place and the product has been tested in the market, giving me the opportunity to adjust the style of the brand without major losses. I am also learning to be more careful about the partnerships I choose to do business with, and have taught myself all the required skills in order to make my own samples in order to cut costs.

The fashion industry is oversaturated, incredibly difficult to break through the big-dollar marketing of the established brands. Each trial and error can be very expensive and production is complicated and after so much investments the dream can become a burden. That is why is important to take time with the preparation and strategy. I learned this the hard way and often been tempted to quit, but during the hard times I connect with other entrepreneurs who are warriors and bring me wisdom, encouragement and inspiration. I take time to simply design and be creative, this process connects me again with my purpose, making me fall in love with my work all over again helping me stay in the course.

There is a sense of power when you decide to pursue a passion of your own. It has taught me to be kind and truthful to myself, trust my instincts, and most important to be grateful. I have met amazing people since I started my brand and have found great support from entrepreneurs that have an inspiring energy, and resilient strength. I would like to think that every fall has helped me be a stronger person to pursue any dream I choose to follow.

www.lizeh.com

Wisdom Is Supreme

MARK EVERHART

I started collecting smarts at a young age. The first job I had was as a paperboy. I delivered to 44 customers on the south side of our town of 3000. The most interesting customer I had was a welder; he operated his small business in a detached garage on a residential property.

In his sixties, Lee operated this small business primarily for farmers needing repair on machinery and fabrication of gates for livestock. He was generally busy; the area in front of the shop was often littered with material.

Within the first month of delivering papers to Lee, I was drawn to the shop as a sinner is to sin. During our first conversation, I could tell he was special somehow. Having somewhat of a hoarseness to his voice, he spoke at a mildly higher pitch. What set Lee apart was how he played with the pitch during conversation, specifically while telling a story.

Lee was a storyteller. Likely the best I have known. He had the ability to describe someone who he did business with in a wildly hilarious way. With several well-chosen adjectives he described my future stepfather before meeting him three years in the future. Lee taught me how to paint a picture with words, and he had a great command of the English language. He showed me a genuine 45 record (the small one with the big hole) with L. Mullinex on the credits for writing the song.

Lee used to spice up his storytelling with a few well-chosen cuss words. This was back when blue collar workers were expected, even encouraged to salt their communication with the common swear words of the day. I never considered Lee vulgar; his favorite expression was that he was 'busier than a cat covering up sh%&'.

One of the first days I visited the shop, Lee asked me the common business questions, "Where was I from," "Who were my parents," etc. A little embarrassed, I let out that my parents were divorced as my dad was an alcoholic. Normally I didn't share that with everyone, but somehow I felt led to do so. Lee let out a quiet sigh and changed the subject.

After giving me a nickel which would buy me a single dip of ice cream up at Noid's Drug, he assured me that I was welcome to stop by and "shoot the sh**" anytime. I told him that I would. And I did. For the next two and a half years until I got the next route over I would always find time to see what was new at the shop. What I was really after was another performance of the English language.

Today, like Lee, I enjoy performing the English language. Not too often, but more than once, I get a comment like "You must think you're really smart using all of those big words." I try to respond politely that the English language is free, it doesn't cost extra to use it. Finding the avenue for good storytelling can be a challenge. Recounting stories of my youth on my Facebook page is a fabulous opportunity. Being invited to contribute to this collection of works is an answer to prayer.

Life continued after moving on to the next paper route. Looking back over the last 45 years, I can see all of the failures and mistakes, all of the lessons learned and forgotten. Lee retired several years after I quit delivering papers. I drove by his house and waved in my car as I finished high school. My brother-in-law bought Lee's pickup truck when he no longer needed it.

I went on through my twenties, putting together a list of schooling and vocations, always seeking more lessons and experience. During this time of my youth, I followed in my father's footsteps and suffered my own addiction. After getting clean and sober at 28, I stopped by and talked to his wife Clara; Lee had passed away a year before. It was then she told me that Lee had been alcoholic. It became necessary for him to be self-employed, although he had finished his life sober himself.

So here I am today, self-employed with a lawn care business. I have learned that the greatest part of my business is the customer relationships I develop. I love to talk to my customers every chance I get. Like Lee, I raise and lower the pitch of my voice when telling stories. Most of the stories I tell involve humor of sorts; other tales seem to have a moral. As my story plays out, I will have my name on the credits in several books. And every day, I remember Lee.

mayloslawn@yahoo.com

The Family Business

KARIN RAFFA

Growing your family and your business at the same time is not an easy task, but also not impossible to do. However, it requires patience and motivation to keep at it. There will be stumbles and occasional setbacks, just like a toddler who learns to walk and every now and then falls. It won't stop her from trying again. I learned to see it this way: there is no failure, only feedback. Here are the seven most important lessons I've learned so far:

1. Learn to say No. Set priorities and learn to say no to things that aren't important. Not everything needs to be done right now. Choose your priorities and say no to commitments you don't want to do. I leaned to say no to commitments which don't contribute to the goal I want to reach. It doesn't mean that you say no to best friends, just evaluate how much you have on your plate already and gently turn down the extras.
2. Don't apologize for having kids. I don't. They are the reason I do what I do to provide them with great experiences. And yes, they sometimes walk into online sessions and jump at me the minute I sit down to talk to a client. I apologize for the interruption while I deal with the "emergency," but not for having kids.
3. Use chunks of time and get organized. This is a big one! I schedule and use time chunks to get work done. I don't always finish the work I set out to complete but I make progress on it. I'm most productive in the early morning and in the evening when the kids are in bed, so I try to complete important tasks during this time. Getting and staying organized is vital for beating overwhelm. Sometimes we have so much to do, and I'm no exception, that we lose track of all the tiny tasks we want to complete. I found great tools to help me stay organized. They need to be easy to use and help you get the job done. Here are my favorites: **Evernote**. I use Evernote for everything: writing, planning, drafting, making lists. **Google Drive**. It allows me to share materials, keep them organized and I can access them anytime I need them. I can create anything I need in Google Drive and have it handy and ready to go in seconds. **Dropbox**. I use Dropbox for larger files, not only as storage space but also for

sharing materials with clients. Audio files tend to be too big to attach to an e-mail. With Dropbox I can share them without delay. These are my favorites. There are lots more available on the Internet. Ultimately, you'll pick one and try it for yourself. As long as it helps you, it's an excellent choice.

4. Have a really good system that supports you and works for you. I have to admit that I didn't have a good system at the beginning. I'm not even sure if I have the perfect system now. It evolved over time. I used to adapt it when something didn't go as well as I had hoped. This holds true for using the right tools but also for surrounding yourself with the right people. I try to keep my environment positive as much as possible. There will be ups and downs which I think is normal. But you don't want a negative environment pull you even more down when things are a bit tough.

5. Try to achieve a balance. Of course, you'll take your business very seriously but you can try a different approach. There are many people who claim that balance is a myth. I disagree. You don't need to work 24/7 even though there is plenty to do. I learned that the work expands to the time you have available. If you only have a two-hour-slot to get the work done you'll make it happen. However, be realistic. If two hours is too short, block two two-hour slots for the work and finish it. I learned to be more efficient with my work and cut out all distractions when I focus on a task.

6. Very good is good enough. It's very easy to fall victim to perfectionism and never share any of your work. Especially because we tend to be our worst critic. I learned that nothing has to be final, everything can be updated and improved. As often as you want. The most important thing is that, at some point, your work is released into the world.

7. Do not compare yourself to everyone else, keep your eyes on your plate. It is very easy to look at other people's achievement and feel paralyzed. I learned that by comparing yourself to others you can only lose because other people's achievements always seem greater. However, keep your eyes focused on what you want to achieve because only that will keep you moving in the right direction.

Even though it seems overwhelming when you start out on your business adventure and growing your family at the same time, it can be done. In fact, there are many successful female entrepreneurs doing it. The pace of your entrepreneurial journey might be a little slower in the beginning but you'll learn vital lessons along the way which will only make you an even more authentic role model for you kids. Always remember: We can achieve great things because of our growing families, not despite them!

www.mygermanology.com

My Debt-Free Journey

MICHAEL CAIRA

Like many millennials, I was in debt up to my eyeballs. $27,500 to be exact. I was your average 23-year-old fresh out of college. I had taken out student loan after student loan and opened multiple credit cards to cover the cost of school. Fortunately, I was able to subsidize some of the cost of college by working different jobs and securing paid internships. But working to pay down my debt didn't just start in college, it started much earlier than that. You see, I've always been a saver. Ever since I was a little kid my parents told me to set aside a portion of whatever money I earned and save it "for that rainy day." I had no idea that starting to save that early would someday help me avoid years of debt payments.

In addition to saving for a rainy day, some other eye-opening words of wisdom once came from a great friend of mine, a nationally recognized author and financial educator named Adam Carroll, who said, "You can have everything you want in life, you can have it all, you just can't have it when you're 22. And if you try to have it all when you're 22, you will spend the next 30 or 40 years trying to repay and dig yourself out of short-term happiness. Right now in today's society you can have the trappings of wealth, but you will leverage yourself way into the future in order to get it, and ultimately to the detriment of your own financial success." You shouldn't level up your lifestyle right out of school just because you've now got a full-time job and see everyone else buying the new car or fancy house, going on trips and spending money like there's no tomorrow. I know it's easier said than done, but the reality is that most of those people are sacrificing their future by living it up today. It takes years and years of patience and discipline to get to a place of financial stability and independence, but I can tell you from experience the journey is so worth it.

Through working numerous jobs in high school and college, years of living below my means, combined with saving and investing, I managed to position myself ahead of the game. Where I could comfortably make more than the minimum payments to my debt and shoot for a payoff goal that was much shorter than the typical 10-year repayment plan. Now, four years after graduating, I have successfully repaid all of my consumer debt and have started focusing in on other financial goals.

I understand the amounts of student loans and credit card vary greatly by the individual, some of us have tens of thousands while others have only a few thousand, though the principles of debt stay the same. Being debt free is a mindset and a process all in one. You have to be committed to the process of getting out of debt and staying out of debt. You have to be disciplined with your spending and have a clear distinction between what is an essential need like food or shelter versus a want such as a new phone, watch, etc. This is the hardest part because we are wired as consumers to spend, spend, spend.

The way you deal with this is deciding what is more important to you, getting out of debt and building wealth or staying where you are in a continuous debt cycle, wasting hundreds, if not thousands of dollars paying interest. As you shift from a spending mindset to a saving mindset, over time you'll begin to see it gets easier to knock out more of your debt. Only buy things you truly need, and if you continue using a credit card, keep your purchases within your budget so that you know you can pay off the balance in full every month. If you want something, set a goal and go after it, save up and make your purchase with cash! If you're not in the right state of mind, with the intentions of becoming debt free, you'll have a much harder time obtaining your goal.

Here's the problem many people run into: many of us don't learn about personal finance until we become mired in financial problems. But don't stress, studying personal finance will enable you to face successfully the financial challenges and responsibilities of life by helping you to acquire financial knowledge, develop your financial management skills, clarify your financial values and goals, and identify specific needs and wants that can be satisfied with your financial resources.

If you're just getting started and looking for a fun and creative method to help you start saving, one that I have personally used to start saving is with the "52 Week Money Challenge." Essentially, the challenge is started in the first week of the year and ends 52 weeks later. In the first week, you put one dollar in an envelope in a safe place. When a week passes, you add two more dollars to the pot, and the next week, you add three more. If you commit to this approach, you will save almost $1400 in one year! (*My suggestion: you could also try doing the challenge backwards by starting off with $52 the first week, $51 dollars the next, and so on and so forth.) Start the "52 Week Money Challenge" to fund an emergency cash reserve or use it to save towards a specific goal!

Throughout the last decade, investing in myself was a huge part of my success, and it still is today. Investing my time, money, and energy into clubs, organizations, and conferences helped me to grow professionally throughout my college career and beyond. No matter where you are in life, you can invest in yourself by getting out there, taking action, and making awesome sh** happen! If you are still in school, all the better! Take advantage of the opportunities that surround you on campus and in your community. Doing so will put you ahead of the game in more ways than one. And you know what they say, if you find yourself in a hole, stop digging. Figure out where you stand by checking your bank and credit accounts regularly. Get into the habit of evaluating your finances weekly if not, monthly. By doing this, you'll be able to see what it is you need to work on and change to become debt free and more money savvy!

Here's my top five things to implement to get yourself on the right track to financial success:

1. Track your monthly expenses; know exactly how much $ is coming in & going out
2. Cut down on non-essential expenses (ex. eating out, cable, other subscriptions)
3. Strive to pay double the minimum payment on your debt and remember "If you can eat it, drink it or wear it, it doesn't go on plastic!"
4. Write down all of your financial goals
5. Start intentionally saving for those goals by setting up automatic deposit into separate savings accounts

To the journey,

-MC
MoneySavvyMike@gmail.com

Did You Ever Get The Call That Changed Your Life?

DANA CIRINCIONE

I remember the moment I got the call. You never think you are going to get it, it's completely unexpected when you do. But there it is, you get the call that makes the world stop and you have to think – what do I do next?

My "change my life call" came in May 2015, when I found out that I very suddenly and unexpectedly lost my mom. The woman who I went to for every life decision, who had been away on vacation enjoying life, and there I was, her only child on the phone with the Costa Rican embassy having a complete stranger tell me that she was gone. I felt like I was on a TV show where someone was going to jump out at me and tell me it was a prank, a sick joke that had gone wrong or that someone was trying to scam me out of money. But it wasn't a joke or a nightmare I couldn't wake up from, it was real life and the world was still moving.

And just like that I had a decision to make.

I felt like I was standing at a fork in the road, two paths in front of me and trying to figure out which one to take. The one of the left probably seems familiar to those who have suffered such a loss, I could have recoiled from the world, trying to understand what exactly had happened and let it consume me. If I took that road I would have just been going through the motions of my day not enjoying what was around me. So I looked to the other path to see what that could hold for me, who I could become and how to move forward from a tragedy on a positive path for life. Most importantly, I thought about the life I wanted for myself and what my mom would want for me. Every time I questioned a decision I would think "what would my mom say to me at this moment?" and I would wait for that voice inside my head, her voice, to help guide me. I never really paid attention before when people said things like we were living on borrowed time. This was the first time I ever began to realize how short and unexpected life can be.

When I started planning her funeral I knew people would send flowers, every time I have had to go to a wake there were always so many beautiful flowers, but I knew that afterwards a lot of the flowers were tossed and many people had spent money on them that could be better spent to do something good. I decided in lieu of flowers I wanted that money to go to something my mom would be proud of, a cause that she would want to support. I started The Marie Frank Foundation in her honor, a foundation that will fund track programs to continue the growth of the program for children ages 5-13, just like the one she coached for over 13 years. It is my dream to grow the foundation to a national level but I know I had to smart small and so the foundation's first goal is to keep the program that she coached funded.

Seven months later I bought my first home, I had always envisioned myself as a city girl but, I gave up the city life and moved closer to the beach, closer to friends and family. At the time I received the call I was an executive assistant, and after being in that role for the past few years I knew I needed and wanted more. I was unhappy in my work life, being an executive assistant meant working long hours, sometimes on the weekend, and I was not enjoying my new home and the life I was trying to build. I had always wanted more so I decided to start taking the steps to get there. I took classes to receive a certification from NYU in digital marketing and began looking for roles which I was passionate about in social media, public relations and marketing. I started going back to a thought I had a few years ago about getting my real estate license but the timing wasn't right. Now there I was re-evaluating my life and I went back to the day that I got the call and thinking about the new path I had put myself on.

So I finally did what I wanted to do, not what someone else was telling me to do. At the end of the week I quit my job, signed up for the real estate class and started my own digital marketing company, DC Interactive. The next week I started my real estate class and two weeks later I thankfully passed the state exam. During the transition I had started talking to everyone I knew or met about my background and my new ventures. I was thankful that through word of mouth and networking I was able to find clients who needed assistance with their social media, websites and digital marketing. I was gradually building both careers and using the skills I had learned from my past jobs to balance my time and priorities with both. DC Interactive was helping to alleviate the fear that I had left the financial security I was accustomed to while I began building my real estate network and then begin to close real estate transactions, which can take anywhere from 60-90 days once an offer is accepted.

Sure it was scary, I was leaving financial security but what I got in return is so much more! The day I walked into my real estate office for my first meeting I had a manager ask me what I feel to have been the most important question for anyone in the field or anyone looking to make a change: "If you had to support yourself for the first 6-12 months could you do it?" It wasn't just a financial question, it was also a question of how strong my support system was at home. I wasn't lying when I responded "Yes." This is what I had wanted for a while, to be my own boss. I didn't just make this decision lightly – I had made a plan, done the research, taken classes and tests, set a budget as I now had to be able to run a household and a business on a limited budget, set expectations and goals for myself for both of my new ventures and had the best support system. I had surrounded myself with those who would pick me up in an instant if I fell down.

Not everyone needs to get a call like the one I did to better themselves but it was the motivation I needed to take the leap. Today I am my own boss working with a wonderful real estate brokerage that supports me, I have my own digital marketing company working with clients who appreciate me and who I enjoy working with, and I have a life that I know my mother would be proud of. It's sad she isn't here to see it all, but she is the reason I am where I am.

So when you get the call ... which path will you take?

Embracing Change Comes With Great Rewards

STACIE WALKER

I'm sure you're familiar with the saying, "The only thing constant is change." No matter how hard you try, you can't stop it. You already know that your life can't stay the same forever. But even though you know this, it can seem a little overwhelming when it happens.

The very thought of changing can make a person uneasy. That's why a lot of people will remain in the same mental place until they're forced to change. Instead of being repelled by change, it would be so much easier to just go along for the ride and let change benefit your life.

Do you get a little annoyed when someone tells you to embrace change? You roll your eyes and think, "Yeah. It's so easy for YOU to tell me to embrace change because you aren't ME. You don't live my life! Is that even possible? Embrace change? Yeah, right!"

Right now, I'm the voice in your head telling you it IS possible to embrace change in your life.

My Near-Death Experience Taught Me to Embrace Change

I became extremely ill to the point of literally being days from death in 2008.

My doctor discovered that I have a small liver that has to work harder to get rid of toxins in my body. To make matters worse, I wasn't the healthiest person at the time. I abused drugs, I barely slept, and didn't eat the right foods. My doctor instructed me to go home, go to bed, and stay there until I was better. He told me that it was the only way my body would bounce back.

That meant I had to make a decision to change. I knew that I had to eat right, sleep, and refrain from putting toxic things into my body. I either had to change or DIE!

I underestimated how long it would actually take for my body to heal. I had been on bed rest for months. I drained my savings, retirement, and paid leave to financially get by. I felt helpless, scared, and useless.

It's amazing how your mind will come up with brilliant ideas, when change is forced upon you. In 2008, I built my first virtual business from the ground up while on mandatory bed rest for almost a year! I didn't have prior experience, knowledge, or connections in the entrepreneurial world.

My near-death experience allowed me to discover a new world of possibilities and live a different life. A wonderful life of selflessness, love, and freedom. It snapped me out of a life of drug abuse, pain, misery, and unhappiness. I'm forever grateful for my wake-up call because I wouldn't have grown into the woman I am today.

How to Embrace Change in Your Life

You may be at a point in your life where you want to change but don't know how to embrace it. Change can be intentional or change can be forced upon you. Either way, it doesn't make the situation easy.

But change isn't supposed to be easy. I can only share some of the things that I have done and currently do to embrace intentional or forced change.

1. Take your brain to the mental gym.
Your brain is like a muscle. You can actually train your brain to handle change in a healthy manner.

Reading every single day will do wonders for your mind. If you haven't read a book since grade school or college, then it's time to hit the books again. It's best to read a variety of books on different subjects. It may be challenging at first but just focus on reading a few pages at time throughout the day. Before you know it, you'll be zipping through an entire book within a couple of days. Reading will stimulate your brain to think differently and solve problems quickly. If you're still having issues reading a book right now, then mix up how you absorb content. You can listen to podcasts and audiobooks.

Your brain is an amazing vessel. Use it or lose it.

2. Find some smart friends.
If the company you keep isn't helping you stretch your mental capabilities, then find smart friends. Ditch people who are enabling you to not get ahead. You know who I'm talking about. This can even mean that you must set some boundaries with your own family. I understand it may be difficult to cut ties with people you have known for years. You'll feel that way until you realize that some of your 'friends' don't want you to get ahead. They want you to stay the same. They will consciously or subconsciously try to bring you down. I've experienced this myself and I'm not the only one. You're indirectly forcing them to look in the mirror.

The goal is to develop strong bonds with people who are interesting, successful, ambitious, and have their shit together.

3. Go to a quiet place and exercise.
Everyone knows that regular exercise is good for the body. Exercise is also one of the most powerful ways to improve your mental health. No matter your age or fitness level, you can use physical activity to feel better and embrace change. You don't have to go to the gym or do some type of exercise you loathe. Figure out what type of exercise works for you. I'm not a medical professional, so it's best to talk to your doctor before you start any type of physical activity.

My favorite types of physical activities are to hike and cycle the mountain trails. There's something about being in a quiet, natural environment during times of change. The quietness gives me a moment to reflect on my life and how much I have changed over the years.

Some people know they need to change but they don't. Even if their circumstances are downright sad, they will stay where they are. They're used to being comfortable in an uncomfortable situation. They will choose to play the victim and not do anything to change their situation.

How about you? Are you choosing to stay where you are because you're afraid to make an intentional change?

Don't be afraid.

If you choose to stay where you are, then you'll never know what an amazing life will be waiting for you.

Part Four

MIND, BODY, AND SPIRIT

Section One: A Sound Mind In A Sound Body

Critical Questions: Trash Or Treasure?

LANA GUERNSEY

Often in my consulting practice I am asked for answers regarding business challenges or next steps when the future is unknown and the path forward unclear. Over the past 20 years, however, I have found that CEOs, entrepreneurs and nonprofit leaders are sometimes impacted less by actual answers from outside advisors and more by simply stated, critical questions that inspire deep thinking within their organizations. Regardless of whether well-framed, inspirational questions come from internal leaders, front-line employees or external consultants, a single question can be your best friend or worst enemy.

Critical Questions Move You Forward

Open-ended, positively-framed questions have the potential to inspire teams to think, innovate, research, dream, and discover. Aspirational prompts provide a team with the opportunity and permission to articulate challenges, pursue opportunities, mobilize resources, shape vision, and even change the world.

Take for example the story of Dr. Gary Heit, a specialist in functional neurosurgery, who now dedicates a significant portion of his personal and professional time to advancing modern healthcare in developing countries. As Medical Director and Co-Founder of Americare Neurosurgery International Inc. (AMCANI), Dr. Heit and his team of healthcare professionals and volunteers deliver high-quality recycled or surplus medical equipment to countries such as Myanmar, where it is estimated that only 30% of the population has access to healthcare and clean drinking water and only 20% have access to electricity, which is often unreliable and prone to dramatic fluctuations.

Traveling to remote areas of Myanmar on river boats, in four-wheel-drive vehicles, and by foot, Dr. Heit and his team visited multiple state hospitals. In addition to finding patients sleeping on the floor when there were not enough available beds, Dr. Heit observed useless piles of once valuable modern medical equipment – now just trash taking up space. By asking questions about the discarded heaps, which included everything from operating room lights to oxygen generators and a microscope, Dr. Heit quickly learned that other non-governmental organizations (NGOs) had donated expensive equipment with the best of intentions, but failed to understand or ask about the dependability of the local power supply. The costly equipment had quickly become trash – discarded clutter burned-out by frequent surges on the 220-volt system.

In contrast, Dr. Heit and his teams prioritize taking the time to ask valuable and detailed questions in conversation with local leaders to understand the obvious and often less obvious issues in context of the community cultures, before they begin to ship donated equipment, arrange local trainings or recommend sustainable new practices.

For example, Myanmar physicians told AMCANI that they really needed X-ray machines. In reality, however, Dr. Heit's professional training and direct experience with the remoteness of the region helped him to conclude that X-ray machines would quickly become futile given the need for additional support systems, such as a required dark room to work with the X-ray films, and the inability to easily and routinely deliver replacement developing agents. AMCANI volunteers soon hypothesized that what the Myanmar hospital *really* needed was not just an X-ray machine, but instead a way to "look inside the human body."

This insight opened up a new realm of possibilities and potential resources and led to a slightly different, more detailed critical question: "How can the Myanmar team best look inside the human body in a more sustainable and cost-effective manner given limited local resources?"

Based on this revised question and the more specific focus, AMCANI now plans to identify, procure, and install $4,000 ultrasound machines instead of potentially useless $40,000 X-ray equipment. The handheld, portable ultrasound machines – powered by a small solar cell and protected by a simple power conditioner with cheap, locally replaceable parts – will deliver a far more effective and sustainable solution with expanded diagnostic capabilities at a significantly reduced price simply because the volunteers were willing to ask good questions and listen to local knowledge before jumping to conclusions.

Imagine the impact on your next retreat, project kick-off or new assignment, if you were able to have a collaborative discussion around one or more of the following questions:

- What outcomes do we want to achieve and why?
- What might wild success look like and over what time?
- What will matter most / have the greatest impact on our target audience?
- If we were to expand our thinking beyond the current potential solutions, how might we achieve the same objectives and more with alternative solutions?
- What immediate next steps can we take to move forward toward our vision?

On the surface, these questions are simple. But in reality, each prompt includes essential characteristics for quality questioning, given that they are:

1. Open-ended (cannot be answered with a YES or NO)
2. Positively-framed (not negative or pessimistic in nature)
3. Thought-provoking (and yet easily understandable)

Constructive questions, appropriately asked of collaborative teams, have the potential to unlock a treasure chest of productive next steps and inspirational opportunities. Unfortunately, the opposite is also true.

Distracting Questions Set You Back

Despite the power of critical questions to move you forward, incomplete or misdirected questions rapidly waste resources and easily distract an organization from its goals. Hiding like a wolf in sheep's clothing, distracting questions often appear worthy of exploration – especially if presented with energy and enthusiasm by a passionate and charismatic individual with a hidden agenda. In reality, however, poor questions pull a project off mission and often result in unproductive analysis wasting time and valuable resources.

Distracting, off-topic tangents can quickly sink a team into a questioning quicksand where obvious follow-up questions, clarifying comments, and clear next steps simply push a team or project deeper down a useless side track and away from the desired goal or outcome. Details and minutiae that should be reserved for implementation issues quickly become the central focus of a strategy discussion rather than the big picture thinking required for success.

At your next meeting, think about what questions are being asked and what has not yet been covered that will really matter most to move the group forward rather than mire it in details.

Will your questions be the trash in the corner or the treasure chest that unlocks a future of productive possibilities?

www.centio.com

Transforming BS Into Dreams

ANAIS BOCK

If you ask me, business is the second largest opportunity for self-development right after relationships with yourself and others. Because nobody tells you that deciding to be an entrepreneur is like taking the following pledge: "I am willing to take full responsibility for my career path, and realize that I cannot blame any boss, copy machine or ridiculous deadline for my feelings of inadequacy, stress or confusion. Everything I reap shall be the direct result of my emotional, procrastinational and thought-based investment, which are in turn influenced by how much I embrace who I am and what I truly desire."

When I launched my first business in the midst of the Egyptian revolution, I realized that my internal state was just as important to business growth as what was going on externally. The political uprising and breaking down of old structures sparked my inner desire for change and gave me the courage to take that scary first step into the business unknown. The bigger discovery was that it works the other way around too – inside to outside. Whatever unresolved issue (or as I lovingly call it, BS) lingers on the inside most definitely showed up in the real world.

For instance, my fear of being too young to be self-employed at 23 resulted in everyone's very first question being "do you mind if I ask how old you are?"

Since yelling "YES I DO MIND" with a German accent and then stomping off wouldn't have been very fruitful, I decided to work on my side of the issue instead – the INside. I labeled what I was feeling as "guru BS" ("thou must have a long white beard and 30 years of experience before being an expert at anything"), which helped me see what was going on as fear or a perceived sense of inadequacy. Rather than believing that fear, I saw it as a state that was holding me back from showing up confidently. I went through a process of active dissociation, which included reminding myself that I am not what I fear and simply naming it when it came up: "hello guru BS, I see you and I will go on anyway." After a year, the acute guru BS was gone. I was so proud that I would go to networking events secretly daring people to raise their eyebrow about the connection between my accomplishments and my age. Of course, nobody asked that question anymore ...

Now, my guru BS only gets triggered when I am in the boardroom with stern men and their white beards and rigid opinions. I say "hello guru BS" with a twinkle in my eyes and then throw myself into the task of shaking up the status quo. It works.

The golden nugget is this: whatever is stuck, feels heavy and out of alignment and keeps showing up in your business probably contains the biggest opportunity for success. Business is always personal and whatever you transform on the inside will have measurable repercussions in your business, bottom line included. Follow the distinct smell of excitement and fear. Dig deep down into the roots of your BS and say a loving, non-judgmental "hello." Transform it by showing up anyway. Booty shaking, power poses and belly laughter all can help because they get you out of that fear-frozen state and into a place of relaxed readiness.

At this point, I could send you off with an inspiring Einstein quote and cross my fingers that this insight will prove useful to you, but I happen to be passionately curious about this subject – to the point that I did a Masters in Organizational Behavior and have conducted qualitative research with hundreds of entrepreneurs. So there is more. Come with me to explore it.

1. We humans are obsessed with HOW. Most of our reasons for not moving ahead with a business dream have to do with our inability to see *how* to make it work, *how* we will get anyone to believe in us, *how* we will find the time or money or support or swanky website, etc. Entrepreneurs who are struggling financially tend to dedicate a disproportionately large amount of their resources (the most valuable being their thoughts and time) to HOW to get clients to love them, much more so than working in and on their business. When how fears come up, the best thing we can do is the opposite of giving up: keep working.

2. Our brain is wired to keep us safe and anything with an unclear HOW feels very unsafe. As a result, many choose safety over artistic entrepreneurial creation or take the entrepreneurial plunge and are then frozen by fear to the point that the most productive thing would be to find a way to finance their life independently of what they are trying to create. Being entrepreneurially productive has a lot to do with finding

the edge of your comfort zone. Scary enough to make you grow, not too scary to freeze you into immobility.

3. Entrepreneurial fears (which often have roots in deeper, more personal fears) do not just mess with our ability to do, they also mess with our ability to dream. And the size of our dreams happens to dictate the size of our courage and thus our accomplishments.

When nothing is working, eliminate all how-related business activities that feel terrible and yield no results, often based on what everyone else seems to be doing. Stop all of it.

Instead dream. Not the desperate kind of "hope I win the lottery or meet an angel that looks like George Clooney" dream, but the "how would being successful look and feel to me personally" and "how can I get into that mental state right now" kind of dreams.

When you are in that mental place of delicious possibility and expansiveness, do your work. Show up and do whatever it is you need to do every day, right at the edge of your ever-expanding comfort zone. Then your BS, whatever it is, will start turning into the stuff of your dreams.

www.meetanais.com

Don't Be Clueless

ERIC HIMEL

"She's a full-on Monet. From far away, it's okay. But up close, it's a big old mess."   —*Cher from* Clueless

What does Alicia Silverstone's musings from a 90's teen comedy have to do with your success? Authenticity. Cher summed it up pretty succinctly: you can put on a good face, phone it in or try to copy someone else, but in the end, you'll be found out. Period.

Which leads me to money. I like money. I really do. It's terrific. As are winning and success. But you know what I like more? Integrity and authenticity – and success and authenticity do not have to be mutually exclusive. Read the news or go and buy a car and you will quickly see that integrity can be fleeting. No matter the industry, the relationships we co-mingle in or our interactions we string together that form our work, the common thread to making them all succeed is authenticity. We are consumers of everything from products to information to experiences. We demand the best and want to be recognized. So no matter what *your* area of expertise is, the experience that you provide, the decisions that you make and the actions and reactions you engage in must be authentic. Genuine.

Me, I am a stylist. A stylist is a consultant who selects the clothing for published editorial features, print or television advertising campaigns, music videos, concert performances, and any public appearances made by celebrities, models or other public figures.

I work in what could be considered two of the most superficial and transient professions: the worlds of fashion and the world of celebrity/entertainment. And I have built a career out of these worlds. I acknowledge I am not solving world hunger, genocide or global warming. In a nutshell, I make people look and feel good. And I am good at it, and I am successful. But being good at something isn't enough. Are you a leader or a follower? Or you an original or do you copy your competitors? Do you always consider your customer or client or do you look out for #1? Are you *authentic*?

Do you ever stop and ask yourself if you are being authentic? This is where my two worlds can collide. The sometimes and very often superficiality of my work leaves ample opportunities to phone it in, be a yes-man and pander to the highest bidder. That's the easy way out – for anyone, in any field. If you feel you may be falling into that trap, stop and ask yourself these three questions:

1. Do my actions hurt me or my clients/customers?
2. Are my decisions the *right thing* to do?
3. Am I being honest to myself and to my clients/customers?

Authenticity means that sometimes you don't make the sale, close the deal, or even get the job, but it allows you to look in the mirror and actually see a soul behind those bloodshot eyes. Not only that, you are giving your clients the best of what you can offer. Authenticity isn't giving a gift, buying dinner, pushing customers into making a deal or a purchase or taking a higher paying gig over a lower paying one just because of the money.

Authenticity is that little inexplicable voice that lives in all of us, some choose not to activate or listen to it, but it's there. It's the thing that represents your essence, the real you, and the right thing to do all rolled up into one. And once you find it and make all of your decisions and choose all of your actions with it, everything turns out right. It feels right to you and everyone else around you. It creates a positive symbiotic energy in your work and in your life that pays off tenfold. Forget about the, "but I should do that" or "someone else will pick up the pieces" or "I don't have time for that" excuses that you say to yourself to try and keep ahead – those actually require *more* time. Once you tap into your authentic self, responding will be effortless, easy and come natural – like breathing.

While our world gets smaller, borders fade and the population grows, there are more people doing what you do, and with that, very little to separate the mediocre from the successful and even less separating the successful from the special. The good news? Being your authentic self at all times is free and available to everyone, and ultimately will separate you from the pack.

So when in doubt, just look in the mirror and make sure what you see at a glance is the same thing you see up close, your authentic self.

Make Friends With Your Mentor Within

ROSEMARY SHAPIRO-LIU

Picture your thoughts. Are they lined up in neat rows like books on a bookshelf? Or are they like a tangled ball of string? Take a deep breath and close your eyes for a moment and really notice what you see.

If your thoughts are tied up in knots it is possible your Monster Within has got the better of you. It is that monster that gets in your way whenever you try to make decisions and take powerful action. Your inner voice is telling you you're not good enough and that you don't know enough. It is asking "who am I to do that?" If this sounds like you, you might be suffering a dose of the Imposter Syndrome.

When your internal monster is louder than your inner wisdom, you know it's time to take action. It's time to turn down the volume of your Monster Within and reconnect with your Mentor Within.

As a coach and mentor, I often see people discounting their inner wisdom, and grasping for answers from people who they see as wiser or more successful than themselves. They have silenced their inner wisdom either as children when they received negative feedback from adults or peers, or as adults by listening to naysayers who doubt their ability. Their Monster Within has taken over and their intrinsic wisdom is silenced. When that monster is active, we lack clarity and confidence and the commitment to do what we know is best.

People are intrinsically wise and, with a little effort, can guide themselves. One way to silence the negative voices in our heads is through Action Learning, a powerful technique to solve dilemmas by asking questions without judgement. The questions are straightforward, open questions. Action learning is most effective in a group where a few people ask one person questions about their dilemma. Without interrupting, and with real curiosity, the group keeps asking questions until the person in the 'hot seat' has a breakthrough. An insight. A realization. A plan that falls into place. This frees the person in the 'hot seat' to make their own decisions based on what they know is right.

Effective questions might be:

- what would be the best outcome?
- what would be the worst outcome?
- what could you do to prevent the worst outcome?
- what are your fears?
- where did you learn that?
- what is the legacy you want to leave?
- can you tell your story as if you have fast-forwarded three years and you are looking back on what happened?

Questions like these are a great tool whether used in a group or one-to-one. Saying "tell me more" after each answer often gets to the root of the issue. Questioning is a powerful way of helping people become unstuck, allowing them to realize that they want to work in another profession, or understand the blocks that are holding them back from being remarkable. Simple questioning can clear the pathway to making a positive impact on the world.

If you are lucky enough to have a coach or mentor, you can get the support you need from them. However, the very best option is to access your Mentor Within. This will help you find clarity, and build confidence. You will become committed to the promises you have made to yourself. When you are in constant contact with your Mentor Within you have a pool of wisdom to draw on, and advice and support wherever you are.

The first step is to have a self-mentoring session every single week which I think of as a "Management Meeting with Self." In this session, you are your own benevolent but firm manager with the wisdom of a great mentor. You will ask yourself powerful questions, just as a mentor or a group would.

1. **Set a time:** calendarize the same time every week, with no distractions. 30 to 45 minutes should do.
2. **Write it down:** take a Mentor Within journal with you. The first half is for tasks, the second half for the bigger questions.
3. **Track your key tasks:** write down the key tasks for the week. The next week check what you have done and what still needs to be done.

4. **Track progress in the key areas of your life:** in the second half of the journal, write down the six areas of your life that you want to track. Some examples would be "work and learning," "health and happiness", "close relationships and family," "spirituality and community-building," "earning," "home." For each area ask yourself what you have achieved since the previous week and set goals for the next week.

5. **Ask yourself powerful questions:** consider what you would like to do more of, what you would like to change, how you would like to feel the next time you meet with yourself. Check in with your Mentor Within about what you know to be right for you.

6. **Stick to some key principles:** in this meeting there is no judgement, only noticing. There is no comparison to others, only to yourself. There is no resentment or regret, just learning from what has happened in the past and what can be done in the future.

7. **Note the bigger questions:** plan a time once or twice a year to ask the bigger questions that come up each week. These are about your ethics, your strategic direction, and your big goals. Make a time once or twice a year to spend time alone (perhaps going away to somewhere beautiful) to have this conversation with your Mentor Within. By noting the bigger questions to answer at an allocated time, your weekly meeting stays focused on the shorter term.

Connecting with your Mentor Within does not replace coaching or mentoring, or soliciting an accountability buddy to help you stick to your promises to yourself. It does, however, offer you the best and most understanding internal voice to help you grow and develop. Think of it as a wisdom muscle: the more you listen to your own wisdom the stronger it becomes and the easier it is to access it when you need it.

Make friends with your Mentor Within. You'll always be in good company.

http://triplewin.com.au

Your Awful Brain

BRANDON LARSON

You have an awful brain. Yep. I said it. But don't feel bad. So do I, and so does pretty much everyone else. It's part of being a human being and there isn't a whole lot you can do to change the fundamentals – sorry. Researchers sometimes call the competing aspects of the mind System 1 vs System 2, Hot vs Cold, Lizard vs Monkey, The Chimp Paradox. For simplicity, let's boil it down to an awful organ that is usually knee-jerk reacting to external stimuli.

So what does this have to do with business? Turns out the better foundation you have as a human, the better set up you are to excel in your area of business or entrepreneurship. Fortunately, the ancient Greeks had it all figured out ages ago: "Know Thyself," as the maxim goes. That is the key to harnessing the power of the awful brain – learning a bit about it.

There are many ways to go about learning about your awful brain. For the sake of this short chapter on it, I'm going to suggest three areas that have been shown through research to have high correlations to high performance in business. They provide a nice foundation to work from. These areas are: Your Personality, Your Emotions, and Your Mental Awareness.

Benefits include developing several traits that are known foundations of happy high performers in business and leadership:

- Being less critical of yourself and others
- Developing an ability to take more responsibility for your decisions
- Gaining higher emotional stability
- Having less personal/work stress
- Managing work/life balance
- Developing a greater ability to endure difficult conditions, also known as Hardiness/Resilience

Be warned: Working on the brain is hard and sometimes requires some uncomfortable introspection. Additionally, there is no such thing as an ideal psychological make-up. Everyone is an individual and everyone can benefit from understanding the value of their own uniqueness. Different traits are useful and valuable in different contexts, but some traits are a bit more desirable to various components of performance in business. If you choose to learn more about yourself and your perceptions don't line up with the learnings – well – that's your awful brain trying to sabotage things again.

Personality

This isn't the DISC or the Myers-Briggs you may be familiar with. We need something more personal, something deeper rooted with behaviors. Have you heard of the Big 5 Personality Traits? This is a well-researched group of traits that consists of scales of Openness, Conscientiousness, Extraversion, Agreeableness, and Neuroticism. They correlate highly to aspects of success in business as well as long term health.

Why do traits matter? Your traits are your stable characteristics, meaning they are generally consistent and long lasting. Traits drive most of your behaviors and feelings. Interestingly, your personality is solidified by about age 7, through your genetics and the environment you grew up in. Many experts believe that your personality is set, but I believe that you CAN, and I've witnessed it many times, develop new habits and behaviors that override your personality type. There is hope for us all!

This programming is what your awful brain relies on to guide your behaviors – the outcomes of your personality. Makes sense to learn about it, right?

Your Mission: Google "Big 5 Assessment" and take it. If you are a more adventurous type then Google "HEXACO Assessment" and take that one. These take around 25 minutes each. Have fun!

Emotions

Emotions are something that we all experience. Highs and lows are a normal part of life. Just like your traits, these emotional states can be shifted to be more desirable in their contribution to your overall being. What is different about a STATE? States are temporary and they generally arise rapidly in reaction to stimuli. Then they pass. An analogy is to think of clouds passing or a storm that rolls in, does its damage, then moves on. Emotions don't last and they don't define you. Don't let emotions define you!

Your Mission: One of the best books on the topic is "Emotional Intelligence 2.0" by Bradberry and Greaves. Additionally, make an effort to be aware of your emotions. Observe, embrace, and learn from them.

Mindfulness and Awareness

Okay – I promise this won't get weird. There can be a stigma around these words, but let's think of them as tools that bring it all together. They are the tools to knowing how your personality traits and your emotional states affect your behaviors. When you learn to reflect on them, you can shift those behaviors to more desired outcomes over time.

What are Mindfulness and Awareness? In an effort to simplify – mindfulness is the ability to observe and not judge – just to notice the things happening in the mind. Mindfulness leads to Awareness. Awareness is the ability to focus your attention on a point of interest and to then reflect on it such that you change the behavior and mind over time. Previously I mentioned learning to *reflect* on your traits and states – it's important to note: there are two flavors of awareness – rumination and reflection. Reflection is where you deeply look into something with an open mind. Rumination is where you check in on something very frequently, almost to a point of anxiety. Reflect don't ruminate.

Your Mission: Imagine a camera following you at a distance. Periodically inspect your traits, states, and behaviors from this third person perspective. Reflect on the things you'd like to adjust and adjust them accordingly.

Let's revisit. You have this awful organ atop your shoulders. If you can wrangle the awful brain and make it work for you – you will be miles ahead of most. Picture the lump sitting above your shoulders that is controlling trillions of events a second, capable of incredible things. Imagine harnessing that power! It's a secret weapon and powerful enough that I have to suggest a more fitting description of awful, the word's alternative definition: awe inspiring. Now go and take your brain from awful to awe-ful.

brandon.m.larson@gmail.com

Self-Belief And Sociability

ADRIANA ALBRITTON

Successful entrepreneurs have a variety of common qualities. However, a couple of core attributes, self-belief and sociability, are vital and massively catapulting. These crucial traits are essential for your business persona, allowing you to have a more profitable business. The entrepreneurial road is not for the faint of heart; it's full of ups, downs, and sacrifice. If these attributes are not in place, your road is just much bumpier, steeper, and twistier. Besides your entrepreneurial self, these characteristics also enrich other areas of your life. Believing in yourself and being more sociable allow you to thrive mentally, psychologically, emotionally, and spiritually.

Self-Belief

Your beliefs are the sum of the cognitive content that you hold as true in your mind. Beliefs are subjective and based on your perceptions, but not all of them are backed by empirical evidence. Positive beliefs about yourself are essential. Self-belief is foundational for your entrepreneurial path, not to mention your personal life. When you have self-belief, you have utter confidence in yourself, in your ability to achieve, and the conviction that outcomes will be in your favor no matter what transpires.

Being on the opposite side of the spectrum, lacking self-belief, harms you and your business. People with poor self-belief present unhealthy thoughts patterns more often. They think in extremes, without considering a middle ground. They take things personally and are more self-centered. Plus, they tend to expect the worse and minimize positive feedback.

Poor self-belief is derived from a low self-esteem. Negative self-beliefs are deeply rooted negative self-conclusions. People with negative self-evaluations tend to scrutinize their actions and attributes, and be highly self-critical and self-deprecating. At the same time, they have biased expectations, generally jumping to negative conclusions about themselves, their circumstances, and their future.

Poor self-belief can have devastating effects on people's relationships, their social life, their health, as well as their business. It causes people to be highly self-conscious, overly sensitive to disapproval, and even needy, increasing the likelihood to be conflictive or over-pleasing. Poor self-belief creates negative expectations, which can act as self-fulfilling prophecies where the person expects the worse, self-sabotages, and consequently delivers the worse. In turn, their pessimistic self-view is reinforced.

There are many ways of raising your self-belief. Start by creating a solid vision of who you want to be and where you want to go, imitate those who inspire you, behave in ways that lift your self-esteem, and, most importantly, act. Action kills apprehension, indecisiveness, and doubt. You should believe in yourself despite external conditions and know that with discipline, self-improvement, and consistent effort you will achieve your desired results. The inevitable truth is that not believing in yourself can immobilize and delay positive outcomes as an entrepreneur.

Sociability

Another great attribute that is highly beneficial as an entrepreneur is being social. When you are social, you continuously make connections, engage others, and build relationships. People are attracted to a friendly, gregarious, and inviting disposition. In order to grow your business persona, it is always desirable to attract others. Being magnetic and attractive widens your reach and helps you grow.

Modern humans are social species. Homo sapiens evolved through various means. Yet, the establishment of communities, language, and cooperation was what mainly allowed us to survive and persevere. This combination advanced technologies and increased lifespans, exponentially augmenting human population. Taking into consideration our evolutionary trend, rest assure that humans thrive when being more social, and entrepreneurs are not the exception.

Taking the opposite approach, being withdrawn, solitary, or standoffish, is detrimental to you and your business. History shows that isolated beings, generally, do not fare too well, in a holistic sense. It is seen that children and adolescents with poor social bonds have more negative emotional patterns and cognitive processes. On the same note, older people with smaller social networks and poor social support express lower levels of happiness. Those with low sociability are, also, more affected by stressful circumstances. And you know that it is not uncommon for entrepreneurs to encounter highly challenging situations regularly. So the lack of sociability can make you more reactive to stress and consequently less prolific.

Even if you are not intrinsically sociable or extroverted, it helps to take steps to increase your sociability. Smiling and greeting others present a more friendly inviting approach. Posting regularly on social media and engaging your audience increase your presence and visibility. Additionally, try to take the emphasis off you and focus on making positive changes in the lives of others. Selfless acts come back to you and help build your reputation. It is also essential to reach out to highly achieving people and connect with them to have a surrounding atmosphere of success. At the same time, it is highly advisable to get a mentor, a coach, or someone who has achieved excellence, at some level, in order to keep bettering yourself. Entrepreneurs achieve greater altitudes when they have available lifelines and far-reaching connections.

Now you know the advantages of believing in yourself and being more sociable, and the adverse consequences of having low self-belief and sociability. Where are you currently standing? If it's not on the positive side, it's time to transition. Ameliorate your entrepreneurial path by believing in yourself and being more sociable. It will propel you to higher achievement.

http://www.fitnall.com/

Bending Time To Your Will

RYAN TWEDT

One sweet day after landing my then biggest client, everything came crashing down through divorce and a weird incident that caused 22 of my V.A.s servers to burn down with everything else lost with it.

While living on a friend's couch, I had my escape. Work. And that was the only thing I knew how to do.

The entrepreneur Work-Grind-Work-Grind and rebuild. So I did. Faster and better than ever. But as the late nights and long days mixed with copious amounts of fatty coffee, Crossfit, and nootropics, I crashed.

BAM-BOOM-POW! Done. And there wasn't anything I could do about it.

My body's hardware broke down and with it, my internal software fragmented. Brought down past my knees and almost dead in my bed. What felt like the end of my life ... I discovered I'd hit adrenal fatigue.

The kryptonite every entrepreneur dreads that reminds us we aren't super human. When I tried to work, it was 3rd grade production. I couldn't think for longer than 3 seconds before feeling fatigued and scattered. Everything I created required countless hours of repetitive "error checking" and I hate error checking!

Being in marketing, my value is expressed through result and I was struggling to be in the right mindset. Broken, I set off to find my unique balance, re-create myself and rebirth anew. So, for the next 6 months I would come to discover a great peace and healing.

I've always heard of meditation. Practiced it here and there. Learned a few different types. But it wasn't until I boiled it down to "software programing" for the human body I unlocked a deeper wisdom. Yet, in today's age I felt the 2,000 year old forms of meditation could benefit from improvement just like technology. So, I set off looking for updates.

For simplicity's sake our "body-ware" works very similar to computers, tablets, and smartphones. From here, I began to work find the controls to use my system differently. I was never formally taught when I was younger. But, I felt it was best to dive in deep and understand the input-output mechanisms of me and through quiet meditation ask and receive deeper insights about my life.

After 10 hours of meditation everyday for 10 days straight, I found, as with many new discoveries, the secret to bending the experience of time and getting more done with less. This simple hack isn't easy but I believe is useful. It works by getting rid of static noise in the body which is good for improving the qualitative noise to signal ratio. And by consciously scanning and flushing the system while mapping out the body we experience improvements in our decision making. Everything flows more smoothly and with proper time and energy investment the more effective it will become at dealing with the buildup of static stress.

With a 100-hour jump start, I began to understand the depth and capacity of my body in ways I could never learn in books. My direct experience of my interverse within me was as great as the universe outside. It was here that the deepest peace I ever felt, washed over me and I came to understand.

When I got home from 10 days in the desert, I found myself surprised by how much more work was on my plate. On Monday, I jumped in started organizing the work based on priority and after 15 minutes of organization, I thought "this is going to take me 3 days to get done."

With my mind saying this should be overwhelming I started the meditation and for 1 hour I defragmented my system and let my unconscious mind organize the work as my body central nervous system wiring was flushed and cleansed.

After the timer went off, it was time to work. What should have taken me 3 straight days, I was able to get done in 3 hours. We are talking technical server issues, website problems, viruses, sales funnel updates, spam, analytics issues and metrics ... 3 hours + 1 hours of meditation and that was it.

I could barely know what to do with myself! So, I went back in for more meditation. This is when I realized the investment made in each meditation session, would generate a very high return on investment in other areas of my life.

And on through life I went. My decision making was accurate and felt guided and true. My production was overly useful and generated higher amounts of success. Most importantly I was clear, my heart was open and soul felt aligned. It was weird to me because I was always torn between decisions and weighing odds all the time which required lots of energy wasted time.

These are real life results I could count on. For an emotional being like myself, time is short, and life was requiring me to make faster decisions. Reality today is stressful for entrepreneurs and if if you don't deal with your system it will deal with you.

The effects of making *better decisions,* has powerful compounding results that move the needle of success. Imagine less second guessing, doubt, worry, or fear while life flowing more fluidly.

So, you are probably wondering, how do you get practical condensed knowledge and training so you can bend time without having to go through such an intensive meditation training program? Practice equals speed, power and knowledge and you will get to the point, where you can take a deep breath, run the programs, and let it do the work on you.

Taking care of your personal tool set, like a CEO taking care of her physical body through exercise, or a software programmer cleaning his computer, we all will get more done in less time by practicing a unique meditation designed for the result.

Section Two: Getting Better Every Day

Begin Your Day Yesterday

COREY B. SCHULER

I have learned that being a high performer in business and life requires keen optimization. And I've also learned that how anything begins is often a good indicator of how the thing goes.

I am obsessed with how things begin. I am a sucker for the first fifteen minutes of any movie. I pay careful attention to the first line of any character of any book I have ever read. The first minute of an interview or a sales call telegraphs the result. Your projects and your business interests do best with momentum typically based on how they begin.

How do you respond to the socially flaccid greeting of "How are you doing?" or some variation thereof?

That's the beginning of a human interaction and it should begin well! I've heard clever yet rote responses such as "If I was any better, there'd be two of me" and "Nearly perfect" and the overly vague "Pretty okay." My standard answer to patients is "I'm alive, awake, alert, enthusiastic!" If that sounds like a 4-H camp song to you, you're not wrong! That's exactly its origin. These surprising responses often bring a smile to the face of the asker. It's not what they are expecting and the trick to comedy, I have learned, is surprise. When a patient interaction begins with a smile, a chuckle, or even a strange look, it often dictates how our visit goes.

While human interactions do indeed need to begin well, so does your entire day. For most people, the day "begins" with awakening and ends with the period of time we call sleep. That makes some sense. We spend productive time and end with a period of recovery. However, what I'm about to share will warp your world. The beginning of a day is arbitrary since we are just riding a continuous rhythm. I have learned that beginning your day after the conclusion of the evening meal is a little-known secret to a happy, healthy, and productive day. Let me explain.

My study of a field known as chrononutrition has also informed my worldview and my perspective about beginnings. Those of us nerds who study circadian rhythms as a part of chrononutrition or chronobiology typically view 24 hour cycles as holy. This is important for you and your productivity because beginning your "day" with things you can control makes all the difference in the world. Follow me.

How you wake up is dependent upon sleep quality, yet you do not actively control the quality of your sleep during the process of sleeping. How you sleep is dependent upon your sleep hygiene, which is your routine of going to bed and the choices you make just preceding sleep induction. Sleep hygiene is dependent upon your state of mind leading into the evening. You can control your mindset. Aha! Finally, something you can control. You can let go of "yesterday." You can move your body, meditate, connect or reconnect with your social support group. Or you can bitch and complain. You can plop yourself in front on the TV or your favorite screen, isolate yourself, and whack out your neurotransmitters and the timing of your melatonin secretion. Your call. Your sleep, your awakening, and your day depends upon it.

Consider the beginning of your day as a sacred period of time. Use it wisely to set up the next 24 hours as a successful contribution to humanity. What about unwinding after a hard day at work? I propose that proactive and active recovery is far superior to passive unwinding with modern and mindless stimulants that disable our natural mechanisms responsible for controlling circadian patterns. Do you have a list of things you wish you could get done each morning? Many people do have such a list and includes many of the aforementioned positive habits. However, doing them all in the morning often leads to earlier and earlier wake times and further restricted sleep.

Begin your day yesterday for improved productivity and outcomes in your career and life. Evening preparation is what we're talking about. You've heard that eating breakfast is the most important meal of the day. According to circadian rhythm research, that's true. But, in order to eat a good breakfast, evening preparation includes setting the intention to have a healthy meal upon rising. It requires determining what you are going to eat and organizing the food itself. You may find it convenient, as I do, to dice or slice any fruits or vegetables that you'll be using for breakfast while prepping the evening meal. A leisurely yet brief walk or bike ride supports your blood sugar and lowers your cortisol helping you have more restful sleep. Have you always wanted to initiate a meditation or personal yoga practice? Your muscles are warm and your mind is clear so you'd be primed for either. Alternatively, a few minutes writing in a gratitude journal provides peace and further helps you adapt to stress. All the books you've ordered and haven't read, they come next in your evening preparation. Make a connection with someone important to you. You can do it all and have time remaining to fold the laundry and fold yourself into bed.

Here's an example of an actionable evening preparation schedule:

    By 6:30 pm finish supper
    6:30-7:30 pm walk and meditate
    7:30-8:00 pm read
    8:00-8:30 pm make a call
    8:30-9:30 pm household chores and bedtime routine

This type of routine minimizes screen time and maximizes your resilience. You may see this and see rigidity. Let me share with you the flexibility it brings. This routine is a "most nights" schedule. The type of tasks is more important than the timeframe of each. "Slotting in" the right types of tasks and activities can help the cadence of your day become effortless.

How anything begins is often a good indicator of how the thing goes. How will you begin tomorrow?

http://gutsensei.com/

The Balanced Entrepreneur

NADAV WILF

The entrepreneurship life: it's all about the hustle, right? And scaling? Sacrificing time with friends and family to achieve the big things most people won't ever achieve. I'm rising and grinding every day, getting up early and killing it all day long. I work nights, weekends, and I am building my business! I'm starting to scale, and I am going to blow this up!

This is how it HAS to be, right? If you want to be successful, this is how you must execute.

How do we know this is so? Because this is what everyone does, right?

Well, then I must be doing it all wrong, because I am a successful, happy and fulfilled entrepreneur with more time and money on my hands than ever before. Just because that is what we've been told, doesn't mean that is the way it has to be.

I wasn't always this way, though. I used to hustle and grind and stress and beat myself up, CONSTANTLY. I built and sold two companies and failed one company. The whole time, although I saw success, I was creating from a place of fear of failing, feeling guilty when I wasn't working, wanting to prove my self-worth by the size of my company. My happiness was measured by my balance sheet.

When I became financially successful, while at the same time realizing I was unfulfilled personally, I started looking to personal development courses and focusing on expanding myself. I did many courses such as Landmark, MITT, Sai Maa, etc., which helped me become more present and focused on what was most important to me. I realized, to me, true success was an equal balance of financial wealth, physical health, mental health, relationships and living in my purpose.

I sensed that there had to be a different way to achieve exactly what we wanted by doing what we wanted to do, not what we felt we had to do. I had this feeling that these beliefs were simply agreements that had solidified in society over time.

I looked deeper into where these false beliefs came from, and I read a book called *Sapiens: A Brief History of Humankind* by Yuval Harari. Harari discusses the different revolutions humanity has gone through recently: the Agricultural, the Industrial, and the Technological Revolutions.

What I found was stunning. When we were hunter-gatherers, we actually worked 25-30 hours per week, in a community-based way, where we would go hunting and gathering in groups. We would return and spend evenings together in the village, cooking, laughing, playing instruments, painting, dancing and having a good time. Sounds fun, right?

The Agricultural Revolution changed the way we grew and harvested food, the Industrial Revolution changed the way we manufactured and produced goods, and the Technological Revolution has changed the way we look at the world and access information.

What each of these revolutions has done is given us an increase in production, but a decrease in quality of some areas of life. We work more hours for money, to pay for the things we think will make us happier, but have less time to do the things we want.

I'm not saying these revolutions were bad by any means, but we can consider that there is a different way. A rebalancing of life priorities and our relationship to time.

- How do you feel about time?
- Can you identify the feelings you don't want?
- What if you could achieve your goals by doing what you want, when you want, how you want, where you want at the pace you want?

You might say "That's not possible!" Consider that this is simply another limiting belief.

Our life experience is shaped by how we feel, so if we feel and believe the ways that I've outlined, of course we will have that correlating experience.

What's awesome about this is that on the flip side, if we become present, and create the feelings of being confident, peaceful, efficient, abundant, trusting, flowing, grateful and believing, we can create new beliefs and change the way we live.

So the beliefs are:

1. My first priority is to feel good. When I feel good, great things come.
2. I deserve to have it the way that I want.
3. I can take my time with my company, I can focus on generating revenue and then scaling the business.
4. I'm in the perfect place at the perfect time.
5. Having life balance is equally as important as my profits, they go hand in hand.
6. When I exercise, my business grows exponentially.
7. When I do what I love, my life improves exponentially.
8. I get paid to live my passion.
9. I'm having fun making the amount of money I want, doing what I want, when I want, where I want.

You may look at these and say that I'm crazy, these won't work.

I ask you two questions:

1. What is more crazy? Feeling stressed and overworked, being fueled by a fear of failure? Or coming from a place of peace, ease, and enjoyment in achieving what you want? That's what I thought.
2. When you read these beliefs, do you want them to be true? If the answer is yes, then it's simply a matter of training yourself to believe them, just like many have trained ourselves to believe the ones we don't want.

It's really this simple: feeling the way you want, believing what you want, and taking aligned action from these feelings and beliefs for long enough to see the results manifest.

This is what I've done with my company Lifestyle Perfected. As opposed to how I operated in the past, focusing on a mass market in the beginning, I created a product that a few customers fell in love with. Once they did, instead of scaling and hustling, I chose to go slow and give those customers the most love and attention I could.

Within two months, I had gotten profitable with barely any expenses and overhead.

Instead of sacrificing other areas of my life, I ensured that I gave these specific areas (wealth, physical health, mental health, relationships and purpose) equal attention. And that inspired my customers and the number of customers increased.

Once I was 100% confident in the product and had testimonials, I started to scale and with the increased revenue, I've now hired an amazing small team, consistently being mindful that we all maintain the level of life balance we want.

The company continues to grow at a pace that feels good and I continue to live a life that feels good, now, not someday, not one day, but now.

I did all of this by maintaining the feelings, beliefs and actions that were most aligned with me and you can as well. Be mindful of the societal expectations we inherited from the Agricultural, Industrial, and Technological Revolutions of the past. We are now ready to live in the Life Balance revolution. Welcome.

LifestylePerfected.co

How Resourceful Are You?

TROY WEST

How resourceful are you? How you answer this question on a scale of 1-10 can completely dictate whether you grow your or kill your business. We've all heard that in life you are either growing or dying. Business is no different.

Before you answer, know that you are limited based upon what you know (you don't know what you don't know), your habits and decisions, and your resources. Where do you want your business to be next year? Where do you want to be personally? What does your lifestyle look like? How does your business add immense value and purpose to your customers, strategic partners, and employees? Now where is your business in relation to where you want it to be? Answer this question now, on a scale of 1-10.

What is the difference between your answer and the perfect 10? If you answered a 6, that's a difference of 4. That means your expectations, known as your business blueprint, is only about 60% of where you want it to be. As you know, business is based on constant improvement and that as how you will close the gap. How quickly and efficiently you accomplish it is based on *how resourceful you are*.

There are different ways to be resourceful. The first is being resourceful in understanding what your business blueprint gap is and understanding what is needed to improve it. Take the number you answered on the 1-10 scale. What would be required to move it up 2 points higher (or to a 10 if you are at 9)? Start with general categories like financial, marketing, operations. What could be better in each area i.e. revenue, budgeting, mitigating taxes, better customers, etc.

Now, break down what are your pure strengths and where you can help your business most and think about where other resources (even if you don't have a name), can or should do better than you. For instance, if you are not great at knowing your numbers, you may need a CPA, financial consultant, or business consultant. What exactly is it that you need? Write it down and specify who would be that resource. As long as you have an idea of what is needed you can go to your network and ask or do something as simple as a Google search.

To be a better business and constantly grow effectively, you must be resourceful in understanding where you are, where you want to be, what the gap is, and where to go in terms of having a team. Once you have that, what are your expectations for each team member? Ensure you communicate what those standards are and have a process in ensuring they get met. Make sure you have methods to monitor progress, so you can constantly adjust.

It is important to note that on a scale of 1-10, you can never be a 10. That means something is perfect, when in all reality, we know nothing is perfect. Indirectly, what you have created is a way of asking, thinking, and processing to constantly improve your business. Some areas may be the finest tuning that differentiated your company from the next or that puts you over the top. Other areas may need a complete makeover or getting a better resource. The point is that *resourcefulness leads to progress and progress leads to a better business, purpose, value, and lifestyle.*

Remember your limitations. If you know you are limited by what you know, then put a system in place to constantly learn. If you know you are limited to your habits, get feedback on how you can improve and put controls in place. If you lack resources in a particular area, do your homework on finding them.

The great advantage you have in being in business or starting one is that you are in control of your destiny *if you set it up that way.* As business owners sometimes we get stuck because we can't see through our limitations and that stops the progression process. By implementing a simple strategy to *always be resourceful you can constantly improve your business.* Sometimes life will happen, however if you are proactive with your resourcefulness process you always find that when you take a step back it will always end up putting you in a better situation tomorrow. When you make a mistake, ask yourself, "What did I learn?" When you reflect on the day, ask yourself, "What can I do better, what opportunities do I have, how do I execute the opportunities most effectively?"

You are your greatest asset and liability, and the face of your business is dependent upon your system of being resourceful. Be the example and not the warning and you will attract quality resources. To live a life of your dreams, take this simple yet crucial lesson seriously. As you succeed, please do the world a favor and pay it forward. You are more powerful than you realize.

A Perfect Waste Of Time

FRANK NATANEK

My wife explained to me that being a perfectionist is a bad thing. Not always bad, getting a child's wound cleaned up and bandaged properly to prevent infection requires a dose of perfectionism. If the context is one of high consequences, perfectionism is valuable. But it may often or even usually be a bad thing in other contexts. Now, you may think you are a super-hero because of your attention to detail, your passion for a project and your determination to finish ahead of schedule and with every specification fulfilled. But, I will argue that my wife is correct about this one.

WHY? HOW?

It mainly comes down to time. The time you spend being a perfectionist about preparing and cooking the best Thanksgiving dinner is time not spent talking with your family members. The time you spend perfectly organizing your plans and strategies for a project or business is time not used to work on the project or build the business. Time that could have used experimenting and learning-by-doing was wasted in an endless and unwinnable attempt to perfect the plan. Even in the high-consequence situations, perfectionism may hinder action, and the delay may cause a bad result.

In my experience as an attorney, manager and business person, I have seen, and fallen into, the trap of perfectionism too often. It sneaks up on you. You think you are being so productive and so smart by obsessively chipping away at the marble statue. Chip...chip...chip... It takes you over and you even feel intense emotions of happiness and pleasure as you think you are perfecting the product, and frustration, panic or anger if you (or your team) don't "get it right." It becomes a drug. If you are lucky the extra effort may have some value or at least may be written off as "risk mitigation" or a "conservative approach." Like I said, sometimes some perfectionism is perfectly appropriate.

But sometimes you are not so lucky. After all the extra work, you might find that the statue is no longer wanted. The customer has changed or the need has shifted. Now you must make a boat or a trumpet or a play. The perfectly smooth statue is dead - useless - weight. As an attorney, I fear losing a deal over endless rounds of negotiation while each side tries to get a perfect contract. Time can kill any deal.

And then there are the truly scary sides of perfectionism. What can happen when you are so focused on a single activity, goal or target that you effectively have blinders on? Imagine a soldier in a trench trying to precisely target his weapon at an enemy position, with all his attention and energy, as the enemy quietly flanks around and gets him or her from behind. Similarly, in business situations you may miss an opportunity or miss a threat. Or, imagine after years of your obsessing over a specific job that your friends, family or co-workers drift away from you for lack of focus on them, isolating you. Imagine your goals never reached because you obsessed so much over the plans or the first steps. In all such situations you won't have time to see all of your goals realized. Eventually we all are dead. Moreover, if you are very deep in focus, you may not even get around to discovering the many other goals that will make you successful and happy as a person.

There is a saying often attributed to the military: the Perfect is the enemy of the Good.

So, what is a perfectionist to do?

You need to learn and practice how to stay observant (of yourself and around you), how to stop and shift gears to other goals or tasks, how to question the goal and the task critically, and how to be present. Learn how to change course when you hit a block. There are a multitude of books on the topics of being present. It is not an easy task. One can look to meditation or various religions for guidance, but there are simpler approaches too. Dan Harris's book 10% Happier is one I recommend. The task of being present comes down to stopping what you are thinking and looking at your thoughts as a third person would. Ask yourself why you are thinking this way, how are these thoughts relevant or helpful to the goal, and what are other the options to your pattern of thought. Maybe your panic over the minutiae is counter-productive or even hurtful.

This leads to a discussion about mistakes and control. Perfectionists try to control mistakes, or control everything to avoid mistakes. Do not fear mistakes. Permit yourself mistakes, accept them and learn from them. Practice, and relish, being imperfect. Spend your time wisely, not obsessively. Spend large chunks of your time with no agenda. The irony of controlling for mistakes is that the more you try to do this the more you are controlled by external forces and irrational emotions. You cede control of your thoughts to the fear of mistakes. True control is to have no fear, thoughtful concern and responsibility perhaps, but not fear. So, again, you need to learn to be present to regain control of your thoughts. Practice the tactics mentioned above, read and learn more about your mind.

Of course, don't try to do any of these perfectly.

fnatanek@gmail.com

Never Say "I Can't"

ALBERT JANS

For my Dad and Mum

My father worked long hours on the farm and my mother run the household. Both of my parents instilled a good work ethic into my siblings and me. After school we were expected to do chores around the home (inside and outside) as well as on the farm. In the weekends and school holidays I could be found on my pushbike going from farm to farm around the district doing odd jobs for the neighboring farmers.

My parents never accepted "can't." They expected me to find a way. Instead of my parents solving every challenge I encountered, they would listen intently, then ask open ended questions beginning with, "Did you consider … ", "What if … ", "What have you tried?" and so on. These questions made me think, helped me break down the problem into manageable parts and guided me to solve the problem myself. It was this thinking and attitude, which gave me the courage to start my first business at the ripe old age of 14 years. Haymaking during this time was very labor-intensive, and required workers with a good fitness level. Farmers found it difficult to find and coordinate a good team to pick-up and stack the hay bales. I saw an opportunity to form a gang of hay workers, so started recruiting my schoolmates who wanted to earn a few extra dollars. Unfortunately my plan had one serious flaw, I didn't have a driver's license!! Remembering to never say "can't," I recruited Mum to drive us from job to job. Thanks Mum.

Zipping forward 10 years, I had been in the workforce for 5 years, but yet to find my passion job. Farming did not interest me, and being a mechanic wasn't fulfilling. So I started looking for a business to purchase. My choice of business was an industrial lunchbar restaurant, because of my interest in cooking. While out with the real estate agent visiting prospective lunchbars we drove past an industrial engraving business which was also for sale. The business interested me, but I had absolutely no experience with engraving, in fact I cannot recall ever being in an engraving shop previously! Remembering my parents' lessons, I analyzed the business and broke it down into manageable parts. During this process I realized, "I can do this!", so I went ahead with the purchase and General Engravers was mine. It would have been a lot easier to say, "I can't," but General Engravers gave me so many wonderful memories and lessons. The business was a stepping stone to greater things.

To say the next few months were hectic would be an understatement. Part of our contract with the previous owners was for them to stay one month after purchase, as a training time, but due to our inexperience we did not request for any funds to be retained until the end of this period. After a couple of days while locking up the previous owner said to me, "If you make $1,000 profit per week you will be doing well," which was slightly more than he was making. My immediate thought was, "I don't want to make $1,000 profit per week, I want to make $1,000 profit per day" (remember this is 1983). That was the last time we saw the previous owners, we were on our own.

Due to our inexperience we worked 16 hours to produce 8 hours of productive work. Many of the items we engraved were very expensive so we would practice on scrap material until perfection was reached. Then we would replace the scrap material with the actual item to be engraved. Some days we would keep up with the workflow, other days I would catch a couple of hours sleep on the sofa at work instead of going home. Every day we were gaining more experience and become faster and more accurate. The cussing and mistakes were getting further apart.

Frustratingly though there was one skill I could not master; engraving silver trophy cups. No matter how much I practiced engraving on used spaghetti tins I couldn't stop the engraving sloping up or down. I needed a solution and I needed it fast because our clients were expecting their trophies ready for upcoming presentation days. Reluctantly I had to admit I needed help and the solution was taking a few trophies cups to a local engraver. While at the engraver, I asked if I could wait while he engraved the trophies, of course all the while watching and learning. James and I struck a good friendship and offered each other reciprocal work. After a few weeks I admitted he had unsuspectingly taught me how to engrave trophy cups. If I saw James today, he would jokingly say, "Hey you owe me $100 bucks for teaching you how to engrave."

The trophy cup challenge taught me a valuable lesson. Was asking for help an admission of failure, saying, "I can't." The short answer is no, because asking for help is part of the solution, but only after all other avenues have been explored and ruled out.

So what are the 5 important things you can do to avoid saying "I can't."

1. *Dream BIG.* Dreams are free; if you want to go to the moon, dream about going to the stars.
2. *Structure and track goals.* Share your goals with the people who matter. At General Engravers we had two graphs in our break room. One for monthly targets and the other for yearly. Our staff took ownership of the targets and were equally upset if we missed (only twice in 6 years).
3. *Ensure everyone profits.* We introduced a profit share system. A staff member could earn a 20% commission by introducing a new client and 10% on every subsequent order. We had clients nationally, Australia and the Pacific Islands because of this system. ROI on this system far outweighed any traditional advertising.
4. *Never say NO.* General Engravers became known as a "go to" business because we never said no. It did not matter how difficult the job was, we would find a way or someone to successfully complete it. In six years we never let anyone down.
5. *PMA.* Always keep a positive mental attitude. Your clients, staff and network will support and understand when things don't go to plan. You can think @#$% on the inside, but smile on the outside.

In conclusion, sometimes saying, "I can't" is the easy thing to do. If you take the mindset of "can" the things that seem impossible today, will become easy tomorrow.

And before I go, yes we did achieve our goal of $1,000 profit a day in our last year of ownership, all due to saying "I can."

www.albertjans.com

Breaking Through All Barriers

SEAN PATRICK

The greatest revolution of our generation is the discovery that human beings, by changing the inner attitudes of their minds, can change the outer aspects of their lives. —*William James, Harvard psychologist*

My first memory of a mental barrier was back in 1999 when my Australian cousin had offered me a contracting job at a large pharmaceutical company in the Greater Toronto Area. All my friends and family members were supportive but offered so many "what's" "if's" and "how" scenarios that had my mind scattered. This put a real wall around my willingness to make the move, and I only had a few days to confirm the job offering and had to stay fully focused on the new life I wanted to create for myself.

During these few days I scoured through my local library to find all the reading I could on pushing through my "so called" limitations and put together the best steps I found and used. What follows below is always my go-to lesson I learned from then and is what I use with my business life here in 2017.

Can you recall a time in your life that had you facing a barrier? We have all experienced some type of limitation or barrier in our life when pushed either physically or mentally – but how often have you actually stretched these barriers to surpass past limitations?

When we come to any barrier, we seem to *merely problem solve* or *shrink to fit the problem*. As an example if someone were to lose their job, they would fall into survival / stress mode – *cutting back, becoming less creative, or simply trying to hurry to the next new job.*

Here are two examples of people in history that did not believe in breaking barriers:

Robert Millikan (In 1923), Nobel Peace Prize winner in physics
   "There is no likelihood that we will ever tap the power of the atom."

Tris Speaker (In 1923), Hall of Fame baseball great
"Young Mr. Ruth has made a mistake by giving up pitching to become a full-time hitter."

Some of the greatest accomplishments in history are marked by their ability to break through the mental and physical barriers to attain remarkable heights and goals. Here are two examples that pushed through their barriers:

Thomas Edison
"How stressful and painful was it for him to fail thousands of times on his way to inventing the light bulb?"

Steve Jobs
"How many trials and tribulations did he push through to revolutionize the tech industry?"

We all share the same common abilities as these great pioneers. The ability to push ourselves beyond what we think we can do.

The first move is that you must learn to *adapt*. Adapting requires you to co-create with life to push your potential. You must look to break through your barrier which activates a powerful inner force that makes us bigger and better, allowing us to use more energy.

You are full of infinite potential, so if you want more to come into your life – you must find ways to let more life come out of you. Your potential is always greater than the problem. If you expand in the face of contraction, and become a big enough, strong enough channel, you become the answer you were looking for.

Both Albert Einstein and Thomas Edison stated
"The brain is a transmitter and receiver of vibrational energy."

Earl Nightingale stated
"We become what we think about most of the time, and that's the strangest secret."

You need to continually think about the outcome of what it is you want –

beyond your inner barrier. Doing so allows you to unlock talent, skill and knowledge with these principles:

1. The Power to Think about the achievement
2. The Power to Desire its achievement
3. The Power to Act in alignment with the achievement

Your powers to think, feel and act are three resources that can instantly begin to move you beyond your barrier. Where action becomes your focus of the day, fear and rejection will be vanished from your mind.

As you continue, your inner energy starts the creative process and begins to travel. By adding the feeling of love into yourself you begin to attract the desire you are looking for. Start believing you can and saying yes to yourself and more so-called "coincidences" will begin to show up in your life.

Every small change creates the confidence for taking additional action. Change in results, of any degree, is the evidence necessary to launch you into an eventual quantum leap. Your first step towards change is to capitalize all on small victories.

Boldness and persistence are expressions of power and genius. Successful people do this. They push away all obstacles or distractions to improve the possibility of future growth.

Trust in your instincts and start. The thought of "Am I ready?" is your signal to begin. Starting is the best way to get ready and the best way to get ready is to get moving.

Have a clear vision of what it is that you what and imagine what it would be like to already have what you desire. Focus on the feeling it gives you, what you will do, what you will see, and how you see your new situation. Hold the feeling of achieving your desire for 3 minutes. Try to act in alignment with your desire. Think, walk and talk as if you already have already achieved your desire.

Practice feeling grateful and in alignment with your desire. Whatever it is you want, be grateful for the things that you already have. Feel good all the time.

Try doing this many times throughout your day. As you focus on what / where it is you want, your daily mental focus you will get the inner feeling of your barrier crumbling and your achievement moving closer to you.

This is the life lesson I have used for my many business achievements.

www.kiksticksafety.ltd

Section Three: Spirit, Source, And Self

Listening To Yourself: Practical Intuition For Non-Woo Entrepreneurs

SARA STIBITZ

My first memorable intuitive experience involved my friend Molly. Molly and I worked together and shared a bite-sized cubicle for eight months. We got to know each other well and shared the fact that we had both experienced depression throughout our lives. Eventually, she decided to move back to Minnesota to live with her parents. On her last day, we walked out to the parking lot together. As I gave her a hug goodbye, I had this certain feeling that I would never see her again. I ignored it.

About a month and a half later, Molly took her life. That day in the parking lot was the last time I ever saw her.

In 2007, my mother had a stroke and was left with severe disabilities. Six years later, I knew she was going to pass away – soon – the moment my eyes rested on her face during a visit to see her. This time I said something about it. I told my step-dad, I told my aunt and uncle. I was emotional, so they dismissed it as, well, emotional, disregarding what I said. Three months later, she passed away.

What could I have said to Molly? And in the case of my mother, how could I have communicated in a way that would be taken seriously, so that she could have seen her brother and sister one last time? I wasn't sure, but I felt bad for not doing or saying more than I had.

Plus, despite these experiences, I considered intuition to be too "woo" to trust. I failed to trust it when my gut was telling me a prospective client was going to be a nightmare. In fact, my gut told me that pretty frequently; it seemed to have a knack for sensing the scope-creepers and the *actual* creepers who would hit on me in the middle of a working relationship. But I still didn't think much of intuition as a quality or a business practice.

That is, until I had a conversation with a particularly successful entrepreneur, someone who seemed to be the opposite of woo (Catholic, married with three kids, dapper, down-to-earth, with a million+ company) told me about how he uses intuition in his business and daily life. One example: when someone or something feels off in a given situation, he'll hear discordant music – almost as if a symphony is playing out of tune. To him, intuition wasn't woo; it was another tool, and he could define it clearly and knew what the signals meant to him.

After this conversation, it was finally clear to me that I needed to pay attention to my intuition, and that I needed to develop a way to understand what it was saying to me – a language, if you will.

Your intuition is your internal GPS, a built-in guidance system meant to help you in your everyday life, including in your business. However, because of our conditioning, our upbringing, our environment, we tend not to trust our inner voice. The fear of being wrong (or hell, the fear of being right) can stop us in our tracks and keep us from voicing or acting on it. We let the moment pass us by, and when our intuition turns out to be right, we tell ourselves, "I knew that was going to happen," ... and we get frustrated about it. The lack of trust in our intuition creates a feedback loop that makes us start to distrust ourselves.

But there's a way to break that cycle. Over the past year, I've interviewed dozens of people about how they use intuition in their businesses and lives for my podcast, **Find Your True North**. Entrepreneurs, doctors, neuroscientists, ex-Navy SEALs, professional speakers, behavioral profilers, paramedics; they were all able to define their intuition and describe how they used it in their work. The results were *fascinating*.

No matter how well-defined (or undefined) the intuitive sense, the people who had the best relationship with their intuition shared the following four traits (just remember AKTT). Here's how you can use these four traits to improve your own intuitive sense.

Awareness. Experiencing and improving your intuition starts with awareness. Clearly, you can't improve until you start paying attention to it, considering it, and reflecting on intuitive experiences you've had in the past. In the busy rush of a day, it's easy to bulldoze right over a nagging feeling or a shiver down the spine. Instead, stop and pay attention. Listen. Ask yourself what your intuition is trying to tell you.

In fact, if you do nothing else, awareness alone will change your relationship with your inner voice.

Know Your Language. We all hold wildly different definitions about what intuition means. Intuition falls on a spectrum; everyone experiences it differently. "Definitions" for intuition could range from pattern recognition to angels whispering in your ear. Maybe you feel butterflies in your stomach when you're onto a good idea, or a nervous feeling when you think about partnering with someone who looks good on paper but feels off. You might get goose bumps, hear words as if someone is talking to you, see pictures as clear as day, or even experience smells.

What matters most are the feelings associated with your experience of intuition. Whether you think this is a logical process or an ethereal one, you have some kind of sensational experience that occurs for you when you experience your intuition. *That* is the language to which I'm referring.

Understanding how your intuition speaks to you is a major key to learning how to act on it.

Trust. Hands down, this is the simplest way to improve your intuition. Trust it. When that inner voice arises, no matter what it's saying, trust it. Ah, but there's the problem, isn't it? Your ability to trust your inner voice is a direct reflection of your ability to trust yourself. And we all know that ain't easy.

Trust takes time to build, but there are some easy things you can do to build it, which leads us to the fourth pillar.

Test. Too often, we have an intuitive experience and then choose to disregard it, either because we don't know what to do with it, there is conflicting logical information, or it makes us uncomfortable – especially when it comes to another person.

There are two approaches to this. When your intuition speaks to you and it affects only you, play with it. If your intuition tells you not to do something, do it anyway and see what happens, or vice versa. Compare your intuitive feeling to the actual event, and then note the outcome.

When it comes to another person, that's a little trickier. Think of it this way: what could I have said to Molly in that moment? That's an uncomfortable conversation, right?

Yes. *And* ... we never know what something we share might do for another person. All we can do is create the space to share, be vulnerable and open about what we experienced, and let the chips fall where they may.

It takes courage to act on your intuition. However, the more you do it, the easier it becomes. And who knows, maybe one day you'll be able to use your intuition to save another person's life – or your own.

When You Quit, You Win

LINDA PHARATHIKOUNE

It goes against everything you've ever been taught, doesn't it? I know, it sounds counterintuitive, but let me explain.

Have you ever felt as though something deep inside was holding you back from your potential and was causing you to self-sabotage, and you just couldn't quite put your finger on what it was that was holding you back?

I felt that way for a long time. In fact, I felt that way for most of my life. Deep down, I ached to "be somebody." The only thing was, I couldn't see what it was that was holding me back from the success I wanted in life. I felt it. I knew it was there, but I could never articulate or say concretely what *IT* was.

I failed plenty. I also quit before I even started. A lot. It was almost as if I was wired to fail, no matter what I did or tried to do, I somehow managed to end up on the short end of the stick.

I felt like a complete loser.

And for a long time, I focused on fixing the external problems I experienced thinking that somehow, if I faked it long enough, success would somehow miraculously find its way to me.

The thing with the fake-it-till-you-make-it strategy was that I felt like a complete fraud.

I know this is a business book and you're expecting to get a business lesson, but when I thought about the one thing I did to finally see success flow to me with near effortlessness, I couldn't pinpoint an experience that didn't ultimately point back to confronting that invisible thing that was holding me back.

You see, I believe success is an inner game; that nothing ever changes in our external experience (a.k.a reality) unless there's an internal shift in how we relate to what's happening *for* us.

And I believe that *IT*, the *thing* that's holding you back, sits squarely between your ears. Fix your thinking, and everything you want (in life & in business) will flow with what seems like effortlessness. Our thoughts, self-talk, and past conditioning corrodes the connection to our intuitive decision making faculties, and if our words (thoughts & self-falk) create our world, which I believe they do, then our ability to manifest our dream lies in our ability to be clear of the shit that's dragging us down.

One day, while listening to Dr. Wayne Dyer's *The Power Of Intention*, something he said finally dawned on me. Regarding whether we're connected to Source, he said, "It's not about whether or not you're connected; it's about how corroded is the link?"

Boom!

In that moment, I asked myself, "how corroded is *my* link?"

It dawned on me that all the negative thoughts, feelings, and toxic garbage I fed my body was validating my low self-worth. My link was pretty corroded. And everything in my reality, was a reflection of that.

I had a plethora of toxic people in my life.
I was in my early 20s and had over $30k in credit card debt.
I went from relationship to relationship, blaming every single one of those men for all the things they never did for me to make me happy.
I hoarded material things that I rarely used and that never brought me any real joy.

So if our words create our world, then our ability to believe in our power to manifest our dream lies in our ability to be unfettered by mental, physical, and emotional clutter.

Something clicked that day and I've spent much of my life since then doing the thing that went completely against everything I was taught, at the risk of being seen as *crazy*: I quit.

I quit everything that no longer served me: TV, debt, social media, unhealthy relationships, alcohol, selfies(!), meat … the list goes on. I even quit my job and sold or gave away all my possessions.

But most important of all …

I quit feeling undeserving, unworthy, and unlovable.
I quit making myself wrong for wanting success.
I quit blaming people for the things they didn't do for me.
I quit being fearful of the unknown.
I quit thinking that there wasn't enough to go around.

I quit enabling the limiting self-beliefs I carried around and adopted new, more empowering beliefs about myself and where I stand in this world.

And since I've quit all those things, my life (and business) has never been better. I am so centered in peace of mind and peace of heart that no matter what happens outside of me, I'm unshakeable.

You're probably wondering how this relates to business. I believe our effectiveness in business stems from our ability to act with clarity, to act with an unshakeable confidence that everything will turn out the way it's meant to; that if we clear out the clutter in mind, body, spirit, and even our physical space, we open ourselves up to inspiration and have the confidence to act in alignment with our deepest desires.

And let's face it, the real reason why we want a successful business isn't because we want to make boatloads of money (although that's a nice byproduct), it's because we want to create a life that's worth living for ourselves and for our family.

How you get to the top of the mountain called success depends on whether you're willing to carry all of your shit with you to get there. Because success isn't about reaching a pinnacle; it's about being the best human you can be while living out your wildest dreams. Your impact on this world hinges on your confidence to act with clarity.

So, how do you actually get clear?

For starters, make peace with your past. If you're still holding on to past hurts, betrayals, and resentments, your suffering over these things will never change what happened. Remember, suffering is optional. (If you're looking for a program that will help you get out of your rut, I highly recommend the Landmark Forum.)

Secondly, commit to your mental, physical, and spiritual health and well-being. Changing the world (with your business) takes time and you've gotta be in it for the long haul. Don't you want to see your plans come to fruition? Your body is the only thing carrying you through this journey, so treat it well. Get good sleep, exercise, read good books, and eat nutritious and healthy food.

Lastly, get your finances in order. Nothing causes us humans more worry than financial stress. Commit to becoming debt free. Quitting debt was the best thing I ever did for myself. Relieving myself of the constant worry created a newfound confidence within.

This will impact how we show up in and for the world and when we operate from freedom from worry about our finances we exude a posture that's congruent with success. And that internal alignment with success is what creates the external experience.

Sometimes you must quit to win. What will you quit today?

www.lindapharathikoune.com

What's Love Got To Do With Business?

CONSTANT LU

As a fledgling dentist more than twenty years ago, I had opened up my own clinic from scratch and essentially started with one front desk person, and no clientele. After a couple of hard-fought years, I also hired a couple of assistants. I was well prepared for the clinical aspect, since I had received intensive training for that during the arduous years in dental school. But I was not as ready to handle staffing problems! One of my assistants was an excellent worker, but had personality conflicts with the other staff. These continued to escalate until I had no choice except to fire her. My inexperience and lack of wisdom got the better of me then, and one evening, in a fit of anger, I fired her over the phone. As you could guess, that was not received well either. In retaliation, I slammed down my receiver. Feeling sad and remorseful in my back office, with the pressure of mounting bills and responsibilities, I called out to God to help me.

What happened next, you could say was mere coincidence, but I believe otherwise. Just then my fax machine turned on in front of me, and a white paper jetted out with large letters saying: "I LOVE YOU." There was no other message on it, and to this day I don't know who the sender was. But that one event marked a turning point in my business. I saw that one of my biggest problems was that I operated more from a basis of fear, not love for my employees, or even for my clients. As the old adage goes, "People don't care how much you know until they know how much you care." Since applying these principles, our office has tripled in productivity, with happier staff who have stayed longer, and happier clients who refer their friends and family. Additionally, I have reduced stress, and have found time to lead a more balanced life. Try the following for your own business, and I believe you will get amazing results:

1. Your team is your most valuable asset

I hire first based on attitude, not just on experience, and ask potential candidates to come on working interviews. Afterwards, I ask the others on the team to give their input on that person. This increases their chances of being able to cooperate as a cohesive group.

Give your team regular positive feedback. A thank you for doing something specific each day can go a long way, in addition to giving out surprise gift items such as gift cards. Team appreciation luncheons or outings held every few months are great for bonding.

If I see an area needing correction, I wait for a proper time, such as a scheduled performance review. Most instances can wait, as often I find myself emotionally upset at the time, and find that communication is much more effective once I have had time to reflect on what needs to be said so the team member will receive it in the best possible way. I will at that time mention at least one or two positive aspects of their performance, and then say, "this area could use some improvement, and I have confidence you are up to the task, since you have such a wonderful ability to adapt." You can use your own words that feel natural to you.

2. Your business is defined by your customers, therefore serve them first

We have used online surveys like SurveyMonkey to get a pulse on what our clients think about the quality of their service, and what areas they would like to see improved.

Each customer is unique and special. Before I go into a room where they are waiting for me, I take a deep breath so I can regain my focus, and thus give them my undivided attention. I then listen to them in empathy, as they articulate their needs and wants, and work out the solutions according to that, not to what I believe they need and want.

We hold monthly prize drawings, and send out "thank you" cards with a gift card for each of their referrals. We celebrate their victories, and mourn their tragedies alongside them. I have personally attended some of their weddings, graduations, and funeral services.

3. A good leader will show courage, character, compassion, consistency, and clarity of vision

To show **courage** is to sometimes take a calculated leap of faith. A few years ago, I merged our office with another, increasing the initial amount of loans I had, but with the ultimate goal of increasing production while keeping the same overhead. It took several years to realize that goal, but the merger proved worthwhile.

To show **character** manifests in various ways: I have had to humble myself by listening to input from both team members and clients that have required me to change my behavior. I have become the better person for it.

To show **compassion** is to understand that everyone is in a different stage in life, but regardless, is worthy of respect and dignity. In our office, we do give significant discounts, and even some donated work, to some clients who are in dire financial situations. I have also volunteered in countries like Mexico, Philippines, Ukraine, and India, and directed volunteers with a local non-profit in our communities to help our homeless and underserved. In fact, I get my greatest sense of fulfillment from such events.

To show **consistency** means you will be fair and impartial to your team members, treating everyone equally, and not playing favorites.

To have **clarity of vision** for our business, I had every team member contribute their own personal vision statements for what they wanted every major quality of the business to look like in three years, and then I would compile their statements into one comprehensive version.

In conclusion, studies have proven that you are able to show more empathy for others, as well as have lower depression rates, less sickness, and improved immune systems, if you believe you are loved by someone else important to you. That's why the fax I received made such an impact on me! I believed that was a message from God; you need to believe in someone special in your life. And your business and life will never be the same again!

www.lighthousedental.net

Your Divine Heart-Mind

MICHAEL ROBINS

My greatest discovery in life was that we have two guidance systems – the human mind and a Divine Heart-Mind. The human mind is the loudest voice in our heads. The Divine Heart-Mind is silent, but it beats the heart, circulates the blood, digests our food, heals our cuts, sustains our life and directs our

soul's purpose, and so much more. Do you think it might be worth listening to its wisdom? However, the vast majority of humanity do not even know that they have a Divine Heart, let alone how to access and listen to it. The human mind is conditioned and limited, and will never lead us to true happiness or fulfillment. The Divine Heart is the evolutionary force that is ever leading and guiding man to ever greater awareness and achievements, and is the sure way out of any trouble or suffering, but only when we are willing to learn how to access and follow it.

That Heart is who we really are, for "'we are made in the image of God, and God is perfect love, but it is sleeping in most of us, thinking it is the body, the senses, and the conditioned human mind. The Bible tells us "to have the mind which was in Christ Jesus." We do, but we must awaken to it. Here is my story of beginning to awaken to it.

"I quit, I'm done," were the strangest words I heard coming out of my mouth. I had been in college for ten, long years, and I had just turned in my doctoral dissertation. I was inches away from the gold when I was told my dissertation needed much revision. That's when those seemingly crazy and defiant words came out of my mouth. What was I thinking? I was shocked. But I wasn't thinking rationally, I was responding intuitively from the leading of my Divine Heart.

And off I went on an adventure that I never would have logically chosen or even thought possible. I lived on the road for 12 years without working, with nothing but the clothes on my back, and no money. It was an awesome adventure of freedom and I loved it. I exchanged stories and wisdom for a meal and a place to sleep, and when it was not an equally desired exchange,

I put my thumb out and was back on the road. I joyfully travelled the United States until my current wife got pregnant. Then, I tried to retreat to freedom many times. I did not want to settle down, get a job, change diapers, and do all the things that normal people did, but there were many subtle, compelling reasons that made me stay.

That's when I dived deeper into the Divine Heart again for that is where true Freedom is, not in any outer circumstances. I began to read and study everything I could get my hands and eyes on in psychology, religion, spirituality, and the art of living, but I didn't want to just believe in what I read. I wanted to know how to live in freedom and joy, regardless of circumstances. And that's what the Divine Heart teaches. It's what we are all here to learn, but not many consciously pursue that quest. It feels safer to stay in the known and familiar, even if it is less than happy or fulfilling. On my travels, I met many old friends who were financially successful, but thought my journey to be a very compelling one. Of course, despite their strong interests in my life style, they could not leave their circumstances and journey with me.

The human mind sees limitation, separation, and is judgmental. The Divine Heart has a perfect guidance system and sees unlimited potential, perfection, oneness, and loves, accepts, and allows all things. They are worlds apart, but the human mind, a very miniscule part of the Divine Mind, is conditioned to stay within its limited framework, even though love, freedom, and happiness are offered to everyone who has the desire and courage to explore the Divine Heart's profoundly helpful and freeing love and service.

I am still a student of the Divine Heart, and have been for over 50 years. It is a very challenging discipline because the strongly conditioned, human mind has to be taught to think and act like the real, Divine Heart, and that is not easy because of how strong a position we have claimed with and for the human mind. My highest hopes are that upon hearing about the Divine Heart, its perfection, and its ability to resolve all of the challenges you are facing, you will become curious and investigate its nature, potential, and abilities. Many lives have been transformed by its benevolent presence, and many more will be. It's plan of perfection will not fail, although our free will may put off its gifts for a very long time. Blessings on the journey.

www.michaelrobins.me

Profit By Consciousness Of Spirituality In The Workplace

LEONARD BURG

In becoming a Soul Therapist, I discovered the limitations of a university definition of "psychology" as "the study of the mind and behavior," whereas etymologically, the root "psyche" is further defined as "the invisible, animating or spiritual principle or entity which occupies and directs the physical body." This has helped me understand why corporations like IBM and Google are successfully integrating spirituality-based activities into the workplace, to enhance the bottom-line well-being and productivity of employee and company.

Ideally, a deeper understanding of the underlying, universal principles of spirit, by individuals and organizations-as-people, enhances and explains the profitable application of spirituality in the workplace.

A common dictionary definition of "spirit" is: "the life force animating the body." Furthermore, spirit is connected to a universal life force (which you may or may not choose to call "God.") In this context, it pays to distinguish between spirituality and conventional religion.

Working as a United Nations representative for an NGO, "A Centre for the World's Religions," I facilitated meditations for delegates, stressing the need to approach "religion" scientifically. In its essence, the *Latin* root of the word religion is *religare*. It means the yoking or "binding back of man's essence to his source" (the root meaning of "yoga"). On the walls of the great pyramids in Egypt, ancients called this, "Man, know thyself." In this context, the spirit or soul is the eternal true "SELF," while the body/mind is the mortal "self."

We need not adopt or change religions to practice *religare*. Everyone can consciously go within, as in meditation, to commune directly with spirit and connect to each other and a Higher Intelligence or Divine force that created and sustains us.

By definition, all forms of meditation empower us to be more "conscious," which is a fundamental faculty of spirit. This enables us to better take advantage of its connection to a Higher Intelligence. Spiritual giants throughout the ages have taught that this enables humans to access "Divine Revelations" as nourishment for the soul. This is the source of creativity, healing, wisdom, problem solving, guidance, development and reduced suffering. **No wonder meditation is increasingly at the center of most corporate workplace spirituality.**

IBM in Australia is just one company known to have incorporated mindfulness and meditation to enhance focused thinking and stress reduction. Following are just a few influential business leaders whom have used meditation to help them reach and maintain high-level success: Ford Motor Company chairman Bill Ford; former Google.org director Larry Brilliant; and Oprah Winfrey, Chairwoman & CEO of Harpo Productions, Inc.

There is general agreement among corporations that at the core of meditation practice in the workplace are spiritual values such as:

- Recognition that 50% of a company's product or service is the development of its workers,
- Having a management service ethic towards employee, not just towards the consumer and community
- Promote the wellbeing of workers as whole persons, with a spirit, mind and body
- Encouraging a safe atmosphere for employees to freely express and dialogue about spirituality
- Promoting activities that link employee personal gifts and life purpose with the company's mission
- Fostering more creative, innovative use of company time, material and human resources
- Conceding the limitations of the technical or "scientific" approach and incorporating more aesthetics (art and culture) in the business environment

One company, with which I am affiliated, that has successfully pioneered the incorporation of spirituality in the workplace is the International Society of Analytical Trilogy. It is an organization of professional psychotherapists, founded by a Brazilian social Scientist, Dr. Norberto Keppe. In over 40 years of clinical experience in Sao Paulo Brazil, they have effectuated the actual cure or remission of mental, physical ailments through what he calls *Analytical Trilogy* – a way of "interiorizing" or "conscientizing," compatible with meditation.

This modality combines science/psychology with philosophy and metaphysics, in a dialectical methodology focusing on the primacy of incorporating the Divine in group and individual therapy. It enables one to gain direct access to the power of the Divine for healing, conflict resolution, growth and development. This spirituality-based approach has led to the creation of worker owned cooperative businesses and residences, a community college, a language school, as well as community service perma-culture and arts projects, wherein group dialogue sessions are an integral part of the business activity. It has also led to the development of an internationally, award winning, ultra-efficient "Keppe motor" based on spiritual principles.

In my own Soul Therapy Coaching and counseling business, I have incorporated meditation and the dialectical methodology of Analytical Trilogy. Both feature an ongoing process of what Keppe calls "Conscientizing" – i.e., being conscious of and truthful about one's thoughts, feelings, and the inherent errors in how one is behaving. (i.e., anger, ego, lust, greed, and attachment). I have found that by conscientizing, "interiorizing" and meditating, my clients see the relationship between what is happening outside of them and what is going on in their inner life. This consciousness or truthfulness opens them up to healing, stress reduction, inner peace and more self-mastery. This can be applied to the general business model.

In summary, companies can, and some are, similarly enhancing profits and productivity by integrating spirituality in the workplace, incorporating some of the following wellness activities, for management and employee:

- Classes, "Lunch and Learn" sessions, retreats and individual or group coaching in various forms of meditation, psycho-spiritual mental health training, conflict management and holistic fitness modalities such as yoga
- Setting aside time and space for employees to engage in individual and facilitated group meditation and dialectic sessions, re workplace issues related to the company mission and individual roles and life purposes

Some companies see work itself as a spiritual path. This increases the likelihood of realizing profits while simultaneously enhancing both the well-being, personal growth and self-empowerment of the worker, as well as corporate social responsibility, community service and supporting a sustainable environment.

www.scribd.com/Linoze

The Immortality Of Integrity

CHRISTINA J. GHEORGIEŞ

In the kingdom of Lions, there will always be Hyenas.

A mere patchwork of others' echoes in this day and age are easily spotted. No pun intended! You will more specifically notice them when you throw anything they could take a few snaps at for themselves to use and consume, and suddenly it begins – the inevitable process of devouring ...

Awaken the Lion Within to serve your True Self. Ask yourself.
Who are You, really? Are you a Sheep, Hyena or a Lion? We all know sheep. They are the consumer that produces only the bare minimum amount towards survival or less.

Often, the consumer mindset is convinced that buying cheap saves them money, therefore, they do not even realize how with this adopted mindset from lack, they buy that item, more often than not, several times that year from the inability of being able to observe the importance in quality in order to deposit their efforts into longevity, instead.

We all want to be Lions. However, when a sheep fears so much of this world, that one can only ascend so far. That self-denied fear subconsciously will transform a sheep through their own limited perception, into a hyena.

Hyenas are no more than a mere Counterfeit.
Being a sheep may be undesired by most. However, NEVER, EVER BE A HYENA ...

When the lion shows, a hyena always ends up running with their tail between their legs squealing away complaints to those pack members willing to listen. They come in packs and leave in packs. They lead through fear imagery, rather than that of self-empowerment.

~The FRUITS of our BUSINESS inevitably stem to the ROOTS of our re-discovered SELF~

Will you choose to consciously awaken to yourself by turning stones to diamonds and bricks to gold blocks or use and abuse by selfishly taking what's given to you, carelessly and advantageously, like a spoiled child? Who does it serve to pretend we're always in control? It appears severely congested and emotionally constipated to someone who has befriended wisdom. How, when, or where can that self-destructive accepted personality find the time or room to grow? ...

There is wisdom in everything as everything collaborates to guide us along in our very creation, by bricks and stone or diamonds and golden blocks alone. How will you Craft Your Own Life and YouNiverse, aiding those who are closely connected to it?

Out of the limited shadow of self-doubt always silently ask your soul on each action's meaning to you.

Both of these consciously chosen personalities, build great characters we ALL can learn beneficial Life Lessons from. However, only ONE is geared for perpetual growth.

Get hurt, try again, skin a knee or two, do all there is to do and then find endless ways to do more, by always remembering the most beautiful thing on earth is the You, which you choose to hide.

For me, it's the one who now speaks the truth she once held in. A free, passionate spirit with experiences of all shades under-belt, and an insatiable thirst towards spiritual ascension ...

How about that "you" in your own element, conducting the orchestra of your own YouNiverse as you craft away at your life. That silly, awkward, too loud, even passionate you.

We have all seen so many of those "I have it all" people all over the world, who are miserable when the lights go out. They are rich, they are poor, they are middle class. They are religious or otherwise. Overweight or underweight. It is not your bank account, religion or your look that defines you. That is an adopted, re-writable mindset.

I remember when my 'brave' would take a lot more coaxing to come through due to the image of a taught common courtesy, as to not make anyone uncomfortable. Respecting elders and titles rather than integrity and dignity, which are all I sift with these days.

It wasn't for a lack of convictions however for a multitude of unreasonable fears which were stemmed from deeply rooted beliefs as a child growing up in the communist country of Romania, during the late' 70's. A culture under a different type of reign.

For some people, the 'brave' one may never come to light even once in a lifetime. Some may never touch that freedom. For others willing to discover, that You is Innocent and Shy. Limitlessly Powerful, Childlike, with that Spark in the Eye.

Only when you let go of what it should look like fully, will your essence take more and more form with time.

Always maintain your childhood enthusiasm!

Not one organically bonded soul on this planet has it fully figured out. However, one of many wisdom holders alike can have the patterns figured out enough to share the Ultimate Truth.

Feel with your intuition. Pause on the flipping through the pages of your mind – these learned techniques and methods, only. Few, perhaps in some realms are buying that "fluff"; and for how long? ... What would you then, be creating?

Real People are attracted to Real People. When Real People experience Real Sh*t, you have to be able to Bleed With them. Cease dependence on these canned scriptures you and thousands of others have heard in similar seminars or read from the same over-read books, which may no longer serve our current time.

There's a deeper lingering essence by Experience Alone, more potent than anything we could dress in words. Transformation isn't a place with sunshine and butterflies. For some, to get to the side where Butterflies hold hope and Sun can pierce its shine through the thickness of other than pitch black, storming clouds, takes what looks like a complete disaster. There's sweat, anxiety, seemingly unending tears, anger fits, denial and confessions you have to be strong enough to hold for someone.

Apathy can rip a soul to shreds and it can tear hearts apart. Be in full acceptance, without handing them some canned by-product inspiration to placate them. Be the guide. You're not a "fixer" of anything, nor are they broken. Their expanding soul is reaching out like a growing child.

~ CREATE a Safe Space of PERMISSION ~
These wild yet undefined emotions need a place to perform their arts of constructive destruction.Your learned abilities have their place. Listen to your client well. Hearing what they are giving freely, equally to what they are holding back.

Learning the process of Transmutation while becoming an Alchemical Catalyst towards everything your life presents you is your most beneficial tool to Crafting the Life you Deserve. This simple process, once fully claimed as one's DNA, with transmutation mastered, all gains you an inter-web of knowledge.

This life lasting processing system perpetually produces results through you, while now organically understanding the process of lasting results through continual ascension.

~ Once PASSION is DISCOVERED, Create INTEGRITY ~
Present space creating, simple techniques while connecting with another soul. Accepting, never projecting while guiding the seeker through his or her own awareness. Serve love to their very soul. Fully grasp the Immortality of Authenticity and Integrity.

There are millions of byproducts in this world. Your best version does not yet exist!

Inhale your Dream,
Exhale your Creation ...

christinajgheorghies.com

Part Five

BONUS CHAPTERS

Understanding The Energetic Dance of Sales

JOLIE DAWN

If I had a dollar for all the times I've felt violated in a sales conversation, I could retire in Bali right now and eat endless acai bowls. Seriously, understanding how to be smooth in sales isn't something that comes naturally to the large majority of people.

Have you started in a sales conversation being 95% sure that you wanted to buy, and then after some sleazy scripts and weird vibes, you were entirely turned off? That's what I'm talking about here. They lost you at some point, they turned you off, and they didn't feel into what you needed, so ultimately, you were a "no."

When I was 16 years old, I was top in sales in my company, a spa/salon chain that had 25 locations. Out of all the locations, I was consistently #1 in sales for my store. I had zero formal sales training, only my ability to connect with and feel people. By 18, I was the district sales trainer, responsible for hiring and training a large staff of women, all older than me. By the time I was 22, I was a full-time entrepreneur, hustling everything and anything. So what is the #1 thing I attribute to my success?

Understanding the energetic dance of sales.

Sales is entirely energetic because you have to FEEL it. It's a dance and it requires the careful presence of a lead, which is YOU. Sometimes you lean in, sometimes you lean out, sometimes you speak, sometimes you listen. It's a delicate dance requiring intuition and faith, sometimes it's specific steps, sometimes you improvise the moves, and I happen to adore it.

Here are some common mistakes that salespeople make in conversation:

- They have an end goal (of making the sale) and are unwilling to feel or see when that goal needs a pivot. They are out of tune with the cues, the subtle hints, the hidden requests of the person on the other side. We all know what it feels like to have the clingy date that is trying desperately to get you in his pipeline.

 – You must make the call personal to the buyer, not just follow a script to get to the end goal.

- They talk too much. The sales conversation should be an 80/20 rule, 80% listening, 20% talking. No one really cares about all your stories and case studies, tune in to the customer, make them feel understood.

 – When the person doesn't feel like you're listening, you've lost them. When you aren't answering their specific questions because you're too busy yammering about statistics, you've lost them. Listen to your customers and change your sales conversations to fit their specific individual needs.

- They don't take the time to build a connection. Rapport is the typical word we hear here. They don't get the likability, the trust, they forget to court the other person. There is a fine line, and you have to figure out how to be genuine, be yourself, be likable, without forgetting the goal of making a sale.

 – You want to be likeable and trustworthy, but not their best friend. Stop making lunch plans and make the sale. Food is for closers!

- They go for the pitch before the other person is even interested. This happens to me so much. I reached out to a graphic designer to get a quote on a simple project I needed, I was looking to spend about $250 or so on it. He sends back "Hey Jolie, my team does entire re-brands for $3000, send me all your stuff ASAP and we'll get started on this right away." Um, what?

 – First of all, I do not operate my business inside of "ASAP." Honestly, I despise that word – which this person would have learned if he'd actually had a convo with me. Secondly, he didn't even ask me what I wanted. I could have easily spent his $3000 price, if he'd taken the time to build the value, show me what he does, and make me want it. He skipped all the steps! I would guess his conversion rate is under 10% with that strategy. Lastly, I don't just share "all my stuff" with random people I don't know and don't know if I can trust yet. Build a rapport, man!

My dear entrepreneur friend, please don't make these mistakes.

If you really want to learn the energetic dance, practice these steps:

- Use your intuition. Pause, let there be spaciousness. Our bodies are brilliant beings that know absolutely everything. Tune into the other person. When they finish talking, ask yourself "What does this person really need? What are they asking for?" and then explain it to them.

- Focus on being of service to others. Instead of having a fixed end goal, ask yourself "How can I give the greatest contribution to this person?" "What service would truly help them in this moment?" Take the time to listen to the customer and their concerns and questions, and drop your attachments and focus on what would be best for THEM, not what would be best for you. If they are clear on their specific needs, address those individually instead of trying to sell them on the most expensive thing that doesn't even solve half their pain points.

- Learn their dance. Instead of forcing the other person into your tango, pick up on their steps. Maybe their pace is more of a swing! Dance to their beat if you want the sale. Like attracts like, people will like you if they feel like you are like them, and if they feel you are trustworthy and likeable.

- Have fun and be yourself! It amazes me how incredibly hard it is for me to just be myself. It took me about 5 years in entrepreneurship to just relax and have fun with my clients. I used to be so stiff and serious. Relax, be you! Enjoy the process! Sell because you believe in yourself, not because you're trying to meet some arbitrary number.

Even though sales is very important in building a business, you are not a used car salesman. You should never come off as stiff, or sleazy, or uncaring. This is your business, your livelihood! Even if you don't think of yourself as a "salesperson," you must be able to sell yourself and your business. How can you be successful, without selling yourself and bringing in money?

The best way to sell is to be yourself. Listen to what your clients are asking for, and then be yourself and be true to your soul. Life is beautiful, don't stress yourself out over sales, just learn to ask for the sale while being yourself and having a beautiful conversation. Because that is what true sales is: a dance, a lovely conversation. And ultimately, we humans desire just one thing, true connection. So find that connection, and dance!

jolie@joliedawn.com

Right And Wrong Social Proof

JASON ECONOMIDES

I've never had difficulty getting clients, but in January 2017 I found myself in a position that I'm not accustomed to: I had more work than I could handle. I had so many clients that I missed the deadline for submitting this chapter by two weeks! And except for the deadline part, this wasn't an accident.

I'm not writing this to brag about my company – I'm British, so bragging isn't something I'm accustomed to. But because this chapter is a public platform, I want to share in it some thoughts on another public platform – the one that got me the influx of clients in the first place.

Earlier in January, I happened to be talking with a business partner of mine, Karl Bryan, and he convinced me to write a post stating how busy I was. It's really not in my nature to do something like this, but Karl assured me that my "followers" like to hear about people succeeding because they believe that success can also be theirs.

I reluctantly agreed, and shortly thereafter posted on Facebook something along the lines of "Apologies, we're currently full. There is currently a 12-week waitlist for one-to-one coaching/consulting with me personally, though my design and development team are still able for done-for-you funnel building clients (my company builds online sales funnels using ClickFunnels)."

Well the response was absolutely astounding. I lost track of the number of comments, congratulations and even some inbound private messages about how excited people were to see me succeed. There were even messages asking for me to get in touch with them when I "free up." Honestly I couldn't believe it. I really couldn't understand why anyone would be interested at all in the state of my business (busy-ness). But apparently it motivates, influences and inspires. As a result I increased my popularity and guru/authority status. Now let's briefly talk about how to keep that status.

We live in an age of social media, where we share all sorts of emotions, feelings and our day to day experiences on the internet. As I write this, Facebook is my primary social media platform that I use for lead generation, though five years from now that may change. Becoming and staying popular on social media doesn't require much other than consistency. However, I do want to share one pet peeve of mine that I recommend that you not do. Do not constantly post about your daily challenges, hurdles, annoyances, how you just got cheated on (either in business or your personal life), how a client just threw you under the bus, how you were short-changed at the supermarket and so forth. Sure, showing the *occasional* vulnerability is fine and can be endearing, but I see some people in my feed who I personally know want to be uber-popular but yet fill their feed with negativity. This is, essentially, the opposite of the post that I made letting people know of my success.

I don't really know if anyone is really interested in what flavor croissant I'm eating today, or how hard my gym workout was, so I tend not to share things like that. But what I do know is that if I share too much about all the bad stuff happening in my life, it will gradually eat away at whatever expert or guru status I have. I mean, as a guru or expert, I'm meant to be keeping it together right? I have my bad days, and my challenges, but if I choose to share them they will be only with my closest friends or in a post where I'm going to give the entire picture. Recounting what happened, why I think it happened, what I learned from it and what I might do next time is far more useful than simply complaining.

Consider this. About 15 years ago my wife and I had a great yoga teacher who came over to our home once in a while to give us private yoga classes. We really enjoyed the classes. Now when you think about yoga teachers what do you picture? Someone who has inner calm, their home constantly burning incense sticks, and they probably go on a yoga retreat to India 3 times a year, right? So this one evening after class, we are all sitting down having a jasmine tea chatting, when suddenly our teacher drops this bombshell about how she has anxiety attacks constantly and is on really high doses of antidepressants!

Now, how do you think we reacted to hearing that?

We can't give our yoga teacher anything other than respect for being so candid and honest with us about her own personal problems and life challenges, but it simply isn't something we wanted to hear from the person who we had elevated in our minds as our "guru" yoga teacher and were seeking balance from at that time. Contrast this with my friend and yoga teacher, Nora Kersten, who lives in Switzerland. Every post of hers on Facebook leaves you with a sense of health, happiness and wellbeing. I'm sure Nora has challenges, but she NEVER posts about them. Nora knows that her followers are seeking bliss and relaxation, not chaos and stress. I actively seek out her profile whenever I need to feel uplifted and energized even though I don't even do yoga anymore.

I don't believe it's being inauthentic, but there is such a thing as TMI. Giving Too Much Information. If you are communicating with your customers and prospects, tell them what they need and want to hear to help them progress towards their goals. This will assist them, whilst at the same elevating your status in the eyes of your tribe. Or to put it another way, share what your audience wants to see, not what they don't.

How To Get Your First 10 Clients And Gain Traction With Your Business

NICK VAN DRIEL

When you're struggling and you need clients now ...

You have to take a good look at your business and look at the assets. ALL of it. Do you have a refined process you take your clients or customers through to get them results, do you have testimonials, if someone walks up to you and asks 'what are the 3 top results you have achieved for someone' are you ready and able to put a big grin up your face and tell a story on how you got him or her there?

It's not just that but once you get some traction, some clients and some experiences under your belt you are in a MUCH better position to actually leverage all your experiences and translate that to the online world and scale that up.

Be honest, who is in a better position to put together a message that will connect with your target audience: the wantrepreneur that is spinning his wheels who is testing a bunch of stuff out, or the person who has done it 3 to 10 times, has case studies, testimonials, results and knows the words that his client is using for the very simple reason he has had dozens of discussions with that exact type of client already?

Now when businesses want to gain traction and actually need a product to sell they build something called a MVP (minimum viable product). This is the bare minimum that you need to sell a product to people, after that you make iterations and improvements and eventually you have the product that you have envisioned for all this time.

Well it's the same thing if you sell services, coaching, productized services, SAAS or anything else for that matter.

You are in a better position to grow a business when you are already working with 3-5 clients, have experience under your belt and have the assets in place to talk with a business owner and show him that you are the right fit since you have the experience, the case studies, testimonials and the results to back up with what your telling.

And that's just on the selling side, businesses are able and willing to pay you for results that you achieve but you also need to have a process in place to quickly and painlessly onboard new clients and get results for them, this all works if you have the right systems and processes in place.

The issue is building such a process takes time to come to fruition, which is tough when you want to get your first 10 clients to build up your results and gain traction.

Here's what to do:

1. Identify a clear problem you can help solve/result you can enable
Do you have special skill, a piece of software, a systemized process you can help your customers or client achieve a specific result? There is a myriad of results you can help with but you have to define what is going to be your superpower on how to help them achieve their goals.

2. Describe the kind of person who likely has that problem/likely wants that result.
Go deep this is where you are sharpening your axe, give him or her a name, put together a customer avatar, a before problem they have and after they use your product or service how does their life look like right now?

3. Make a list of 100 such people. (Your Dream 100 List)
This is the list that of people that you WANT to work with you know them inside and out, you follow them on twitter, you are in the same LinkedIn groups and you have a way to connect with them.

Then:

1. Connect with them, email them, call them, have a very human-to-human conversation with them. Do they have that problem? Do want that result? If you do connect with them and once they feel you understand them, then.

2. Make them an offer that's easy for them to say "yes" to, it could (and probably should) be a small starter project. Something that will have them experience the beneficial result of having you onboard, you can help them either in full or in part as long as they reach a goal. I've found a lot of success by offering two free trial weeks of my services – yes I've had to put in free work up front, but by giving that much value I've been able to build a lot of traction.

Side Note: if you are in the sales conversation and you have that self-talk about doubt, that's okay, we have all been in that position and that's where this process comes into play, cause you're building up all your assets that will help you down the line. It's hard asking for a $1,500 a month contract when you KNOW you can get them results but you don't have anything to back it up, but it's an entire different conversation when you have already achieved the results 5 times already, proven case studies, have testimonials and a proven process for them to walk through. You can even create a case study video or cheatsheet and promote it on social media channels – this will help you attract people who are interested in that topic itself before you send them to the web pages that sells them on your help.

Once you get at a certain point where you have helped 5-10 big clients and you want to take it to the next level put together a few web pages together that focus on explaining your process and how you help that ideal client reach their goals, this is how you achieve that:

1. Coaching/Services Sales Page
On this sales page you introduce yourself, show your results and testimonials off, show how you can help them (everything you worked for leads up to this) and ask them to apply (on this page ask for just the email of the person).

Here is a very simple headline that you can use: "Do You Need Help With X (X being the main thing you help your clients with)?"

2. Application Intake Page
On this page go a bit deeper in what you're looking for in a client. This is where you qualify them, ask the interested prospect to fill out step 2 of the application process. This is also where your research of your ideal customer will shine since you have different qualifications to work with you than the next person.

3. Thank you/Homework Page

Thank them and give them homework and other steps they need to take. This can be as simple as "Hey, connect with me on LinkedIn" or "call me on my cell," up to "fill out this 5 page questionnaire" (this all depends on your own business and what you would like for your clients to do).

Getting traction is the most important thing, because it's hard to generate customers. But think about it like this: it's MUCH harder to go from 0 to $5,000 in your business then it is to go from $5,001 to $10,000 (for example). The most important element is that by having a system that will bring in not just your first clients but have a strategy in place for you to bring in multiple clients going forward, will make you in a much better position to grow your business. This is not easy, it takes a lot of work and it will take you a couple of tries to have this going – but the moment you do it will change your business.

Moving Forward With Health And Wellness

ERICA COLLINS

The best business lessons are to master knowing when to move on while making your health and wellness a priority first.

Unlike our Baby Boomer parents' generation believed, keeping a job or business forever is not true success. Since 9/11, the path for Generation X's success was challenged in business to go against everything they were taught by their baby boomer parents. The invention of the internet and now social media has changed the way we do business leading to a Gen Y or Millennial business world of collaborations, from marketing communications to targeted marketing, from e-commerce to algorithm commerce, and from emotional intelligence to artificial intelligence.

The Baby Boomer model is credited with the fall of the economy based on greed and waste. I am sure the youth of the Civil Rights Movement, Women's Right Movement, and Hippie generations never thought this is the legacy they would leave behind.

Recent election corruption and scandal through technology has led us right back to a time capsule mixed with generations trying to make sense of an unknown future. The matrix became a mirror and cracked into several pieces. As we cut ourselves and argue on whether to glue the pieces back together or get a new mirror, one thing is true: the reflection will be forever changed.

Yes, the audacity of hope and change. This is why the best business lesson you could ever master is knowing when to move on because success will depend on how well you adapt to change. During the dot-com era, I met a woman who seem to always know when to leave her job on a high note and grab a great new high paying job. She was in sales. Now, we would probably ask her for a webinar or mastermind session on her brand as a sales specialist. The most important observation is how she mastered knowing when to move on and preserving her health and wellness.

Women of color way too often stay in jobs or businesses because it takes them longer to acquire a new job, and a business seems like that one opportunity to make it or it will break you. Recently, Business Insider reported on an increase of 322% of new African American women business owners and 224% of Latin American women business owners. The challenge will be shedding the mindset of racism, sexism and realizing that your brand and experiences have value to the world. If a client or group is still stuck in the physical world of business clouded by social issues of race and gender, the key will be simply to move on and meditate on the next plan of action.

Now, we have access to a world of business opportunities in every industry. There is an emphasis on access to capital for women and women of color, but what will capital really look like in the future? What will a successful career or business look like? Many of us admire the business mogul Oprah Winfrey. Will we one day think it was silly that a person made billions of dollars as a talk show host? When everyone will become their own talk show host expressing their brand and collaborating in a new economy, it's possible.

As many know and from personal experience, traditional media bred an abusive environment in so many ways especially for women and women of color. As the access to broadcasting has turned to webcasting and now streaming, it seems haunting that the plight, quest and sacrifices to be a part of this industry has worn our health and wellness down mentally, emotionally and physically. How many generations of media professionals have put their lives on the line for a story, suffered heart attacks and strokes from stress, or developed cancer and mental health issues from what some label as an industry with "cool perks but thankless." Was your health and wellness worth the use and abuse in an industry now done from the comfort of people's homes or anywhere at any time?

As Simon Sinek points out, the social, emotional and biological issues the millennial generation in business. There is one very important observation: when millennials are uncomfortable, they move on; they challenge authority's healthy living standards and work/life balance. They question whether the use and abuse of brands man-made and created enslaved our free spirit with the comfort of a career or business that forever stunts our intellectual growth. For example, people who had cozy jobs for 20 years and developed mental, emotional and social routines suffer mental illness trying to adjust to change. So much time and energy wasted in resisting and processing change instead of embracing it and evolving from it.

So reflect, release, renew, and move on to the next business that creates work/life balance resulting in improving or maintaining your health and wellness. The best business lesson I ever learned was that every opportunity is a lesson to take you to the next level in your life. Embrace it – don't hide from it or deny it. Empower yourself with it. Let the negatives and positives both make you stronger. Express the lesson. Evolve from it, and find your next level.

I-Am-Erica.com

How To Increase The Commitment Of Your Team

PABLO GARCIA DE LA FUENTE

I was just coming out of a depression after breaking up with my girlfriend in Vietnam. Six months before I had moved to live in Hanoi after living for two years in Ho Chi Minh, a city with tropical weather. The reason was that I wasn't at all motivated with the job after the failure of a personal business project, which left me with less than two thousand dollars in my bank account and with important expenses to cover in the next weeks. The move meant to break with my past. All my world had collapsed and vanished. I was in a city which welcomed me with a hard winter.

I was the fifth person who had taken the post which I had accepted. The construction project had a delay of almost a year, more than 340 days. The team was formed by a Spanish architect, two Filipino engineers, and twelve local Vietnamese, including a secretary and a very good translator. She was my savior, because the English level of all the members of the team wasn't good enough to have smooth communication to work with each of the member of the team. She was really busy.

There was also the suspicion that some of our engineers were giving out important and confidential information about our client, which was something management worried about. Distrust was very important between locals and foreigners. Our client complained about our "useless" reports and meetings all the time. One of the engineers at the end of the day always said: "One day less in Hell."

After six months in that hell and in Summer, my parents came to visit me in Hanoi. I enjoyed their company while we discovered new places around the city under the hot weather. I pretended that in the last six months my life there had been great. I didn't want my parents to know what was going on in my personal and professional life at that time.

When my parents returned to Spain, I made a decision. It can't happen again. My mother could not see me like that again. I had to do something.

When have I been the happiest in the last years? – I asked myself. Immediately I knew, it was finishing my first Olympic Triathlon in Vietnam. I remembered that when I started to prepare it, I found a report of the Phuket Triathlon. It was on a list of the 20 best triathlons of the World. I told myself "Someday I will do it." That day had arrived. It was the perfect reason to get fit, to start every day with energy and the most important, it was something that I could control. It helped me leave behind my sad days. **No more excuses.**

I started to feel better. I arrived at the office with a lot more energy after my morning training. I was capable of transmitting that energy and joy as I worked and to the team.

Then I asked myself – **How I can be a better Project Manager? How can my team improve?**

I found the book *"The 7 Habits of Highly Effective People"* of Stephen R. Covey. It inspired me to make the change which I had been looking for, for both me and my team. I decided to put it into practice, because common sense doesn't mean common practice.

The first stage was to do a small questionnaire with three questions to each member of the team.

1. **What is the Mission of our team in this Project?**
2. **What are your goals in this Project?**
3. **What do you need to achieve them?**

I gave them a week to answer. Then we put all our answers in common. We had 30 minute meetings daily from 12:30 to 13:00 before lunch. We needed to have other kind of communication in our team. These 30 minutes were so important to work on the business values of our company. These values could be aligned with the values of the team and each of the members.

These blocks of time were also used to have personal interviews with each one of them. I searched using coaching techniques a way in which to empower each member of the team, listen to their proposals and grow as a team. So, we got everyone to express themselves, collaborate and feel important. The commitment and communication grew incredibly.

The result of the process resulted in an **Action Plan** with the following points:

- **A Clear Mission of the Team Signed by every member of the Team**
- **Goals and Needs of each of the Members of the Team**
- **Planned Actions**
  - _ Team and Individual
  - _ Monthly Review
  - _ Reviews every four months (New Objectives of the Next Period)
- **Budget and Schedule**

Each day I got to the office with much more energy and joy than before, thanks to my training. I got to share with all members of my team, so all were more motivated and committed than ever before.

And Yes, I did my Phuket Triathlon.

What did I learn in the process?

- You have to change first before others changes around you. You are a role model, if you want or not.
- You have to take care of your people; they will take care of your Project. I spent years taking care of costs of concrete and steel rebar, schedule and drawings. I have to focus on people.
- Commitment Increased as high as I've ever experienced before.
- Social Corporate Responsibility is not about giving money to charity, NGOS or collect rubbish on the beach one time a year. It's about taking care of your people and THE SUCCESS OF THE PROJECT WITH REAL VALUES.

You will be surprised about what your team can do if you listen and empower them.

It showed me the power of Coaching in teams. It made me study deeper in this area in order to be a better Project Manager and Help more People.

Why you don't you give it a try in your team?

pablogarciadelafuente@gmail.com

Everything I Know About Business, I Learned In High School

PHIL STODOLA WITH KRISTEN STODOLA

All I have learned about business I have learned during my time in high school. Those four years were some of the most valuable years of my life. One important lesson I learned in high school was that no matter how hard I work, I need to put time aside for fun. I have made sure to incorporate that same rule into my daily life as an adult. Sure, things have changed since high school, but I have maintained the same work ethic and ways of accomplishing tasks as I had in high school. As a business person, I have learned that creativity and uniqueness are pivotal to success. Looking back on my high school years, I can definitely say that I had used these skills to further myself and accomplish all that I had accomplished. High school included a good mixture of all the ingredients one needs to succeed in life, and I have continued to foster these ingredients in myself so that I can be the best individual I can be.

When I was in high school, I worked hard. I had a passionate interest in basketball, and joined the team as a freshman. Basketball was my life. My dad and I would get to school an hour and a half early each day to open the gym so I could practice. I gave it my all every single day. I pushed myself to be the best basketball player I could be. If I was given critical feedback during practice the day before, I made sure to work on that aspect of my game 100 times more than I would have otherwise. I worked hard to play hard. Giving up was never an option for me, and I still live by that rule today. No matter what task I am given or what I am working on, I give it my all and never give up. I use my resources and talents to give life my best shot (no pun intended).

I belong to a team. We work hard, and we play hard. We could not have gotten where we are now if we had tried any less. Just as my high school basketball team performed as a unit, I make sure my business team does the same. When one person falls, we all fall. When one person succeeds, we all succeed.

As members of a team, we have to be there for one another to keep each other accountable and help each other grow. My talents would be futile if not utilized to their fullest extent. If there was one lesson I learned in high school, it was that one's talents and abilities are best manifested when used in conjunction with others. The world is my basketball court, my colleagues my team. If we all kept our individual talents to ourselves, how would we ever get a point, much less win a game? Some players are better at defense, some at offense, some at free throws. In order to successfully play a game, we need to each use the talents we have and work together. That is the mentality I use toward life itself.

My work ethic may have truly manifested itself in high school but began developing when I was a child. Sure, I procrastinated on assignments at times, but I made sure to use all my resources to complete the task at hand. It may have seemed to others that I was putting the assignment off until the last minute, but I began thinking of ideas for the paper or project starting on day one. My method was not as conventional as most, but neither is my life today. I have never done things in a conventional manner. That is okay, though, because my non-conventional method has always worked for me. While some follow the exact rules by the book, I create my own rules. This does not mean I am a complete rebel; I have just been able to be my own person while accomplishing the tasks of life necessary to succeed.

My childhood friend Eric and I used our creativity to work together and develop ideas for our own little club, P&E. We were an unbreakable unit, and helped each other grow as individuals. We used our own passion for life to help the other enhance his talents. Eric and I understood each other on a deeper level than most adults do. He helped me get to the point I am now, and I have hopefully done the same for him. We worked hard together, and we played hard. He is the one childhood friend I still talk to today. We continue to help and inspire each other to become better people.

Just as Eric and I have inspired each other and helped each other grow, I try my hardest to do the same with every individual I encounter. Every friend, team member, person I meet on the street deserves to be inspired. We are all given the opportunity to help one another and offer our talents to each other. Just as my high school basketball team worked together to become the best unit we could, each one of us as individuals can help each other become a better society. This goes beyond my work as a business person and further speaks to my role as a human being. The good old days of high school are long gone, but I can still apply the lessons I learned in those years to my life today.

philstodola@gmail.com

The Hero Whispers

(Notes to college girlls on how to slay dragons in the real world)

JEANNE MCPHILLIPS

For the Girlls.

To my faves, the college coeds, trying to find your way. Footloose and fancy free as a young babe … you inspire me. You have the world by the balls. It's your time. And because we are all sisters – we're all in this together.

SuperGirlls was born out of this commitment to you. The mission is to inspire you to be your own hero, believe in yourself, listen to your own voice, go forth and slay dragons. Know your power. Rule the world. Know yourself, accept yourself, BE yourself.

THE SECRET SISTER CODE:
GET GOOD: know and love thyself. GET GIRLS: rock the sisterhood. GET GOING: slay dragons.

Start here. Basic building blocks. Take what you like, leave the rest. Put your hero to the test. Sent with love from me to you, lessons I learned along the way, tied up in a bow, and gifted. XOXO

Mariah grabbed my heart with this ballad. It's THE BOMB.

HERO
And then a hero comes along
With the strength to carry on
And you cast your fears aside
And you know you can survive
So when you feel like hope is gone
Look inside you and be strong
And you'll finally see the truth
That a hero lies in you

Get Good

"Know thyself." —Socrates

First things first. Buy the sketchbook. GET READY to design the most important project in your life: YOU.

Do whatever it takes to know yourself and love that girl with all your heart. LISTEN to your voice.

Get to know yourself. Spend some time alone, thinking, being with your best self. Know her inside and out. Break down your life into 4 parts: head, heart, soul, body. Be able to talk about what you like, love, hate. What inspires you? What fires you up? What if you were being interviewed for your own show? Get good at talking and thinking about yourself, your needs, your desires, your wildest dreams, your fears, your nightmares, your darkness. Face it all girl. Embrace it and STRUT, don't walk, toward life. Be clear and vibrant about what your best self looks like. And don't worry ... this will change. For sure.

1. WHAT ARE YOUR PURSUITS?? ... Dreams? Goals? Desires?
2. WHAT ARE YOUR PASSIONS?? ... in your heart? Loves? Values? Can't live without?
3. WHAT IS YOUR PAIN? ... Fears? Nightmares?

I learned that in order to BE A TRUE BYOTCH IN LIFE you must follow your own voice. ME ... I got lost listening to everyone else ... "get married," "have babies," "work a corporate job." As a young babe, I didn't have the courage to hear and follow my true calling – to inspire, to entertain. I married young and I wasn't ready ... I didn't know myself yet. How could I possibly know love if I didn't know myself? I was reckless, restless, and we ended up divorced. I traveled a road that was not my true calling, and it has taken me years to find my true path. DON'T DO THAT!

Get Girls.

"Maybe our girlfriends are our soulmates and guys are just people to have fun with." —Carrie Bradshaw

Respect the sisterhood. Find your tribe. Never let them go.

There is just something magical about GIRL POWER. Something indescribable that just nourishes our souls. That emotional bond that is simply unbreakable. You know what I mean. Life is better with our girlls. It just is. They cry with you, laugh with you, pick you up when you are down, dream your dreams with you, kick ass for you, and hold your hand. I never would have made it through my divorce without my mom, my sister, and my BFF who lived with me and supported my business travel by taking care of my little man! Thanks to these babes I emerged from the dark years–happy, healthy and hopeful!

"Girl Power" doesn't go away when you graduate. It only gets BIGGER BADDER BETTER. You will launch into life with millions of us, and if you are smart, you will work the girl mentor opportunities to make you stronger and more successful through life's bumpy road. Because TRUST ... it WILL be bumpy and sometimes painful. Your girls will get you through. You can count on it. Call on your guardian angels anytime.

Get Going.

> *"The moment God put a dream in your heart, the moment the promise took root, God not only started it, but He set a completion date. God will bring your dreams to pass. Now do your part and break out of anything holding you back." —Joel Osteen*

Slay your goals. And anything standing in your way.

Have faith. Listen closely to your inner voice BITCHES ... the dream that is calling ... the adventures that are waiting ... the passion that is burning inside of your heart. Make sure you do not ignore the calling for too long. This is LIFE. Not a dress rehearsal.

Okay. You dreamed. You learned. You bonded. Now get out that sketchbook again. Keep it simple. Baby steps, short term and long term goals. What's the vision? Clarity will come once you write. You can achieve all that you desire. Keep the plan close to your heart always. Stay open. It's all happening for you. You got this. Be focused and ALWAYS listen to your own hero.

Go for it.

I get it. You can barely think about tomorrow, never mind the rest of your life. I hear you. But force your badass self to vision ... this year, 5-10-20-50 years. Life is a journey; savor every single breath.

Superheroes make a plan to crush the bad guy. They don't always know how it will happen, but they KNOW their target. Write it down. Broad strokes of the brush. IT IS OKAY to pivot. Just Get Going. There is a higher power at work. TRUST.

My journey in life was an emotional roller coaster. I lived on the edge, to the max. All the adventures are what empowered my hero. Last year I moved 3000 miles for an amazing opportunity and before I even knew my zip code, the whole thing blew up. I left my family and friends back east for a fantastic adventure. But when it all fell apart, all that was left was ME. That's what inspired SuperGirlls ... to take on my own destiny, create my own wealth, and inspire all of you.

Life will no doubt kick you in the ass. Probably when you least expect it. Take it as a sign that you should be someplace else. There is something greater for you out there. Don't dwell on the sadness for too long. Find your hero. Fight the good fight. It's not how hard you fall, it's how you pick your pretty little ass up and slay those dragons. Take risks, skydive, jump high ... but use your supergirll weapons to break your fall. Bring your best girl hero. YOU.

"You have all the weapons you need. Now fight." —*Sucker Punch, 2009*

supergirlls.com

Behavior Economics: Moving To A Service Economy Too Quickly

KENNETH T. DAVIS

Understanding economics and market trends is essential before starting any business. Historically the international community has boiled down the global workforce in order to make it easy to process and understand. The traditional first world, second world, third world categories are often used to help administrations, politicians, and school teachers to help members of society comprehend who is doing well and who is struggling. This is, of course, a terrible way to classify nations, but nevertheless the need for a quick comprehensive category is useful.

The International Monetary Fund's (IMF) World Economic Outlook (WEO) is a publication focused on the status of nation's development. They use this three-classification system dividing the world into three non-even groups labeled with advanced markets, emerging markets, and developing markets.

The United Nations Development Programme (UNDP) adds one more category to the labeling of countries. Their four labeling categories are very high human development, high human development, medium human development, & low human development. These four categories make up what is called the United Nations Human Development Index (HDI). The UN's HDIs use access to healthcare and education to help define human quality of life in addition to income alone. It is generally seen as a better system of labeling compared to Income alone.

The World Bank's labeling system has recently changed and is now a four-classification system. It labels the global labor force by nations into low-income economies, lower-middle-income economies, upper-middle-income economies, and high-income economies. This is focused on the Gross National Income which has limitations to the quality of these labels. They have recently stopped using the label developing country as all nations are "developing" in one way or another. The use of this labeling system is not surprising when the organization lends money to governments and the precept of income or ability to pay back the loan is a concern.

With only 3 or 4 labels to address the behavior of these nations, the usefulness of these traditional labeling systems is limited. Gross domestic product or Gross national income are easily collected and do indicate over time if some progress is being made. But it is only a sample window of progress and for this reason has generally not been agreed upon by the international affairs community as good ways of labeling the now 7 billion people and approximately 200 nations or political societies.

The Journal of Business and Behavioral Sciences (volume 26, Number 3, ISSN 1099-5374, fall 2014, K. Davis) shows a great new labeling system promoting a new behavioral economic model with 9 classification labels. With twice the labels, like a microscope, we can get a more specific look at new groups and their behavior to get a better understanding of development or progress both forward and from time to time backward progress. The article was named after this new behavioral economic model and is called the Behavioral International Economic Development Growth Path Model or (BIED-GPM). The first study in 2014 identified 15 growth paths over 2002 – 2012. Now we have the ability to look at not only a label but other nations that are "developing" in similar ways. The trend is to move from an agrarian dominated labor force to an industrialized/manufacturing labor force, and ultimately to a services-dominated labor force. Using only a three-category labeling system makes the groups too large to see subtle differences. With the BIED-GPM we can now see both positive and negative growth. We can also see those that move through labor force by sector (agriculture, industry, service) along with movement through Gross Domestic Product (GDP) through (agriculture, industry, service). Using GDP by composition of sector on the y axis and labor force participation by sector on the x axis, we get nine unique classifications. Over time we can see who moves to a new classification and identify 15 new BIED-GPM Growth Paths. Of these new growth paths we identify four BIED-GPM Growth Path Clusters. Based on behavior these Growth Path Clusters are (1) Non-Transitional (Steady) States, (2) Positive Transitional States, (3) Split Transitional States, and (4) Negative Transitional States. While you might think these four classifications look like the four-tiered World Bank or UNDP classifications, they do not.

The 2014 Study adds four new products to the database. The first and second product is new BIED-GPM development stages for each nation for both 2002 and 2012. This puts all the identifiable nations into one of nine categories from the BIED-GPM. What we learn is that a disproportional number of nations are imitating post industrialized nations without perhaps being ready to do so. This means they have most of their labor force in the service sector and perhaps most of their income coming from the service sector but compared to the UN or WB labeling systems still are lacking in education, health, or other human development priorities.

The third product is the identification of BIED-GPM Growth Paths. While 15 new classifications are identified, studying them helps to get a clearer understanding of movements. This has the potential to support stronger more accurate models. Using more categories allows us to see more specifics and a clearer picture is possible.

The fourth product of the 2014 study is the identification of the BIED-GPM Growth Path Clusters. Seeing four distinct groups that are based on behavior gives the international development community a better understanding of national movement, predictability, and forecasting. This is particularly important when several other models do not account for negative growth. So for example, after the fall of the U.S.S. R. when several satellite countries slide in development, accounting for this movement was problematic. The new BIED-GPM clearly identifies both negative and positive growth to make for better measurements.

In 2016 a second major study was done using the BIED-GPM. It can be found in the BIED Society Review: The works of International Affairs & Foreign Relations (Autumn 2016, ISBN 978-0-9982870-0-3, K. Davis) in this article titled Labeling Matters: the United Nations Development Programme (UNDP) and the Behavioral International Economic Development Growth Path Model (BIED-GPM). All business owners thinking about investing should seek to understand their economy, market forces, and labor influences first.

www.biedsociety.com

Imaginal Cells: Planetary Metamorphosis And Evolved Entrepreneurship

DAVID WEBER

Capitalism and caterpillars have a lot in common. The state of our global economic paradigm closely reflects the condition of a bloated, immobilized caterpillar entering its chrysalis. We are living at the climax of the extractive era of "business as usual," and it appears as if the entire economic system is teetering on the verge of collapsing before our eyes.

This systemic failure is evident across many industries, and it's clear that a great turning is upon us. Our planet is in a critical crisis, defined by the rampant destruction of our ecosystem, vast social inequality, and the hyper-militarized state of global political affairs. This problematic paradigm is a powerful catalyzing impetus for transition and transformation on a local, regional, and planetary scale. Do you feel it?

Patterns in nature hold timeless wisdom to inform and guide human evolution. Let's pretend, for the sake of metaphor, that the post-Industrial Revolution world economy is a hungry caterpillar. Throughout the caterpillar's life-span, it has one job: to grow constantly by consuming as much food as possible. In one day, it can eat up to three-hundred times its own body weight in plant matter. Economic trends over the past two centuries have mirrored the life of a caterpillar – progress measured by non-stop growth at any cost.

An objective analysis of simple statistics regarding environmental degradation and basic human quality of life on this planet yields the obvious conclusion that we have an abundance of inexplicably tragic, complex planetary problems on our hands. Our economic system is failing 99% of the population, our Earth is dying, and billions of people are devastated and destitute. Like the caterpillar, our prevailing global system has exhausted its life-force consuming everything in its path and is set to breakdown in the confines of the cocoon (chrysalis) to be wholly changed and reborn.

Here in the West, it's been easy to allow our mass engineered apathy and collective cognitive dissonance to repress the otherwise natural response of visceral empathy and compassion for the tragedies of our world from surfacing and distracting us from our busy, comfortable lives. However, as the severe symptoms of core systemic malignancy continue to emerge, more and more of us are waking up to the undeniable fact that massive change is urgently necessary, and that we as empowered creators must do something about it. Enter – Imaginal Cells.

Imaginal cells are the visionary catalysts inside the body of a caterpillar that hold the evolutionary genetic blueprint of the butterfly. They remain dormant until the caterpillar has become a cellular soup inside of the chrysalis, upon which they awaken and activate the codes to initiate the metamorphosis.

At first, the cells are seen as foreign organisms and are identified as threats to the body of the caterpillar. In a misguided attempt to protect themselves, the normal cells attack the imaginal cells, only to be inoculated by the evolved consciousness they carry and converted. As the imaginal cells gain strength in numbers, they clump together and symbiotically cooperate with the nutritive soup of caterpillar cells to fuel the metamorphosis from caterpillar to butterfly.

The remarkable rise of "conscious capitalism," "for-benefit businesses" and "evolved enterprises" illustrates the narrative within which evolved entrepreneurs are emerging as "imaginal cells" in the realms of business worldwide. This diverse spectrum of impact-driven individuals and companies are actively using business as a force for good to help solve some of the most dire issues facing humanity today. By building benevolent business models that are designed to solve problems while generating profits, these highly contagious imaginal agents are spreading a positive virus that is shifting our current paradigm and redefining a new era of purpose-first, triple-bottom-line business that demonstrably values people, planet, and ethical profit.

In his critically-acclaimed book *Evolved Enterprise*, Imaginal Council partner and Maverick1000 founder Yanik Silver presents this call to action: "It's time for Maverick entrepreneurs, visionary creators, change makers, and impactful leaders to wake up and step fully into an accelerated entrepreneurial evolution. What serves the collective whole also serves you. Business is the biggest leverage for making a significant difference, and you can be a beacon for others following your path. You're being asked to step up with your talents, capabilities, and gifts to open up a new era of capitalism. You're needed as an ambassador to lift and transform the notion of what business looks like in the 21st century." Those are the words of a fully embodied "imaginal cell" articulating an evolutionary narrative for business in the 21st century.

A true luminary thought-leader and voice for the future of business, Silver paints a picture of an entrepreneurial evolution that facilitates a transition from transactional business, to transformational business, to fully transcending business as we know it today. Perhaps that 'transcendence' will mark the pivotal shift from an extractive system that chronically concentrates power and resources by design to one that is more distributed, reflective of real, tangible value, and in resonance with what's in the highest collective good for the Earth and humanity as a whole.

One thing is for certain – we are in the chrysalis of transformation. To the untrained eye, this could easily appear to be the end of the world, at least as we know it. Just as the rotting fruit falls away to reveal the new seed, the caterpillar must die unto itself to be reborn anew into its most majestic form. Thus, we look to the wisdom of nature and allow its metaphors to guide our path and inform our work as we step faithfully forward into the unknown future.

Only time will tell how and when the butterfly will emerge. The real question is – who are you, and why are you here? The Imaginal Council of evolved entrepreneurs is actively striving to catalyze collective evolution and planetary metamorphosis. We invite you to add your voice and imagination to the revolution of evolution. Be your imaginal self, through the vehicle of your Evolved Enterprise. Together, we'll rewrite the rules of business as usual.

Conclusion

We hope you enjoyed reading this book half as much as we enjoyed creating it for you. The value in this book is immense. A repeat read is highly recommended. Each time you read it, you will learn and discover many new things. We also recommend being a good friend. If there's someone in your life that could benefit from this material, please share it with them.

Thank You To Our Sponsors

Founded by Adventure Capitalist Jaret Henhoeffer, Penguin Power exists to help passionate entrepreneurs acquire, build and exit visionary businesses.

We serve as Exit Strategy and Acquisition advisors, Angel Investors, Project Leaders, interim C-Suite executives and Board Chairs, or any other roles necessary to achieve greatness and execute happy endings.

We serve select visionary entrepreneurs who live life fully and are willing to get dirty, roll up their sleeves and take immediate action.

We operate on a "Hollywood" business model, bringing together the best producer, director and script writer for you to star in a blockbuster.

With over 150 deals closed, we know how to get you across the finish line.

If you are on an epic entrepreneurial adventure and are seeking guidance, wisdom and talent to pivot, transform, acquire or sell, give us a call.

Jaret Henhoeffer, CEO, Penguin Power
16 Gerber Court, PO Box 667
Milverton, Ontario, Canada, N0K 1M0
jaret@penguinpower.ca
www.penguinpower.ca
Office: 1-888-900-4535; Cell: 519 274-2179

D&D AUTOMATION
www.ddauto.com

Intelligent Solutions – D&D Automation Inc. is a controls integrator. We are a contracting firm that designs and implements PLC based control systems for industrial machinery, manufacturing lines, process environments and other automated facilities. D&D is a leader in integrating both the hardware and the software with the client's existing facilities. We will provide the services required for a complete turnkey installation but also offer all of the individual elements of an automation project such as consulting, programming, electrical contracting and panel construction.

Creative Innovation – D&D partners with key clients in the act of starting something for the first time, of introducing something new. We work to develop innovative ideas for our clients to help maximize and minimize. We maximize throughput and quality. We minimize downtime and costs. Ask our team to put their experience, expertise and energy to work for you today.

Our Mission – "We will be the best company to do business with."

The success of our mission is measured by the success of:

- Our Employees
- Our Clients
- Our Suppliers
- Our Community

Our Purpose – Inspiring others to do things they didn't know they could do.

Michael McCourt
President
t: 519.273.7282
c: 519.404.7730
f: 519.273.7431
mmccourt@ddauto.com
www.ddauto.com

Leave A Review And Join AU

If you enjoyed the book, please leave a review. It really helps! Also, if you want to get in contact with all of the Authors, join our community here: https://www.facebook.com/groups/TheAuthorsUniteLounge/

We look forward to meeting you.

650 BET

The better business book : volume 2.

05/04/20

CPSIA information can be obtained
at www.ICGtesting.com
Printed in the USA
LVHW041533010320
648616LV00010B/528